Disrespected Neighbo(u)rs

Disrespected Neighbo(u)rs:

*Cultural Stereotypes
in Literature and Film*

Edited by

Caroline Rosenthal, Laurenz Volkmann
and Uwe Zagratzki

**Cambridge
Scholars**
Publishing

Disrespected Neighbo(u)rs: Cultural Stereotypes in Literature and Film

Edited by Caroline Rosenthal, Laurenz Volkmann and Uwe Zagratzki

This book first published 2018

Cambridge Scholars Publishing

Lady Stephenson Library, Newcastle upon Tyne, NE6 2PA, UK

British Library Cataloguing in Publication Data
A catalogue record for this book is available from the British Library

Copyright © 2018 by Caroline Rosenthal, Laurenz Volkmann, Uwe Zagratzki and contributors

All rights for this book reserved. No part of this book may be reproduced, stored in a retrieval system, or transmitted, in any form or by any means, electronic, mechanical, photocopying, recording or otherwise, without the prior permission of the copyright owner.

ISBN (10): 1-5275-0868-4
ISBN (13): 978-1-5275-0868-2

TABLE OF CONTENTS

INTRODUCTION viii

USA

CHAPTER ONE 2
Mexicans on the American Screen: The Discursive Construction
of Ethnic Stereotypes in Contemporary Film and Television
Christoph Schubert

CHAPTER TWO 23
Remember the Alamo: The Persistence of Cultural Stereotypes in Literary
and Filmic Representations of the Mexican American Borderlands
Jutta Zimmermann

CHAPTER THREE 41
Racial Stereotyping and Performing Blackness: Branden Jacobs-Jenkins's
Neighbors as Post-Black Play
Frank Obenland

CHAPTER FOUR 62
Between the Need to Fit in and the Desire to Stand out: Race, Gender,
and Sexuality in Celeste Ng's *Everything I Never Told You*
Brygida Gasztold

CANADA

CHAPTER FIVE 80
The Palestinians and the Jews: "Disrespected" Neighbo(u)rs
in Jason Sherman's *Nathans Plays*
Albert Rau

CHAPTER SIX 97
Gold Mountain and the Yellow Peril: Literary Representations
of Chinese Canadian Relations
Eva Gruber

GREAT BRITAIN

CHAPTER SEVEN 114
Anti-Irish, Welsh and Scottish Propaganda in Eleventh- and Twelfth-Century Anglo-Norman Writings
Katarzyna Jaworska-Biskup

CHAPTER EIGHT 127
"Grand though it might seem in one way, all of it was petty": Sectarian Conflict and Neighbourly Relations in Short Fiction about the Irish Troubles
Eva Orth

CHAPTER NINE.. 140
Of Foreigners and Friends: Music, Art and Militarism
Alan Riach

INDIA

CHAPTER TEN 156
History and Memory: Gendering the Other in Jyotirmoyee Devi's *The River Churning* and Amitav Gosh's *The Shadow Lines*
Nandini Saha

CHAPTER ELEVEN 173
"Dwindling into symbols": The Politics of Stereotyping after the Indian Partition and 9/11
Christoph Singer

EUROPE

CHAPTER TWELVE... 188
Good and Bad Neighbours: Metaphors and World Making in U.S.-American, German, and Polish Literatures
Paula Wojcik

CHAPTER THIRTEEN 202
Between (Semi-) Orientalisation and (Imaginative) Colonisation: On Othering the Ally in Polish Wartime Recollections
Joanna Witkowska

CHAPTER FOURTEEN 223
The "Other" in Contemporary Slovene Literature from the Trieste Region:
A Case Study of National Stereotypes in Minority Literatures
Ana Toroš

CHAPTER FIFTEEN 234
Female Rebels Undoing Otherness in Fatih Akin's *Auf der anderen Seite*
and *Gegen die Wand*
Funda Bilgen Steinberg

CONTRIBUTORS 245

INDEX 250

INTRODUCTION

The present volume probes the liminal spaces of the construction and perception of stereotypes in literary and media representations and also investigates the interplay between both. The collected essays shed light on how such representations both react to and impinge on the spheres of cultural, political, and economic practice. This is the third volume in a series focussing on constructions of the Other in cultural stereotypes. While the two previous volumes dealt with common features of stereotyping as seen from different academic disciplines (2009) and with shifts in literary and media representations of the Other after 9/11 (2011)[1], this collection specifically focuses on *the textual mechanisms* employed to pit a self against an Other in neighbourly relations. Neighbourly relations here refers to relations between nations or within various cultural groups of a nation. Our racial, ethnic, social, or gender identities are created in demarcating ourselves from others who differ from us in culturally significant ways. These processes of identity formation are often spurred by stereotyping the Other. Sometimes these stereotypes take the form of humorous teasing or satirizing critique. Often, however, stereotypes turn into petrified value judgements of others and lead to discriminatory acts, violence, and sometimes culminate in warfare and genocide.

Disrespect for the immediate neighbour based on stereotypical preconceptions and cultural bias may lie dormant for a long time and then, activated by changes in the economic and political macrocosm, surface instantly and fuel economic exploitation, political suppression, destructive propaganda and, ultimately, pogroms. What had up to this point been recognised as a familiar neighbour, who was defined through linguistic, cultural, and religious distinctions, now not only transmutes into the unfamiliar, but the disrespected and, finally, hateful, Other.

This volume comprises contributions reflecting on these processes and thus shares its particular research focus with numerous publications in recent years of global crisis. Among them are George Tzogopoulos' study *The Greek Crisis in the Media. Stereotyping in the International Press*

---

[1] Two conference-related volumes – *Us and Them-Them and Us: Constructions of the Other in Cultural Stereotypes* and *Ideological Battlegrounds – Constructions of Us and Them Before and After 9/11* – came out in 2011 and 2014 respectively.

(2013) and Perry Hinton, *The Perception of People: Integrating Cognition and Culture* (2016), which unquestioningly raised issues instrumental in shaping the concept of the conference. Since then Claude Fields' volume *Stereotype and Stereotyping: Misperceptions, Perspectives and the Role of Social Media* (2016) has shifted the research emphasis to a new specialisation in accordance with the present study.

A more detailed look at the rhetoric of recent conflicts around the globe related to religious fanaticism, economic crises, racism, or sexism reveals deeply entrenched pre-conceptions of the gendered, ethnic, or social Other. Gendered stereotyping has been an object of analysis in Sara Mills and A.S. Mustapha, *Gender Relation in Learning Material: International Perspectives* (2015), and Linda Seidel, *Mediated Maternity: Contemporary American Portrayals of Bad Mothers: Literature and Popular Culture* (2013), while Jesper Svartvik, *Religious Stereotyping and Interreligious Relations* (2013), has emphasized another significant source of Othering. Such stereotypes are shaped and disseminated through fictional and non-fictional texts, television, and the Internet as well as in everyday cultural practices. As the contributions to this volume show, stereotypical representations of the Other in texts and media products such as films and TV series feature prominently in producing, disseminating, and maintaining cultural difference in ideologically effective ways.[2] Degrees of covert or overt forms of disrespect range from conventional hetero-stereotypes (e.g., Southern laziness, African inertia, Polish cunning, Greek economy, Scottish meanness, Irish drunkenness) in everyday encounters to open de-humanisation (axis of the evil, unbelievers, terrorists) in times of heightened ideological or military tensions.

The present volume[3] conceptualizes and contextualizes the uses and effects of stereotypes in literary and filmic representation within various theoretical discourses, among them critical discourse analysis (Fairclough 1995), ideology-critique (Althusser 1976, Eagleton 1990), critical theories of representation (Hall 1997), discursive practices of power/knowledge (Foucault 1981), and practices of exclusion (Macherey 1978, Foucault 1981) as well as theories of Othering (Said 1995). All of these theories share the assumption that discourses are the product of certain notions about reality and simultaneously produce versions of reality. Discourse

---

[2] On TV studies see also: Kathleen M. Ryan, *Television and the Self: Knowledge, Identity and the Media Representation* (2013).
[3] The editors would like to cordially thank Florian A. Wagner for his diligent, conscientious, and efficient proof-reading and formatting of this volume.

never is an isolated collection of statements or utterances, but consists of groupings of words, sentences, and statements which are always shaped by and enacted within a social context. Crucially, this seemingly natural order of the world is created through its linguistic description, and humans understand – as discourse analysis argues (Foucault 1981, Fairclough 1995, Macherey 1978) – objects through the way they are constructed linguistically.

For the theoretical framing of our undertaking in this essay collection, it seems essential to take into account the insight gleaned from Stuart Hall (1997: 5) about the nature of cultural representations: "Representation is [...] defined as [the] production of meaning through language, signs or images." In the very process of creating representations, the meaning of cultural concepts is generated in the minds of readers through three interrelated strategies: first, the projected assumption that what the recipient reads represents an authentic, mimetic representation of reality; second, the strategy of working with binary oppositions in creating meaning; and, third, the strategy of Othering, that is establishing asymmetrical relationships between culturally different representatives.

One objective of this volume is to investigate how the dichotomies of Self and Other are constructed in and through representational practices. As to the strategy of creating a sense of authenticity, it is, according to Roland Barthes (1957), not so much the degree to which a character's ethnic or racial background corresponds to real-life scenarios, but rather the impression generated by textual strategies such as genre modelling (in a fictional autobiography, for example). In other words, the seeming authenticity of a text has little to do with whether a text actually offers a one-to-one representation of reality, but rather whether it succeeds in convincing its readers that it offers an accurate rendition of, for example, a character's racial or ethnic characteristics and traits. To create this mimetic effect, a text on the one hand needs to present its authentic "raw material" in a manner that it appears as authentic; on the other hand, it needs to offer concepts of reality that readers can integrate into their own cognitive needs, prior knowledge, understanding and expectations concerning the text.

How, then, is meaning structured in a text? Structuralists since de Saussure's *Cours de Linguistique Generale* (1916) have explained the essential contribution of difference to the creation of meaning. This insight into the role of binary oppositions is shared by Stuart Hall, who argues that meaning is only perceived in terms of relational differences, since we can only know what constitutes "black" if we can contrast it with "white" (cf. Hall 1997: 234). As Hall continues to argue, meaning is always dialogic and evolves through contrasting opposites, which means that we can only define "us" if there is a "them" or "not-us." As a result of these binarisms, Stuart Hall (1997) and critics like Mikhail Bakhtin (1982) state that we can only learn what "us" means if we engage in a dialogue with the "other" in an effort to know the "other," for only if we know the "other" do we know the "us."

However, the plea for "dialogism" (*sensu* Bakhtin) or a dissolution of binary oppositions as simplifications has often been neglected in favour of practices of Othering and exclusion. Discourses are organized around dichotomies, with clear-cut hierarchies and asymmetries. Here two strategies exist: one magnifies differences to the benefit of "us" and the detriment of "them" through stereotypical or even prejudicial representations; the other, less obvious and more oblique strategy being that of exclusion, which also comprises linguistic exclusion. As to the first strategy of Othering, stereotypes appear as an exaggerated way of representation; as Hall (1997: 258) explains, they "take hold of the memorable characteristics, reduce them, exaggerate them, and simplify them without change or development to eternity. So stereotyping reduces, essentializes, naturalizes, and fixes differences." Such discourses are essentially organized around practices of exclusion. These mechanisms of exclusion have a tendency to make the act of exclusion appear as self-evident and natural, something which is almost unsayable. Michel Foucault (1981: 56) has famously described this as a "prodigious machinery designed to exclude." In his ground-breaking study *A Theory of Literary Production*, Pierre Macherey elaborated on the concept of literary texts as not just containing multiple gaps and indeterminacies which the reader has to fill with their imagination (as reader-response theories describe). Macherey (1978: 154) also admonishes literary critics and asks them to look for what a text does not say or cannot say. A literary text

> [...] exists above all by its determinate absences, by what it does not say, in its relation to what it is not. Not that it can conceal anything; this meaning is not buried in its depths, masked or disguised; it is not a question of hunting it down with interpretations. It is not in the work but by its side; on its margins, at that limit where it ceases to be what it claims to be because it has reached to the very conditions of its possibility. It is then no longer constituted by a factitious necessity, the product of a conscious or unconscious intention.

To sum up, what is essential to all critical approaches to analysing and interpreting literary texts is the assumption that there is no neutral use of language but that all linguistic expression is socio-culturally formed. Dominant ideologies, such as those about race, ethnicity, and gender define the hierarchical and asymmetrical modes of encoding and decoding culturally shaped textual signs. Detecting and exposing those textual strategies of creating binary oppositions, of Othering, through what is said in a text or not said in a text (*sensu* Macherey) implies reflecting on frames and silent presuppositions which are rooted in certain ideologies. Such suppressive ideologies consist of "a falsifying collectively held system of ideas and beliefs that interpret the world […] in the interest of those who are in power, covers up contradictions and conflicts in society" (Meyer 2011: 182) in order to maintain and legitimize the status quo. In our context, intersectional differences such as race, ethnicity, gender, class, and nation should each and all be regarded as a "significant social and cultural construction, which has been used to classify others as subordinate and legitimize social, economic and political practices, such as segregation, exploitation and disenfranchisement" (ibid.: 196). Therefore, the critical approach adopted in this volume is aligned to critical studies of race, class, gender, and nation and aims at uncovering the ideological underpinnings of these concepts and the role literary and filmic representation play in these processes.

*

This volume looks at various instances of Othering across different media, times, and spaces. Dealing with ethnic groups and neighbourhoods from three world areas as well as genres and media instrumental to their respective cultural stereotyping, it includes chapters on the production of stereotypes in US literature, theatre plays, and films; Canadian ethnic writing and theatre; on strategies of "Othering" in Anglo-Norman, Irish, and Scottish texts; and on stereotyping in the literatures and cultures of India. Moreover, this volume presents an array of reflections on European cultures, ranging from Polish and German literatures, Polish wartime recollections, Slovene minority literature to Turkish German feminist films.

In the US literature and media section **Christoph Schubert** and **Jutta Zimmermann** analyse strategies of Othering in telecinematic discourses. Whereas Schubert, supported by critical discourse analysis, focuses on a US American crime drama series and drug-cartel films featuring the stereotypical Mexican villain "to raise an awareness of how mainstream media discursively construct stereotypes by means of specific communicative patterns," Zimmermann scrutinizes representations of the historical battle of Alamo in US literature and films "as manifestations of cultural memory whose function it has been to express the American nation's self-image." Her line of analysis proceeds from the making of the myth to recent challenges of its inherent binarisms with respect to American and Mexican cultures and the Texan Mexican borderland. Despite challenges and revision, Zimmermann argues, the stereotypes constituting the myth remain unchanged at heart. **Frank Obenland** in his contribution tackles a new turn in contemporary African American drama. "Post-blackness," according to Obenland, "seeks to revisit the complex relationship between theatrical representation of blackness and the long-standing discussion of what constitutes a 'black play'." For him, Branden Jacobs-Jenkins's *Neighbors* serves as an example to reveal the limitations of post-black concepts, since disconnecting the staged racial Other from the assumptions and notions underlying the ideologies required for the creation of the stage characters entails the continuation of cultural and racial stereotyping. He thus reads the drama as a "satire on the performative construction of 'post-blackness'." In her contribution, **Brygida Gasztold** centres on the idea of difference in Celeste Ng's novel *Everything I Never Told You* (2014) as it appears on the levels of race, gender, and sexuality. On the surface depicting a Chinese American mixed family drama, the text encapsulates the overarching complexity of identity construction for interracial marriages in 1950s America.

Albert Rau in the section dealing with cultural stereotyping in Canadian literature expands the notion of the disrespected neighbo(u)r when he discusses *Nathans Plays* by the Jewish Canadian playwright Jason Sherman. Not only does Sherman respond to the Arab-Jewish conflict in Palestine as a conflict between neighbours, but he also puts his diasporic Jewish Canadian protagonist, who eagerly seeks to construct his Jewish identity, in a "disrespected" relation to the Israeli/Zionist mainstream. Probing into the literary representations of Chinese Canadian relations on the basis of three disparate ethnic texts, **Eva Gruber** points out moments in the texts under consideration when the disrespected Chinese neighbours "seem to turn into enemies within." From here, she argues, revealing the hidden violent essence of stereotypes about disrespect, it is just a little step to where they actually "hurt in the most literal of senses: physical violence."

Great Britain and Ireland are represented by three contributions. On the basis of a selection of works **Katarzyna Jaworska-Biskup** delineates xenophobic views in early Anglo-Norman prose describing not only strategies of Othering the Welsh, Scottish, and Irish counterparts evolved for the implementation of power structures, but also when the concept of "Englishness" was initiated. **Eva-Maria Orth** highlights the role of short stories in the depiction of sectarian divisions during the Irish Troubles. Exemplified by two stories from both religious sides of the Troubles she illustrates "the significance of the private" for both authors. By merging the political and the private in the stories, "neighbours" and "neighbourhoods" come to have a metaphorical power and "serve as signifiers of division and social exclusion." **Alan Riach** makes a plea for a re-negotiation of established binary oppositions via the ambiguous arts originating in the "national" and disseminating beyond: "national identity is strengthened and enriched by the recognition of difference. And the creative arts are the best ways in which that foreignness may be mediated internationally." Thus binarisms of "nation" and "foreignness" – us vs. them – tend to lose their dichotomous, rather antagonistic character and are replaced by a recognition of their creative potential. Consequently, foreignness turns into "a matter of curiosity, of optimistic enquiry."

The section on India commences with **Nandini Saha**'s study of the generation of cultural stereotypes in Indian literature caused by the 1947 Partition and the 1971 War of Liberation in Bangladesh. Her main focus is "how in several ways the construction of the 'other' is gendered and how such social constructions then get reflected in literature." She illustrates her thesis by references to two novels which, though differing in their feminist and post-colonial modes of narration/representation, draw identical conclusions with respect to the gendering of the "Other." **Christoph Singer** looks into contemporary Partition of India narratives in popular culture and demonstrates how they construct and deconstruct stereotypes, intersect with cultural memory and finally misuse an "existing trauma" for other – political and commercial – ends.

The concluding section on Europe covers literatures and films from different European cultures. Conceptual metaphors theory lies at the centre of **Paula Wojcik**'s considerations. She argues that "literature can violate the common way we use conceptual metaphors or disturb the seemingly evident connection between a particular metaphor and specific social groups." Four examples from U.S. American, German, and Polish literatures are taken to prove that metaphorical concepts are related to cultural stereotypes and to what extent literary language can interfere with the habitual use of conceptual metaphors. **Joanna Witkowska** deals with Polish World War II recollections of the Polish-British war alliance. She reads them as evidence that though the British were allies of the Poles the habits towards their junior partner "bore the traces of a colonial discourse" close to orientalisation as stated in Edward Said's seminal study of 1978.[4] British, that is Western, Othering of the Poles, that is the entire Eastern Europe, in consequence rests on familiar binary oppositions like civilisation vs. savagery/barbarity. Polish counter-narratives strove to

---

[4] See also Laetitia Nanquette, *Orientalism versus Occidentalism* (2013).

subvert the binarisms in the process of constructing new ones in order "to reclaim dignity" and "to protect their (Western) identity." **Ana Toroš** puts her emphasis on the existence of national stereotypes in contemporary Slovene Triestine literature compared to Italian Triestine literature. Her primary concern is with "the reasons for their conception, longevity and unrecognisability of their construction." She concludes that "symbolic dialogues" between various regional Triestine literatures contribute to collective "Triestine memories" which may result in understanding the cultural Other. **Funda Bilgen Steinberg** sets the films of Fatih Akin against stereotypical Hollywood representations of women to retain male power relations. Deconstructing Gustav Jung's theory of archetypes, Akin creates counter-archetypes that "display anima and animus [...] but in a subversive manner, thus creating images of femininity which disturb the patriarchal order and are opposed to the male (cult) hero." This becomes most visible when challenging the mother-archetype, as shown in two of his films under consideration in the article, where not only the mechanisms of male power structures are exposed, but are also replaced with feminist counter discourses.

As stated above, for better use this essay collection is primarily organised around world areas and specific regions within which diverse approaches reflect upon specific practices and productions of cultural stereotypes. However, the individual essays also form various transverse structures. Beyond a specific area or socio-cultural group they share a concern for political questions of representation and participation, of colonialism, repression, and dominance, of racism, sexism, and nationalism. Next to their subject matter, the essays may also be read according to how they deal with the means and manner of representing stereotypes and cultural differences in the differing genres of films, short stories, dramas, poems, memoirs or music. All of them show that what we need in today's increasingly globalized world is an awareness for the mechanisms and processes of how cultural difference is not only reflected but made in daily conversation and textual representation.

Secondary sources

Althusser, Louis. 1976. *Essays on Ideology.* London: Verso.
Ashcroft, Bill, Gareth Griffiths and Helen Tiffin. 1989. *The Empire Writes Back: Theory and Practice in Post-colonial Literatures.* London and New York: Routledge.
Bakhtin, Mikhail 1982 [1935]. *The Dialogic Imagination.* Austin: University of Texas Press.

Barthes, Roland. 1957. *Mythologies*. Paris: Seuil.
Eagleton, Terry. 1990. *The Ideology of the Aesthetic*. Oxford: Blackwell.
Fairclough, Norman. 1995. *Critical Discourse Analysis: The Critical Study of Language*. London: Longman.
Fields, Claude, ed. 2016. *Stereotypes and Stereotyping: Misperceptions, Perspectives and the Role of Social Media*. New York: Nova Science Publishers.
Foucault, Michel. "The Order of Discourse." [1971] 1981. In: Robert Young, ed. *Untying the Text: A Post-structuralist Reader*. London: Routledge & Kegan Paul, 48-78.
Gonerko-Frej, Anna, Malgorzata Sokol, Joanna Witkowska and Uwe Zagratzki, eds. 2011. *Us and Them - Them and Us: Constructions of the Other in Cultural Stereotypes*. Aachen: Shaker Verlag.
Gonerko-Frej, Anna, and Malgorzata Sokol, eds. 2016. *Ideological Battlegrounds – Constructions of Us and Them Before and After 9/11*. Vol. 2: *Perspectives in Language*. Newcastle upon Tyne: Cambridge Scholars Publishing.
Hall, Stuart, ed. 1997. *Representation: Cultural Representations and Signifying Practices*. London: Sage.
Hinton, Perry R. 2016. *The Perception of People: Integrating Cognition and Culture*. London: Routledge.
Macherey, Pierre. 1978. *A Theory of Literary Production*. London: Routledge and Kegan Paul.
Meyer, Michael. 2011. *English and American Literatures*. 4th ed. Tübingen: Franke.
Mills, Sara. 1997. *Discourse*. London / New York: Routledge.
Mills, Sara, and Abojali S. Mustapha, eds. 2015. *Gender Representation in Learning Materials: International Perspectives*. New York / London: Routledge.
Nanquette, Laetitia. 2013. *Orientalism versus Occidentalism*. London: Tauris.
Ryan, Kathleen M. 2013. *Television and the Self: Knowledge, Identity and Media Representation*. Lanham: Lexington Books.
Said, Edward [1978]. 1995. *Orientalism*. Harmondsworth: Penguin.
Seidel, Linda. 2013. *Mediated Maternity: Contemporary American Portrayals of Bad Mothers in Literature and Popular Culture*. Lanham: Lexington Books.
Svartvik, Jesper. 2013. *Religious Stereotyping and Interreligious Relations*. New York: Palgrave Macmillan.
Tzogopoulos, George. 2013. *The Greek Crisis in the Media. Stereotyping in the International Press*. Farnham: Ashgate Publishing.

Witkowska, Joanna, and Uwe Zagratzki, eds. 2014. *Ideological Battlegrounds – Constructions of Us and Them Before and After 9/11*. Vol. 1: *Perspectives in Literatures and Cultures.* Newcastle upon Tyne: Cambridge Scholars Publishing.

USA

CHAPTER ONE

MEXICANS ON THE AMERICAN SCREEN: THE DISCURSIVE CONSTRUCTION OF ETHNIC STEREOTYPES IN CONTEMPORARY FILM AND TELEVISION

CHRISTOPH SCHUBERT

1. Discursive Othering in Media Representation

"You make us immigrants look bad!" With these words, Arizona Sheriff Ray Owens, played by former California governor Arnold Schwarzenegger, accuses and arrests the fiendish Mexican cartel boss Gabriel Cortez in the 2013 action film *The Last Stand* (1:26:02). This critical statement can be decoded at the meta-fictional level as well, since it may aptly be applied to the often one-sided representation of Mexicans in American film and television at large. Although Sheriff Owens, who is marked as a foreigner by his distinct Austrian German accent, puts himself in the same category of "immigrants" as the Mexican citizen, Schwarzenegger's character is the brave and well integrated law-enforcer, while the Latino is the ruthless and criminal Other. Owing to such discriminatory practices, the representation of ethnic groups or nationalities in the US entertainment industry is a crucial topic for Critical Discourse Analysis (Fairclough 2001; Wodak et al. 2009), since TV series and films not only reflect existing categorisations but also support and perpetuate biased perceptions in the collective memory of a given culture. Accordingly, through an investigation of linguistic Othering, this article intends to raise an awareness of how mainstream media discursively construct stereotypes by means of specific communicative patterns.

In accordance with well-known conflicts on the common border, Mexico and Mexicans play a notorious role in contemporary US-American television series and feature films. One central ingredient of stereotyping is the affiliation of Mexico with drug trafficking through tightly organised cartels, continuing the common *bandido* image of numerous Western and adventure films of the 20th century (Berg 2002). In order to deconstruct this persistent stereotype in detail, this paper focuses on the portrayal of Mexicans in AMC's crime drama series *Breaking Bad* (Vince Gilligan 2008-2013) as well as in the contemporary drug-cartel films *Traffic* (Steven Soderbergh 2000), *Savages* (Oliver Stone 2012), *The Counselor* (Ridley Scott 2013), *The Last Stand* (Kim Jee-woon 2013), and *Sicario* (Denis Villeneuve 2015).

For an in-depth investigation of stereotypes, cognitive-linguistic prototype theory provides a fruitful theoretical foundation (Taylor 2003; Geeraerts 2007). In order to make sense of everyday experience, human beings generally rely on the construction of cognitive categories, which are marked by a prototype as the most typical representative. While prototypes are principally neutral and non-judgemental, stereotypes, which can be triggered by mass media or other sociocultural factors (Schneider 2004), convey a biased and disparaging image of ethnic groups, potentially fostering social exclusion. Hence, through a comparative analysis of the popular films and the TV series, characteristic attributes of the stereotypical Mexican villain will be identified.

As regards characterisation strategies, Jonathan Culpeper's cognitive model (2001) will be employed, which combines bottom-up effects of discursive clues with top-down inference processes based on the recipients' prior world knowledge. Owing to the multimodal quality of telecinematic discourse (Piazza, Bednarek and Rossi 2011; Wildfeuer 2014), the study will occasionally also consider visual aspects of representation, whenever they enhance or contribute to the one-sided verbal depiction. A qualitative and exemplary analysis of key scenes involving Mexicans or Mexican Americans will demonstrate that the Other, typically represented by vicious drug lords and their henchmen, ultimately serves the function of highlighting various facets of the US protagonists' personalities. Moreover, it will be shown that the series and films employ ideological stereotypes in order to meet the cultural expectations and preconceptions of a mainstream audience for the sake of economic success.

2. Characterisation in Telecinematic Discourse

Television and film can be subsumed under the heading of *telecinematic discourse* and are thus defined as "integrated multimodal (verbal and visual) fictional narratives" (Piazza, Bednarek and Rossi 2011: 1). As regards the communicative situation, these genres belong to the category of "screen-to-face" discourse (Bubel 2008: 64) at the level of producers and viewers. Within the fictional plot, this level is complemented by verbal interaction between the different characters (Bednarek 2010: 16). The inter-character dialogues are closely intertwined with the multimodal features of cinematography, music, and the audio track of sound effects (Wildfeuer 2014: 22-31). As Claudia Bubel argues, the film and TV production team will carry out an "overhearer design" (2008: 68), anticipating expectations and knowledge resources of their target group in order to create an appealing narrative. With respect to stereotyping, this means that scriptwriters and directors will to some extent choose well-established and preconceived ideas and images that overlap and harmonise with their audience's world knowledge.

In order to examine the construction of stereotypes, it is essential to take into account telecinematic characterisation strategies. Jonathan Culpeper (2001) has developed a suitable cognitive model of characterisation, explaining how "a representation of character [is] constructed in the mind during the process of reading" (2001: 34) or watching a film respectively. Accordingly, comprehension is regarded as a combination of two processes, which are (a) top-down inferencing based on the recipients' prior world knowledge stored in their long-term memory and (b) bottom-up effects of clues in the film discourse, including verbal and nonverbal communication of the characters as well as cinematographic devices. The two sides dynamically affect and correct each other, for "what you see influences what you know, and what you know influences what you see" (Culpeper 2001: 36), so that stereotypes are continuously reinforced. According to Norman Fairclough, Critical Discourse Analysis assumes a similar procedure of interpretation through viewers, arguing that textual cues cognitively activate so-called "members' resources" (2001: 118), which comprise ideological and culture-dependent preconceptions. As a result, characterisation processes are closely linked to the construction of biased images among audiences.

As far as discursive clues are concerned, it is useful to refer to the well-established distinction between direct and indirect characterisation. While "direct" or explicit characterisation manifests itself in traits attributed to characters by other characters or by the narrator, "indirect" or implicit characterisation relies on the characters' own linguistic choices and discursive strategies (Baldick 2008: 52). In the present telecinematic data, Mexicans and Mexican Americans are occasionally described by other persons, but they are chiefly characterised through their own utterances. Stereotypes, however, are ultimately constructed not on the inter-character plane but at the screen-to-face level of communication.

While the series *Breaking Bad* consists of five seasons that comprise 62 episodes with an average length of about 45 minutes (Thomson 2015: 84-91), the running times of the five feature films *Sicario*, *Traffic*, *The Last Stand*, *Savages*, and *The Counselor* range between 102 and 141 minutes. Hence, the series and films in total add up to over 56 hours of telecinematic discourse, allowing for valid observations on ethnic stereotyping. They all deal with drug-related crime at the Mexican-American border, featuring a variety of American protagonists with different professions. *Breaking Bad* tells the story of a high school chemistry teacher who is diagnosed with lung cancer and seizes the opportunity to financially provide for his family by producing and selling crystal meth to drug lords operating in New Mexico. In *The Last Stand*, an upright and tough small-town sheriff, who formerly worked for the Los Angeles narcotics department, arrests a notorious Mexican cartel boss that has just escaped from a federal prison. In *Traffic*, the head of the Office of National Drug Control Policy fights the war on drugs at the national level, so that high-ranking Mexican officials are involved in the plot as well. In *The Counselor*, a shady American drug-cartel lawyer unwittingly becomes the target of his former Mexican clients, who suspect him of embezzling their money. In *Savages*, the two young Californian drug dealers Ben and Chon decline the Baja Cartel's offer of cooperation, which leads to a violent conflict across the border. The protagonist of the film *Sicario* ("hitman") is the idealistic FBI agent Kate Mercer, who belongs to a task force fighting the Mexican Sonora cartel. Towards the end of this film, the cartel boss is assassinated by the Mexican killer Alejandro, who has been hired by the American authorities. With the help of numerous relevant examples, it will be shown that the Mexican antagonists are constructed as stereotypical villains through the recurrence of characteristic features.

3. Categorisation, Prototypes and Stereotypes

From a cognitive-linguistic perspective, the centre of a mental category is realised by a prototype, which serves as the most representative example, so that prototypes function as "reference points" (Taylor 2003: 45) for other potential members of the same category. Accordingly, less typical members are located in the periphery of a category, which implies that the boundaries between different categories are principally fuzzy. Conceptual categorisation fulfils significant functions for human beings, such as linguistic economy through the use of superordinate concepts which cover a wide range of entities. Moreover, prototypicality supports language users in their perception of the world and the recognition and classification of newly experienced phenomena (Croft and Cruse 2004: 74).

If a specific category contains visually perceptible physical objects, the respective prototype can be determined by the "similarity approach" to prototype theory (Croft and Cruse 2004: 82). With regard to the visual representation of ethnic groups in telecinematic discourse, this approach could focus on the prototypical outer appearance of a Mexican, including aspects such as clothing, hair style, and skin colour. Alternatively, a prototype can be defined by a list of attributes, so that "[t]he centrality of an item in the category depends on how many of the relevant set of features it possesses: the more it possesses, the better an example of the category it will be" (Croft and Cruse 2004: 81). As a result, this approach is highly relevant whenever the prototype is more abstract, as in the case of characteristic Mexican discursive behaviour. Along these lines, the present study compares the verbal behaviour and communicative strategies of fictional Mexicans in the data in order to isolate salient attributes. Although such a list of attributes is always changeable, open and expandable (Ungerer and Schmid 2006: 26-27), the identification of recurrent attributes allows revealing insights into current conceptualisations. It is important to note that a prototype is not regarded here as a specific individual but as a "mental representation" (Taylor 2003: 64) that is discursively constructed.

Although social stereotypes also locate persons and entities in conceptual categories, they differ from prototypes in two main ways. First, while prototypes are basically neutral and unprejudiced, stereotypes are "typically associated with evaluative features" (Croft and Cruse 2004: 81). Hence, they may result in derogatory labels for social or ethnic groups, which construct social actors in a discriminatory way, as disclosed by Critical Discourse Analysis (Reisigl and Wodak 2009: 94). Second, while the cognitive construction of prototypes takes place in an unobtrusive and unconscious manner, social stereotypes are often used consciously and strategically for the sake of ideological argumentation. Accordingly, since stereotypes are closely intertwined with "cultural expectations, they tend to be exploited in advertising and in most forms of popular entertainment" (Lakoff 1987: 85). In particular, thus, fictional film and television may employ well-known stereotypes in order to meet preconceptualisations and beliefs of their target audiences. Stereotypes can be established in life through personal experience or through culture-specific socialisation processes, as conveyed by education, parents and peers (Schneider 2004: 23), yet the influence of the mass media has continuously grown over the past decades.

4. Conventional Stereotypes of Mexicans as Cognitive Cultural Models

Stereotyping of Latin Americans has a long tradition in the USA, as corroborated by the monographs by Arthur G. Pettit (1980), Frank Javier Garcia Berumen (1995), Oscar J. Martínez (2001) and Charles Ramírez Berg (2002) as well as by an extensive chapter in Benshoff and Griffin (2009). In particular, as regards the representation of Latinos in Hollywood movies, Berg (2002) identifies six main stereotypes, which are defined according to both gender and dramaturgic roles in the movie plots. The criminal and illegal agenda is realised by the images of "*el bandido*" and "the harlot," while the comic roles are the "male buffoon" as well as the "female clown," and romantic or erotic functions are fulfilled by the "Latin lover" and the "dark lady" (Berg 2002: 66). Since the present dataset exclusively consists of examples from the crime drama and thriller genres, this study concentrates on the first of these three categories, the depiction of Mexican outlaws. In the conceptual category of Latino villains, their stereotypical outer appearance has changed in the second half of the twentieth century from the dishevelled, gap-toothed and begrimed bandit of Western movies to the elegant and well-groomed drug dealer in an expensive suit, displaying status symbols such as a luxurious hacienda, a private yacht or stylish prostitutes. In sum, however, until today the outwardly transformed gangsters remain "the same inarticulate, violent, and pathologically dangerous *bandidos*" (Berg 2002: 69).

In contrast to other ethnic minorities in the US, Mexicans on the American screen are associated with a relatively restricted geographical area, located "in the Southwest, in Texas and the states carved from the territory ceded in the Treaty of Guadalupe Hidalgo" (Pettit 1980: xv), through which California became a part of the United States in 1848. Due to the regional proximity of these states to Mexico, there is a tendency in films to place Latinos from other countries such as Colombia or Cuba, which are also frequently associated with crime, in the same category as Mexicans. Moreover, almost needless to say, Mexicans and Mexican Americans are hardly kept apart in American mainstream movies. In addition, Mexicans are not only subject to geographical restrictions but also to limitations with regard to film genre. In particular, the Mexican Other looms large mainly in "Westerns, social problem films, and the more recent urban violence films" (Noriega 1992: xv), among which the latter type is alternatively labelled the "gangster movie" (List 1996: 22). Such genres are marked by recurring conventions in the design of plot and characters, so that "by limiting the representation of Chicano identity to specific genres, Hollywood perpetually reproduces the stereotypes" (List 1996: 22).

On a historical note, the nineteenth century already saw American reporters, explorers and historians constructing pejorative images of the Catholic Mexican Other (Martínez 2001: 56). The ethnocentric American idea of Mexican inferiority was significantly fostered by the dominant ideology of Manifest Destiny (Benshoff and Griffin 2009: 143). With the establishment of silent films in the early 20th century, Mexicans appeared in cinemas mainly in the form of the so-called "greaser" character, which referred to the disrespected profession of greasing the axles of vehicles. With the help of an attribute list, a stereotypical greaser can be paraphrased as "a swarthy, dishonest, corrupt, conniving, incompetent, and sleazy individual" (Martínez 2001: 58). A few decades later, in the 1960s, atrocious Mexican bandits gradually replaced bloodthirsty Native Americans as the hostile Other in mainstream Western movies (Benshoff and Griffin 2009: 153). As the analysis of contemporary film and television will underline, such denigrating images have survived until today.

Since such stereotypical conceptualisations have been persistent over decades and even centuries in the USA, they constitute "cultural models," seminally defined by Dorothy Holland and Naomi Quinn as "presupposed, taken-for-granted models of the world that are widely shared [...] by the members of a society" (1987: 4). In other words, such models are culture-dependent "stored cognitive representations" (Ungerer and Schmid 2006: 49), referring to social beliefs, norms and categorisations. Cultural models form the foundation of common perspectives on social and discursive practices in ethnic groups (Kristiansen and Dirven 2008: 9), distinguishing the in-group from the out-group represented by the Other. As such, they have a decisive influence on audiences' top-down inferencing and interpretative processes (Stockwell 2002: 33). Hence, the perpetuation and enhancement of cultural models in the mass media may have significant sociopolitical consequences:

> Nightly news reports about violence and drugs along the border, as well as films like *Traffic* (2000) and *Bordertown* that center on such issues, may also be contributing to anti-Hispanic sentiments among some Americans. (Benshoff and Griffin 2009: 160)

Thus, as Critical Discourse Analysis argues, different types of mass communication constitute alternative forms of "social practice" and are therefore likely to construct biased images in an interdiscursive and mutually reinforcing manner (Wodak et al. 2009: 8). Along these lines, Donald Trump's xenophobic election campaign in 2015 and 2016 could also benefit from enduring and firmly established Mexican stereotypes (Schubert 2017a: 49-53). Metaphorically speaking, popular movies and television series can be regarded as a "powerful public textbook" (Cortés 1992: 91), since they subliminally convey attitudes and ideologies that may have actual effects on the everyday behaviour of individuals. In consideration of these premises, it is crucial to create an awareness of these mechanisms and to deconstruct prejudiced conceptualisations. This goal can be achieved by identifying their basic building blocks, as they manifest themselves in the form of specific characteristics.

5. Contemporary Attributes of Mexicans in American Film and Television

Through an analytical comparison of Mexican and Mexican American villains in the present telecinematic data, it is possible to isolate a number of distinctive attributes typical of this ethnic Other. Correspondingly, the more of these features an individual character in the series or films possesses, the closer he or she is to the *Stereotypical Mexican Villain*, henceforth abbreviated as *SMV*. Along these lines, the fundamental fuzziness of categories, as commonly highlighted by varying degrees of "birdiness" in the category *bird* (Ungerer and Schmid 2006: 27), applies to the *SMV* as well. As the distribution of distinctive attributes will demonstrate, different characters may show diverse degrees of *villainy*.

(a) *The SMV is greedy and corrupt.* When the series or films feature shady individuals belonging to the Mexican administration or police force, these officials are usually depicted as corrupt, neglecting their duties in favour of an additional illegal income. In this way, crime is associated not only with the obvious drug dealers on the street but also with civil servants supposed to uphold and enforce the law, which makes the situation in the country even more threatening. In *Traffic*, for instance, the Mexican general Arturo Salazar informs the US politician Wakefield, played by Michael Douglas, that the fight against drug trafficking is "a very difficult task because of the corruption in the police force [...]" (1:25:41). This is a case of direct characterisation of Mexican police officers, but in contrast to the general's American conversational partner, the film viewers are informed that Salazar himself works for the Juárez Cartel. Hence, this statement also indirectly characterises the general not only as criminal but also as hypocritical, with the consequence of dramatic irony at the producer-audience level. An earlier scene in this film confirms Salazar's bleak assessment, when in Tijuana two anonymous American tourists report their car stolen. After they have addressed police officer Javier

Rodriguez, he gives them the phone number of an enigmatic man and advises them to call him:

> FEMALE TOURIST. How is this guy gonna know who has our car?
> JAVIER RODRIGUEZ. The police will tell him.
> MALE TOURIST. (*Scoffs.*) Why will they tell him, and they won't tell us?
> FEMALE TOURIST. (*To her husband.*) Because we pay him, stupid. (*To Rodriguez.*) Right? And he pays the police, and suddenly our car appears.
> JAVIER RODRIGUEZ. (*Nods and smiles.*) Es – es – es correct. Es correct. (*Traffic*, 0:20:06)

The police officer, here embodied by Benicio del Toro, is linguistically marked as the Other by a distinct Spanish accent as well as by interlingual code-switching ("es correct"). As far as corruption is concerned, the police have obviously found a treacherous way to hide their illegal activities through the introduction of a mysterious middleman. The attribution of corruption is here less direct than in the words of Salazar, but the female tourist's paraphrase and Rodriguez's confirmation leave no doubt about the police's lawlessness.

In *Sicario*, the Mexican-born hitman Alejandro Gillick, who works for the US authorities and is also played by Benicio del Toro, warns the FBI agent Kate Mercer of the Mexican police when they arrive in Juárez, advising her to "keep an eye out for the state police. They're not always the good guys" (0:30:44). In this direct form of characterisation, the Mexican officers are vaguely labelled as criminals, which not only entails corruption but also other felonies. Throughout the film, the truth of this assessment is corroborated by the corrupt Mexican police officer Silvio, who secretly works as a drug courier for the Sonora Cartel. Similarly, in *The Last Stand*, the Mexican drug boss Gabriel Cortez comments that "in my country the police say *gracias* after being paid off" (0:36:25). Thus, here the Mexican antagonist directly characterises Mexican police officers as corrupt and at the same time indirectly frames himself as a villain who habitually bribes officials. However, when Cortez eventually offers money to the principled sheriff Owens, this paragon of virtue declines with the words "my honor is not for sale" (*The Last Stand*, 1:29:46), foregrounding American moral superiority.

(b) *The SMV is aggressive and brutal.* In addition to corrupt and fraudulent behaviour, the Mexican Other is very frequently marked by both physical and psychological brutality, commonly used by villains to gain material wealth or to exercise power. In *Breaking Bad*, for example, the drug distributor Tuco Salamanca serves as the epitome of irrational and unpredictable violence. After killing his own bodyguard No-Doze at a junkyard with his bare hands under the influence of crystal meth, he frantically shouts "damn, man! Look at that! Look! Whoo! That's messed up" (*Breaking Bad*, episode 1.07, 0:43:52). His actions and words thus reveal a complete neglect for human life and imply a threat towards his new business partners Walter White and Jesse Pinkman, so that he is indirectly characterised as a dangerous and narcissistic psychopath. When Walter and Jesse are abducted by Tuco but finally manage to overpower and kill him, Walter directly characterises the Mexican as an "insane, degenerate piece of filth" (*Breaking Bad*, episode 2.02, 0:40:10). Such bottom-up clues of characterisation by Walter and Jesse mutually reinforce each other and can easily be integrated in viewers' preconceptualisations of Mexican violence, as acquired through news media or other fictional representations.

In *Savages*, the enforcer Lado, again impersonated by Benicio del Toro, is a similarly sociopathic personality, mercilessly murdering enemies of the Mexican Baja Cartel. In one scene, before he kills a disloyal American lawyer, he sadistically shoots his victim in both kneecaps and informs a fellow criminal on the phone: "Oh, we're just making gringo-lawyer soup here in the kitchen" (*Savages*, 0:18:38). Like in the case of Tuco, Lado's lexical choice shows a cynical disrespect for human beings, since he uses the racist label "gringo" and figuratively equates the American with "soup." The mapping of the two domains implies that through the blood loss the victim's body is being liquefied to resemble soup, and since this dish is usually a starter, the metaphor foreshadows further killings. Accordingly, the physical activity of murder and the verbal utterance jointly characterise Lado as a barbarous killer in an indirect way. Since the actor Benicio del Toro is a ubiquitous face in drug-cartel thrillers, experienced viewers of such films will add this fact to their genre knowledge. As a consequence, such audience members may use this information in the process of top-down inferencing, so that the image of the shady Mexican killer is also supported through the strategy of typecasting, associating individual actors with specific roles.

In *Savages*, the attribute of brutality manifests itself not only in male characters but also in the posh cartel boss Elena Sánchez, who in one scene has dinner with her American hostage Ophelia. While eating, Sánchez threatens to murder her two friends with the words "I like talking to you, Ophelia. But let me remind you that if I had to, I wouldn't have a problem cutting both their throats" (*Savages*, 1:30:28). This utterance, which exemplifies verbal and psychological violence and hints at physical butchery, has a shocking effect, since it stands in stark contrast to the otherwise civil and polite dinner table conversation. Correspondingly, negative stereotyping here is immanent to the ethnic group of Mexicans but transcends the borders of gender, thus expanding the stereotype of the Mexican criminal.

In *The Counselor*, cartel members do not frequently appear on the screen, so that their cruelty is voiced mainly in explicit utterances by Americans. For instance, the dubious American businessman Westray informs the eponymous counsellor about cartel atrocities including decapitation, snuff films, and necrophilia, drawing the following bleak conclusion: "the point, Counselor, is that you may think there are things that these people are simply incapable of. There are not" (*The Counselor*, 1:04:41). This type of inverse characterisation, based on the negative prefix *in-* and the particle *not*, opens room for unlimited speculation about further abominations by the Mexican cartel gangsters. This expansion of the perspective from Mexican individuals to larger groups is also present in *Sicario*, when a convoy of American DEA and FBI agents arrives in the city of Juárez. One American officer looks out of the car window and provides his colleagues with a gloomy historical flashback, accompanied by eerie and threatening music:

> AMERICAN FEDERAL AGENT. There she is. The beast, Juárez. You know, nineteen hundreds, president Taft went to visit president Díaz. Took 4,000 men with him. And it was almost called off, 'cause some guy had a pistol. Wanted to walk right up to Taft and blow his brains out. But it was avoided. 4,000 troops. Think he felt safe? (*Sicario*, 0:25:00)

This brief narrative sequence dominantly foregrounds the diachronic dimension of stereotyping. In addition to the personification through the feminine personal pronoun *she*, the city is metaphorically labelled a "beast," which highlights the dangerous and savage character of its inhabitants. Moreover, the juxtaposition of "4,000 men" on the American side with "some guy" on the Mexican underlines the tremendous potential for violence represented even by single members of the Other. This impression is further enhanced when the federal agents see mutilated bodies hanging from a railway bridge, upon which the Mexican-origin CIA official Alejandro sarcastically comments to Kate Mercer: "welcome to Juárez" (*Sicario*, 0:27:40). This expressive speech act of ironic welcoming implies that such inhumanity is characteristic of Ciudad Juárez. As far as the imagery of *beasts* is concerned, drug kingpin Gabriel Cortez in *The Last Stand* drives a tuned Corvette, which is labelled by an American police officer a "monster on wheels" (0:24:25), so that the Mexican driver is placed in the same menacing category.

(c) *The SMV places tremendous emphasis on family ties.* In many scenes, Mexican criminals use the importance of family ties as an argumentative strategy, either to enhance social coherence in their own community or in order to threaten opponents. In *Breaking Bad*, for instance, cartel boss Hector Salamanca uses ruthless methods to teach his nephews Leonel and Marco the lesson "la familia es todo" ("family is all"): after Leonel had uttered that he wished his brother was dead, Hector keeps Marco's head under water until Leonel starts to hit his uncle (*Breaking Bad*, episode 3.07, 0:02:51). This is a symptomatic scene that represents the stereotypical Mexican amalgamation of family values with brutality.

In *Savages*, when hitman Lado tortures his former colleague Alex to get a confession of treason, he threatens to slaughter Alex's wife and children. After the brutally enforced admission of guilt, Lado concludes that "a man takes care of his family, and I respect that. I'd like to give you a better death. But it would set a bad example" (*Savages*, 1:42:04). In this way, Lado instrumentalises and ultimately mocks Alex's responsibility for his family, reducing the positive connotations of "respect" to absurdity. Similarly, as cartel boss Elena Sánchez learns about the ménage à trois of their Californian drug producers Ben and Chon, she tells Lado on the phone: "interesting people, Americans. I think I found their weakness. Is she pretty?" (*Savages*, 0:38:10). Accordingly, she orders her henchmen to abduct Ophelia, the female member in the love triangle, while at the end of the film the two Americans likewise kidnap Elena's estranged daughter in California, beating the cartel boss at her own game. In this way, the film plot suggests that Mexican methods of abduction and extortion are inevitably imported into the US. Along these lines, it is also noteworthy that the film title of *Savages* is ambiguous. On the one hand, the Americans consider the Mexican cartel members as barbarous because of their bloody acts of violence, as Chon comments that "savages don't make deals" (0:56:57). On the other hand, Lado calls Californians "savages" for their sexual promiscuity and liberal lifestyle (*Savages*, 0:35:25). However, Lado is indirectly characterised as a hypocrite, since his utterances on family ties and tradition are called into question by the fact that he frequents prostitutes.

In *The Last Stand*, Gabriel Cortez finds sadistic pleasure in destroying American families, which appears particularly threatening in view of the stereotypical Mexican abundance of children. After escaping from prison, he deliberately shoots the police officer McKay with the words "baby on the way, right?" (*The Last Stand*, 0:21:09), and when he takes the young female agent Ellen Richards hostage, he warns her superior on the phone that he will dismember her body: "how are you gonna explain to her parents why their daughter is returning home in plastic bags?" (*The Last Stand*, 0:30:54). This threat serves as a metaphor for the stereotypical Mexican disintegration of familial and societal structures in the US. In *Sicario*, the hitman Alejandro surprises the Mexican cartel boss Alarcón sitting at the dinner table with his wife and two young sons, facing him with the words "every night, you have families killed. And yet, here you dine. Tonight should be no different" (*Sicario*, 1:41:00). Since Alarcón had Alejandro's wife and daughter murdered, now the latter shoots Alarcón and his entire family. This scene not only shows the unscrupulousness and inhumanity of cartel bosses and Mexican hitmen, it also stereotypically underlines the blending of private family matters with the merciless business of drug trafficking.

(d) *The SMV is unpredictable and opaque.* A highly salient feature of members of the Mexican Other is their impenetrable and inexplicable culture and mindset from a US perspective, as highlighted by Alejandro addressing FBI agent Kate in *Sicario*: "listen, nothing will make sense to your American ears. And you will doubt everything we do. But in the end you will understand" (0:22:14). This assessment chiefly refers to his idiosyncratic methods of tracking down the Mexican Cartel boss Alarcón, as legitimised by US officials. At the same time, the statement meta-fictionally addresses the viewers, who are informed about Alejandro's personal vendetta not until the finale of the film.

In many scenes, the aggression of the *SMV* manifests itself in subliminally threatening allusions and innuendoes, which at the producer-viewer level have the function of enhancing suspense. For instance, when hitman Lado pays the corrupt police officer Dennis a visit at his home, he explains that "I was driving by your neighbourgood [*sic*] and noticed that your yard needs some trimming. My crew would like to give you a free haircut today" (*Savages*, 1:45:48). Since the audience is aware of how Lado previously tortured and murdered an American lawyer, the metaphor of the "haircut" implies violent action. Similarly, in *The Last Stand*, after a dangerous stunt in a race car cartel boss Gabriel Cortez opaquely advises his accomplice "don't try to see death coming. You won't" (0:51:44) and eventually throws her out of his car while driving. In *The Counselor*, the protagonist receives a phone call by Jefe, a senior cartel member, who verbally tortures the counsellor with ambiguous information about his abducted fiancée and challenges him with the question "do you love your wife so much, so completely, that you would exchange places with her upon the wheel? And I don't mean dying, because dying is easy" (1:32:36). When the counsellor consents to this proposition under tears, Jefe tells him that the exchange is impossible since the counsellor himself is responsible for the situation through his past actions. In *Breaking Bad*, Don Eladio, the head of the Juárez cartel, indirectly warns the Chileans Max Arciniega and Gustavo Fring, who are the owners of a chicken restaurant and drug distributors, not to get in the Mexican cartel's way:

> DON ELADIO. Your chicken, it's so zesty, piquant. But it does not taste like a Mexican style.
> MAX ARCINIEGA. It's a recipe I learned in Chile which I've modified a bit for the Mexican palate.
> DON ELADIO. I bet we like a little more chilli than you Chileans. We Mexicans like a good hard kick! (*Breaking Bad*, episode 4.08, 0:35:20)

By establishing an opposition between the "Mexican style" and Arciniega's recipe, Don Eladio already indicates his dislike for the Chileans as representatives of the South American competitors in the drug business. Through the pun based on the homophony of "chilli" and "Chile" in collocation with the comparative quantifier "more," the national distinction is further supported. Finally, in this short extract, the metaphor of the "good hard kick" may not only refer to the taste of the chicken but also to physical violence employed with an aggressively intimidating intention.

Apart from such indirect and equivocal discursive strategies, the Mexican Other is also marked by opaque communication forms that further support the menacing aura. In *Savages*, for instance, the voice of Elena Sánchez is distorted and her face cannot be seen during a Skype conversation, in which she forces the American drug producer Chon to take a gun and "stick it in that vulgar mouth of yours" (0:48:44). Since the pitch of her voice is lowered, it is not even clear to the addressees that they talk to a female cartel boss. In *Breaking Bad*, Hector Salamanca's twin nephews Marco and Leonel, who work as contract killers for the cartel, do not speak at all but exclusively use nonverbal communication, such as nodding to each other in agreement. Owing to their minimal use of facial expressions, the twins appear like merciless killing machines that are in no way inhibited by second thoughts.

The most opaque and cumbersome way of communication in the telecinematic narratives is employed by the character Hector Salamanca, who sits in a wheelchair and has lost his ability to speak due to a stroke. As a consequence, he uses a small bell attached to his chair in order to answer *yes/no* questions and to spell out utterances with the help of an alpha-numeric card handled by his geriatric nurse. In the following scene, DEA agent Hank Schrader and other officials under the leadership of agent

George Merkert try to retrieve information from Hector at the police station:

> HANK SCHRADER. So, Mr. Salamanca, you got something you wanna tell me? (*Hector rings bell.*)
> GERIATRIC NURSE. (*Moving her hand across the alpha-numeric card.*) A, E, I, O. (*Hector rings bell.*) Row O. P, Q, R, S. (*Hector rings bell.*) First letter S. A, E, I, O, U. (*Hector rings bell several times.*) Second letter U. A. (*Hector rings bell.*) B, C. (*Hector rings bell.*), A, E, I. (*Hector rings bell.*) J, K. (*Hector rings bell.*), A, E, I. (*Hector rings bell.*) J, K, L, M. (*Hector rings bell.*), A, E, I, O, U. (*Hector rings bell.*), Row U. V, W, X, Y (*Hector rings bell.*)
> GEORGE MERKERT. All right. That's enough. Thank you. (*MERKERT shows written note "SUCK MY" to HANK.*)
> HANK SCHRADER. Yeah, thanks. I can spell. (*Breaking Bad*, episode 4.13, 0:23:35)

In suspenseful anticipation, a great number of police officers in the interrogation room expect valuable inside information on drug trafficking. However, they are disappointed by the first two words forming the vulgar imperative "suck my," which can easily be complemented by the predictable linguistic collocation *dick*. By means of the very slow and tiresome spelling process, Hector not only wastes the police's time but also ridicules the US authorities. In this way, he is indirectly characterised as a cunning and aggressive wretch who refunctionalises his communicative disability as a weapon against law enforcement.

(e) *The SMV is deficient in moral and linguistic ways*. In the telecinematic dialogues, interlocutors of Mexican ethnicity are framed not only as different from Americans but also as deficient in various ways. In *Traffic*, for example, the cultural distinctiveness on both sides of the border is established already in the beginning of the film through the technique of colour-coding, since Mexico is cinematographically depicted in grainy yellowish hues, while America is portrayed in different shades of blue. This visual differentiation can be equated with American rationality and professionalism in contrast to the dusty and chaotic Mexican wasteland. Accordingly, at the El Paso Intelligence Center, the politician Bob Wakefield asks the question "who has my job in Mexico?" and receives the answer "your position doesn't exist over there yet" (*Traffic*, 1:04:39), which foregrounds the stereotypical deficiency and carelessness of authorities south of the border. In a subsequent meeting with General Salazar in Mexico, Wakefield mentions American financial support for Mexico in the war on drugs and inquires about Salazar's views on the treatment of addicts. To Wakefield's consternation, Salazar replies that "addicts treat themselves. They overdose, and then there's one less to worry about" (*Traffic*, 1:25:39). Hence, Mexican authorities appear utterly indifferent to serious social problems and completely unwilling to invest energy in their solution.

Apart from this deficiency in moral standards and sociopolitical activity, Mexicans and Mexican Americans appear inferior also due to their lower linguistic proficiency in English. Since characters such as Gabriel Cortez in *The Last Stand* or Lado in *Savages* speak with a pronounced Spanish accent, this can be interpreted as a metaphor for both Otherness and intellectual limitations, which supposedly make it impossible for Mexicans to compete with American resourcefulness (Berg 2002: 68). Accordingly, Hector Salamanca's inability to speak and to engage in complex conversations, as outlined above, further enhances the stereotype of Mexican linguistic incapacity. In *Breaking Bad*, the stereotypical slang of uneducated Mexican drug dealers is contrasted with the eloquence of chemical scientist Walter White, who adopts a professional approach to the drug trade. This becomes clear in the following dialogue towards the end of season one, in which Walter White and Tuco Salamanca negotiate the terms and conditions of their illegal business cooperation:

> TUCO SALAMANCA. (*Shouts.*) What, you're gonna argue? You got something to say? You're doing business like a couple little bitches (*turns to go*).
> WALTER WHITE. I want all of it. Seventy grand.
> TUCO SALAMANCA. What did you say?
> WALTER WHITE. You like this product, and you want more. Consider it a capital investment.
> TUCO SALAMANCA. Loco bald motherfucker. (*Breaking Bad*, episode 1.07, 0:12:30)

Walter's discursive strategy is marked by technical terms from the domain of economics, such as "product" and "capital investment." In contrast, his Mexican business partner in drug trafficking prefers aggressive threats containing expletives and vulgar insults such as "bitches" and "motherfucker," complemented by the Spanish adjective "loco" ("crazy"). As a result, Tuco's utterances exclusively show the informal and colloquial register of Mexican gangster talk, which indirectly characterises him as cognitively limited and verbally deficient. Thus, in contrast to the academic Walter White, who has at his disposal a wide range of situationally adequate linguistic levels (Schubert 2017b: 44), the Mexican thug Tuco is not able to switch to the technical register of business communication.

6. Concluding Remarks on Mexican Stereotyping and Chicano Resistance

To conclude, Mexicans and Mexican Americans are frequently depicted in one-sided and deprecating ways in American fictional film and television covering drug trafficking at the common border. Through a comparative investigation of popular and successful examples of telecinematic representation, it is possible to identify five main attributes that constitute the stereotype of the Mexican villain (*SMV*) through direct and indirect characterisation. The *SMV* is (a) greedy and corrupt, (b) aggressive and brutal, (c) highly emphatic about family ties, (d) unpredictable and opaque, and (e) deficient in moral and linguistic ways. Accordingly, the more of these attributes a specific character on the screen has, the closer he or she is to the disrespectful stereotype constructed on the American screen. In telecinematic discourse, the process of verbal Othering is additionally supported by cinematographic techniques such as colour-coding.

As Mexican villains fulfil various professional and societal functions in the domain of drug trafficking, the stereotype manifests itself in four more specific substereotypes. First, there is the violent Mexican drug dealer, who is epitomised, for instance, by the choleric Tuco Salamanca in *Breaking Bad*. Second, the mysterious and equivocal Mexican hitman appears, for example, in the form of Alejandro Gillick in *Sicario*. Third, the eloquent and malevolent Mexican cartel boss is prominently portrayed through Elena Sánchez in *Savages*, undermining male dominance in the villain stereotype. Fourth, telecinematic narratives feature the treacherous Mexican official, who surreptitiously cooperates with cartels, as depicted, for instance, by General Arturo Salazar in *Traffic*.

In several cases, the American protagonists, such as Walter White, the eponymous counsellor, or the two drug dealers Ben and Chon in *Savages*, also pursue a criminal agenda. However, in contrast to the Mexican villains, the American main characters are constructed as complex and multi-faceted antiheroes with whom the viewers can empathise, since their social circumstances and psychological motives are made transparent and the plot is presented from their personal vantage point. As a consequence, the narrative function of the often one-dimensional Mexican antagonists is to characterise the American protagonists by highlighting different facets of their personality. At the communicative level of producer and audience, the stereotype of the Mexican villain is employed by scriptwriters and directors in order to link in with biased ideas entertained by the target groups.

The dissemination of pejorative images of an ethnic group in fictional telecinematic narratives may have serious sociopolitical consequences, since established stereotypes form cultural models that can be utilised in political rhetoric, as seen in Donald Trump's 2015 and 2016 election campaign. Thus, telecinematic discourse contributes to the construction of cognitive templates that can be filled with ideological meaning and may be employed for the sake of partisan argumentation. It is therefore unsurprising that already in the 1960s the "Chicano Movement" (List 1996: 3) put up resistance against distorted representations of Hispanics by the mainstream Hollywood film industry. A more recent example of an influential Mexican American director is Robert Rodriguez, who has been a highly successful Hollywood filmmaker subverting and countering conventional preconceptions since the 1990s (Benshoff and Griffin 2009: 157). For instance, he co-directed the farcical action movie *Machete* from 2010, in which Danny Trejo impersonates a tough and principled former Mexican police officer who fights a corrupt, treacherous and xenophobic Texas State Senator. Even more recently, cinematic resistance is offered in the form of a counter narrative in the crime thriller *Desierto* from 2015, directed by the Mexican filmmaker Jonás Cuarón. This film tells the story of a group of migrant workers from Mexico who cross the border with the hope for a better life but are ruthlessly hunted down and shot by an American vigilante killer.

Occasionally, mainstream Hollywood movies by non-Mexican directors throw a satirical light on the conflict at the border, such as Roland Emmerich's 2004 disaster movie *The Day After Tomorrow*. In this film, a catastrophic climate change results in a renewed ice age in North America, so that US citizens are forced to seek refuge in Mexico as the southern neighbour. It is also worthwhile to mention the Spanish-language remake of *Breaking Bad*, entitled *Metástasis*, which was produced in 2014 by Sony Entertainment Television Latin America in cooperation with a Colombian TV company. It features Colombian television actors and is set in Bogotá, Colombia, so that the protagonist, here named Walter Blanco, is Latin American. However, although the process of Othering is thus undermined and resistance may be part of the agenda behind this remake, it seems that the main objective was to address new audiences in Latin America.

It would be desirable for future research to thoroughly explore multimodal cinematographic means of ethnic stereotyping and to investigate the ways in which other telecinematic genres utilise misrepresentations of Mexicans in order to meet audience preconceptions. For instance, it could be illuminating to examine the image of Latina domestic servants in rather humorous films such as *Spanglish* from 2004 or in the successful American television series *Devious Maids*, which aired from 2013 to 2016. From a critical discourse-analytical perspective, it is crucial to make audiences aware that even highly acclaimed films and cutting-edge television series in the realm of quality TV may perpetuate very conventional stereotypes of ethnic groups. It remains to be seen whether the anti-Mexican agenda of President Donald Trump will have an impact on the representation of Mexicans on the American screen, possibly provoking increased resistance or furthering pejorative stereotyping.

Filmography (DVDs)

Gilligan, Vince, prod. 2008-2013. *Breaking Bad: Seasons 1-5*. Culver City, CA: Sony Pictures Television, Inc.
Jee-Woon, Kim, dir. 2013. *The Last Stand*. Los Angeles, CA: Di Bonaventura Pictures.
Scott, Ridley, dir. 2013. *The Counselor*. Los Angeles, CA: Twentieth Century Fox.
Soderbergh, Steven, dir. 2000. *Traffic*. Los Angeles, CA: Initial Entertainment Group.
Stone, Oliver, dir. 2012. *Savages*. Los Angeles, CA: Universal Studios.
Villeneuve, Denis, dir. 2015. *Sicario*. Los Angeles, CA: Black Label Media.

References

Baldick, Chris. 2008. *The Oxford Dictionary of Literary Terms*. Oxford: Oxford University Press.
Bednarek, Monika. 2010. *The Language of Fictional Television: Drama and Identity*. London: Continuum.
Benshoff, Harry M. and Sean Griffin. 2009. *America on Film: Representing Race, Class, Gender and Sexuality at the Movies*. Chichester: John Wiley & Sons.
Berg, Charles Ramírez. 2002. *Latino Images in Film: Stereotypes, Subversion, Resistance*. Austin: University of Texas Press.
Berumen, Frank Javier Garcia. 1995. *The Chicano/Hispanic Image in American Film*. New York: Vantage Press.
Bubel, Claudia M. 2008. "Film Audiences as Overhearers." *Journal of Pragmatics* 40.1, 55-71.

Cortés, Carlos E. 1992. "Who is Maria? What is Juan? Dilemmas of Analyzing the Chicano Image in U.S. Feature Films." In: Chon A. Noriega, ed. *Chicanos and Film: Representation and Resistance.* Minneapolis: University of Minnesota Press, 74-93.

Croft, William and D. Alan Cruse. 2004. *Cognitive Linguistics.* Cambridge: Cambridge University Press.

Culpeper, Jonathan. 2001. *Language and Characterisation: People in Plays and other Texts.* London: Longman.

Fairclough, Norman. 2001. *Language and Power.* 2nd ed. Harlow: Pearson Education.

Geeraerts, Dirk. 2007. "Where Does Prototypicality Come from?" In: Vyvyan Evans, Benjamin K. Bergen, and Jörg Zinken, eds. *The Cognitive Linguistics Reader.* London: Equinox, 168-185.

Holland, Dorothy and Naomi Quinn. 1987. "Culture and Cognition." In: Dorothy Holland and Naomi Quinn, eds. *Cultural Models in Language and Thought.* Cambridge: Cambridge University Press, 3-40.

Kristiansen, Gitte and René Dirven. 2008. "Cognitive Sociolinguistics: Rationale, Methods and Scope." In: Gitte Kristiansen and René Dirven, eds. *Cognitive Sociolinguistics: Language Variation, Cultural Models, Social Systems.* Berlin: Mouton de Gruyter, 1-17.

Lakoff, George. 1987. *Women, Fire, and Dangerous Things: What Categories Reveal about the Mind.* Chicago: University of Chicago Press.

List, Christine. 1996. *Chicano Images: Refiguring Ethnicity in Mainstream Film.* New York: Garland Publishing.

Martínez, Oscar J., ed. 2001. *Mexican-Origin People in the United States: A Topical History.* Tucson: The University of Arizona Press.

Noriega, Chon A. 1992. "Introduction." In: Chon A. Noriega, ed. *Chicanos and Film: Representation and Resistance.* Minneapolis: University of Minnesota Press, xi-xxvi.

Pettit, Arthur G. 1980. *Images of the Mexican American in Fiction and Film.* College Station: Texas A&M University Press.

Piazza, Roberta, Monika Bednarek, and Fabio Rossi, eds. 2011. *Telecinematic Discourse: Approaches to the Language of Films and Television Series.* Amsterdam: John Benjamins.

Reisigl, Martin and Ruth Wodak. 2009. "The Discourse-Historical Approach (DHA)." In: Ruth Wodak and Michael Meyer, eds. *Methods of Critical Discourse Analysis.* 2nd ed. London: Sage, 87-121.

Schneider, David J. 2004. *The Psychology of Stereotyping.* New York: The Guilford Press.

Schubert, Christoph. 2017a. "Constructing Mexican Stereotypes: Telecinematic Discourse and Donald Trump's Campaign Rhetoric." *CADAAD Journal: Critical Approaches to Discourse Analysis across Disciplines* 8.2, 37-57.
—. 2017b. "Constructing the Antihero: Linguistic Characterisation in Current American Television Series." *Journal of Literary Semantics* 46.1, 25-46.
Stockwell, Peter. 2002. *Cognitive Poetics: An Introduction*. London: Routledge.
Taylor, John R. 2003. *Linguistic Categorization*. 3rd ed. Oxford: Oxford University Press.
Thomson, David, ed. 2015. *Breaking Bad: The Official Book*. Toronto: Sterling.
Ungerer, Friedrich and Hans-Jörg Schmid. 2006. *An Introduction to Cognitive Linguistics*. 2nd ed. Harlow: Pearson Education Limited.
Wildfeuer, Janina. 2014. *Film Discourse Interpretation: Towards a New Paradigm for Multimodal Film Analysis*. London: Routledge.
Wodak, Ruth, Rudolf de Cillia, Martin Reisigl, and Karin Liebhart. 2009. *The Discursive Construction of National Identity*. 2nd ed. Edinburgh: Edinburgh University Press.

CHAPTER TWO

REMEMBER THE ALAMO:
THE PERSISTENCE OF CULTURAL
STEREOTYPES IN LITERARY AND FILMIC
REPRESENTATIONS OF THE MEXICAN
AMERICAN BORDERLANDS

JUTTA ZIMMERMANN

1. Introduction

Allegedly, "Remember the Alamo" is the battle cry with which Texians – American born Mexican citizens who had settled in the northern borderlands of Mexico –went into the battle of San Jacinto in 1836 under their leader Sam Houston. The Americans won a triumphant victory against the troops of Mexican general Santa Anna and gained Texas its independence. Nine years later, Texas joined the United States of America and became the 28th state. "Remember the Alamo" has since often been invoked to remind Americans of the need to defend democracy and freedom against the supposed threat of tyranny. The historical significance of the Alamo lies in the effect it had on Texians and American settlers in Texas. The Alamo provided them with time to unite their forces and to prepare for the military confrontation with Santa Anna's army. According to the monument erected at San Jacinto, the battle changed world history: almost a third of what is United States territory today was won at San Jacinto. Besides the military actions taken by General Sam Houston, the determination of the Americans and their allies to take revenge for the defeat at the Alamo is said to have been the factor which turned the tables in favor of the Americans.

The battle cry "Remember the Alamo" and the continued presence of the event in American popular culture and public discourse underlines the significance that cultural memory and cultural stereotypes have for the construction of a national collective identity. Cultural memory, as defined by Jan Assmann, refers to the function which representations of the past serve in establishing and affirming a collective identity. According to Assmann, cultural memory is "the body of reusable texts, images, and rituals specific to each society in each epoch, whose "cultivation" serves to stabilize and convey that society's self-image" (Assmann 1995: 132). In a similar vein, Mieke Bal emphasizes that cultural memory – in contradistinction to history – is not so much concerned with the past and with historical truth than it is about the present and future needs of a community. "Cultural memorization," Bal argues, is "an activity occurring in the present, in which the past is continuously modified and redescribed even as it continues to shape the future" (Bal 1999: vii).

In the context of a volume entitled "Disrespected Neighbors," the Alamo provides a perfect illustration of the processes by which a wedge is driven through a community thereby turning what used to be neighbors into citizens or full members of a group on the one side and into outsiders who are bereft of their individuality and humanity and become invisible on the other side. The phrase "disrespected neighbors" seems somewhat of an oxymoron that highlights the divisive function of identity discourses, such as, for example, nationalism which constructs a homogeneous imagined community and from the divisive moment on, treats those who do not fit the criteria as outsiders. Typically, this social exclusion is performed by rhetorical acts of dehumanization, such as, for example, referring to all those who do not fit the criteria for belonging to the imagined community as "foreign elements." The numerous retellings of the Alamo thus have an important function in affirming and legitimizing the nation-state – first Texas, later the United States. A narrative of defeat (cf. Flores 2002: xiv) is turned into a myth that naturalizes the establishment of the modern nation-state as the victory of democracy over tyranny, a process which Anibal Quijano characterizes as "the formation of structures of power":

> [...] the nation-state began as a process of colonization of some peoples over others that were, in this sense, foreigners and therefore the nation-state depended on the organization of one centralized state over a conquered state of domination. [...] It began as an internal colonization of peoples with different identities who inhabited the same territories as the colonizers. (Quijano 2000: 558)

In the following, I will analyze representations of the Alamo over the last 180 years as manifestations of cultural memory whose function it has been to express the American nation's self-image. Literary and filmic representations of the historical battle of the Alamo range from a poem published in the same year as the battle over John Wayne and John Lee Hancock's Western movies to contemporary films and historical novels published after 2000. The focus will be on the question of how a battle whose historical significance has often been doubted could become an American myth and how this myth has been challenged in recent decades. Most of the retellings since the 1980s have a revisionist agenda and are meant to challenge the cultural stereotypes of freedom-loving, self-reliant Americans against authority-prone and morally weak Mexicans that were established at the time when the battle of the Alamo took place. Similarly, whereas earlier representations imagine Texas and Mexico as sharply divided imagined communities, more recent representations challenge this binarism and present the borderlands as shaped and constituted by complex and intersectional relations along categories such as race and class, gender, and sexual orientation. However, while each individual retelling challenges and revises earlier stereotypical representations, it also paradoxically reaffirms and perpetuates these stereotypes, if only be evoking and calling them to mind.

2. Johnny Cash, "Remember the Alamo": The Alamo as Mythical Narrative

Johnny Cash's rendering of the song "Remember the Alamo" best illustrates the mythic quality of the Alamo narrative. At a live performance of the song at a concert in Madison Square Garden in 1969, Johnny Cash introduced the song as a "history lesson" thus foregrounding the relevance of this past event for a nation that was engaged in the Vietnam war:

A hundred and eighty were challenged by Travis to die
By the line that he drew with his sword when the battle was nigh.
Any man that would fight to the death cross over,
But him that would live better fly
And over the line went a hundred and seventy-nine
Hey Santa Anna we're killing your soldiers below
That men where ever they go,
will remember the Alamo.

Bowie lay dyin', but his powder was ready and dry
Flat on his back Bowie killed him a few in reply
And young David Crockett was singin' and laughin',
With gallantry fierce in his eyes
For God and for freedom, a man more than willin' to die
Hey Santa Anna we're killing your soldiers below,
that men where ever they go,

will remember the Alamo.

> And then they sent a young scout from the battlements bloody and loud,
> With the words of farewell from a garrison valiant and proud
> "Grieve not little darlin' my dyin', if Texas is sovereign and free,
> We'll never surrender and ever with liberty be"
> Hey Santa Anna we're killing your soldiers below,
> that men where ever they go, will remember the Alamo. (Cash 1963)

The song presents a stripped-down version of the battle of the Alamo. It opens with a reference to an event that might or might not have taken place. Allegedly, when it had become clear that no reinforcements could be expected and the defense of the fort would mean certain death, commander William Travis drew a line in the sand and gave each man a choice either to escape under the cover of night or fight to the last man. According to legend, all but one man crossed the line. Besides Travis, two other individuals are named. These are the legendary frontier heroes James Bowie and Davy Crockett. History is here turned into myth as the song reduces a very complex history of conflicting interests into a battle between hero and villain, good and evil.

Like the three individuals mentioned in the song, thousands of Americans had moved to what was then part of Mexico. The Mexican government had invited American settlers to help defend the sparsely populated area against Indian tribes, yet by 1830 tried to put a stop to the influx since Americans had become a majority in the region and started to pose a threat to the Mexican control over the region. A violent conflict broke out when the government tried to tighten its hold over the province. Besides the American-born Texians, many of the Mexican Tejanos who had lived in the region for generations joined the Americans in their opposition to the central government under General Santa Anna. A number of Tejanoswas present at the Alamo, a fact that often remains unmentioned.

Another issue that the Alamo myth glosses over is the treatment which the Tejanos were subjected to after Texas gained its independence. In a recent study which argues that "[a]lmost everything Americans have been taught, or think they know about the Alamo is not only wrong, it is nearly the antithesis of what really occurred" (Tucker 2010: vii), Phillip Tucker argues that not only has the role of the Tejanos been misrepresented – "respected Tejano Texas Revolutionary heroes eventually became villains, while Anglo-Celtic real-life tyrants became heroes" – but Tejanos were systematically driven from their land once Texas had gained its independence: "Existing for hundreds of years, legitimate ancient Spanish land grants were routinely dismissed by white judges. Additionally, state and local government raised taxes to force foreclosure of Tejano properties, which were then eagerly gobbled up by large white ranchers" (Tucker 2010: 324).

Traditional accounts of the battle in the U.S. have also mostly left unmentioned that slavery was a source of contention between Americans and Mexicans and that at least two of the three alleged heroes – like the majority of the Americans settling in the area – were Southerners and owned slaves.Considering the position on slavery, the chorus of the song gives expression to what Edward Morgan has called "the central paradox of American history": "The rise of liberty and equality in this country was accompanied by the rise of slavery" (Morgan 1972: 6). The story turns history into myth as it reduces the complexity of the historical situation. Not only does Cash's song reduce the complex relations between Mexicans and Americans, Texians and Tejanaos – who for decades had been neighbors in the region – to an opposition between heroes and villains but it also "strategically forgets" (cf. Sturken 1997: 7-8) that, legally, the territory at the time was part of Mexico and that Mexico had abolished slavery in 1829.

While Cash's song forgets the presence of Tejanos and African Americans, it proudly remembers the valour of the American defenders whose position he identifies with when he has them collectively refer to their killing of Mexican soldiers as a defence of freedom and as an act of resistance to tyranny. The implied audience is expected to sing along because the values defended at the Alamo are considered universal – "men wherever they go" will associate the battle with self-sacrifice for a higher cause, freedom. Three individuals, Travis, Bowie and Crockett are singled out as embodying the defiance of the enemies and an insatiable desire for freedom.

Like the Alamo narrative, Johnny Cash's particular performance of the song at Madison Square Garden in 1969 is a manifestation of the American paradox. Before he delivered the song, Johnny Cash directly addressed President Nixon and asked him to compare the Alamo to the Vietnam War: "180 Americans against 5,000. Mr. President, that's the kind of odds we got today." While the comment is generally read as Cash protesting against the war, this protest is double-edged. After all, the call to remember the Alamo is directly related to the events that resulted from it: the ultimate victory over the Mexicans and Texan independence. Johnny Cash's song – although not explicitly – inscribes itself in a representative tradition in which the cultural superiority of Americans over "racial others" is established and emphatically affirmed.

3. The Earliest Representations of the Battle of the Alamo (1836)

The earliest source of the Alamo myth, as Manuel Peña has pointed out, is a public proclamation issued by the citizens of Nacogdoches on March 26, 1836: "They died martyrs to liberty; and on the altar of their sacrifice will be made a vow that shall break the shackles of tyranny" (Peña 2012, 125). In the same year, only a few months after the battle, an anonymous poem "The Fall of the Alamo" was published in one of the leading literary magazines, the *Knickerbocker* in New York:

> Then force assumed another form:
> Protracted siege was turned to storm,
> Upon this fatal day.
> Yet, as a loathing, trembling craven
> The herd-like mass was onward driven,
> To dare the fearful fray.
> In front, three columns dense and dark
> Of shuddering escaladers mark
> The force apart for storming set;
> While rearward, ranks of horsemen stand,
> Charged escopets, and sword in hand,
> To drive them o'er the parapet. [...]
> Tried veterans they, in part – in part
> A herd, without or hand or heart:
> Such beings they, for whom – nor few –
> To emptied prisons thanks were due;
> A squallid crowd, in couples chained, Felons with crimes unnumbered stained.
> From Yucatan to Santa Fé,
> Each province swelled the grim array:
> Puebla's olive lineage here,
> The Zacatecas mountaineer,
> Brown herdsmen drawn from Potosi, Talisco's thralls to slavery –
> Saltillo's brood, blown into flame,
> By hatred of the Texian name – Campeachy's lowlanders, and ranks
> from Rio Grande's farther banks –
> In mingled mass are marshalled now,
> To 'make the stiff-necked rebels bow.'
> From pure Castile to black Japan,
> All shades of skin the eye might scan:
> The sable Ethiop and the brown,
> The copper-colored Indian's frown,
> Mulatto and Mestizoe's hue,
> With olive, marked the mottled crew. (Anon. 1836)

The poem refers to a whole number of Alamo defenders by name, whereas the Mexican soldiers are represented as an anonymous mass that consists to a large extent of criminals and men that had to be forced into service. The speaker compares them to cattle which had to be driven into battle. The Mexican victory is attributed solely to overwhelming numbers. Historical analogies with Leonidas and the 300 and the Battle of Thermopylae suggest that the battle demonstrates what free men, even if few, can achieve against an autocratic system which forces men into battle. The main reason for the Mexicans' lack of fighting spirit, the poem suggests, lies in the soldiers' "racial inferiority" as the numerous references to skin colour and the terms "Mulatto" and "Mestizoe" show. In the racial discourse of the time, mixed racial origin – "hybridity" – is considered the cause of degeneration (cf. Horsman 1981: 208-228).

The cultural stereotype of the Mexicans as "lazy, ignorant, bigoted, superstitious, cheating, thieving, gambling, cruel, sinister, cowardly half-breeds, incapable of self-government or material progress" (Weber 1988: 159),which David J. Weber sees manifest in American travel narratives of the first half of the nineteenth century, is reflected in "Fall of the Alamo." According to Weber, this stereotype is based on an even older stereotype and can thus be seen as "an extension of negative attitudes towards Catholic Spaniards which Anglo Americans had inherited from their Protestant English forbears" (1988: 159). Spanish governments in the eyes of British colonists in North America were "authoritarian, corrupt, and decadent" (Weber 1988: 159). This older notion is now coupled with a notion of the Mexicans' racial inferiority as a result of centuries of racial and ethnic mixing between Europeans, Indians, and Africans. The simultaneity of the conflicts over the settlement of Mexico's northern borderlands and the emergence of a racial ideology is no coincidence. According to Reginald Horsman, the territorial expansion of Americans into Mexico was "the catalyst in the overt adoption of a racial Anglo-Saxonism" (Horsman 1981: 208).

In 1845, in an article on the annexation of Texas, John O'Sullivan coined the term "manifest destiny" as a shorthand for the historic mission of the Anglo-Saxons on the North American continent (O'Sullivan 1845: 5). A few years earlier, in 1839, he had published an article in which he calls the United States the "nation of futurity" and an example to the world. He distinguishes American democracy from the "the tyranny of kings, hierarchs, and oligarchs," and imagines America to "carry the glad tidings of peace and good will where myriads now endure an existence scarcely more enviable than that of beasts of the field" (O'Sullivan 1839: 430). The passage clearly resonates with the dehumanizing representation of the

Mexican soldiers in the 1836 poem. Whereas O'Sullivan focuses on the American democratic institutions and self-government, other writers of the time foregrounded the racial difference. James Buchanan, senator, secretary of state and President between 1857 and 1861, argued in favor of the annexation of Texas because in his view, "our race of men can never be subjected to the imbecile and indolent Mexican race" (cf. Horsman 1981: 217). Ed A. Muñoz sums up the cultural stereotype that emerges in the conflict over Texas: "Mexicans, with their mixed racial and cultural background and adherence to feudal and Catholic traditions, were the antithesis to emergent American core values" (Muñoz 2009: 327).

The Alamo narrative is reduced to a few binary oppositions, or "racialized [...] binaries," as Deborah R. Vargas states: "Texans/Mexicans, brave valiant heroes/ruthless uncivilized cowards, [...] and freedom/tyranny, to name just a few" (Vargas 1997: 11). In depicting the territorial expansion and the violent subjugation of racially inferior Indians and Mexicans as historically inevitable, the Alamo narrative is embedded in a larger mythical constellation, the frontier myth. In three volumes, Richard Slotkin has traced the relation between the colonization of the continent and the ideological concept of the frontier by which Americans have perceived and interpreted this history. *Regeneration Through Violence*, the title of one of Slotkin's books (1973), captures Frederick Jackson Turner's famous thesis that violent conflicts with the indigenous population account for the continuous regeneration of the American nation which is thus protected from becoming over-civilized and degenerate. The myth finds its most ideal articulation in the genre of the Western, the national epic. The Western genre pits the protagonist – the sheriff, cowboy, or pioneer – against hostile Indians against whom the former often single-handedly has to defend and protect the settlers – among them women and children–who come from Europe or the civilized East coast. To prevail in the violent conflicts, the protagonist needs to take recourse to forms of violence that are beyond what is considered civilized interaction.

4. John Wayne's Western *The Alamo* (1960)

Since representations of the Alamo belong in the mythical context of the American frontier it is no coincidence that John Wayne, the actor who like no other during the 1940s and 50s shaped the image of the Western hero in Hollywood, turned the *The Alamo* into a Western. In the Cold War context of 1960, John Wayne considered the Alamo a narrative that would present America as the model of freedom that O'Sullivan had in mind: "[T]he eyes of the world are on us. We must sell America to countries threatened with

Communist domination. Our picture is also important to Americans, who should appreciate the struggle our ancestors made for the precious freedom we enjoy" (Thompson 1991: 80).

Wayne considers the Alamo a symbol of freedom and individual self-determination that is meant to remind Americans of what is at stake for America. In this film, the category "gender" is used to naturalize the hierarchy between Americans and Mexicans. *The Alamo* uses gender in ways that both break with and affirm stereotypical representations. The racial hierarchy between Anglo-Saxons and Mexicans is often conveyed through a triangular constellation. A white woman embodies the feminine virtues held in high esteem among the middle classes until the 1960s: selflessness, altruism, purity. A Mexican woman, often a prostitute, competes with the white woman for the attention of the Western hero, yet ultimately accepts her rival's moral superiority (John Ford's *High Noon* is a good example). In contrast, Wayne's *The Alamo* presents a courtship plot in which Davy Crockett protects a young Mexican lady against an aggressive Anglo businessman who wants to force the woman into marriage to gain control of her property. For obvious reasons, the romance between the two cannot materialize. Nevertheless, in their final conversation, Crockett teaches the young woman an important lesson:

> Now I may sound like a Bible beater yelling up a revival at a river crossing camp meeting but that don't change the truth none. There's right and there's wrong. You got to do one or the other. You do the one and you're living. You do the other and you may be walking around, but you're dead as a beaver hat. (Maddrey 2016: 84)

The language reflects the hero's folksiness, simplicity, and common sense. Freedom and self-determination are more important to him than life itself. *The Alamo* here continues the tradition of the anonymous poem and presents the sacrifice of the defenders as transcending death. The Mexicans are presented in a much more favourable light than in earlier representations. The difference between the opposing groups is not depicted as racial difference, yet the gendered hierarchy between Davy Crockett and his protégé clearly affirms and naturalizes the hierarchy between Americans and Mexicans. One of the most striking scenes in the film shows Davy Crockett manipulating his men into choosing fight over escape by forging a letter from Santa Anna. His men react impulsively and declare their determination to fight Santa Anna. When the decision has to be made, Davy Crockett reveals to his men that he had manipulated them, but this revelation does not make them change their mind. The film suggests that the Americans' desire for freedom and the aversion to authority is innate, an expression of their Anglo-Saxon origins. Despite the obvious revisions of the racial stereotypes that had dominated the 19th century discourse on the Alamo, John Wayne's *The Alamo* nevertheless perpetuates the cultural hierarchy between superior Anglos and inferior Mexicans that is established and naturalized by the courtship plot.

5. Revisionist Alamo Narratives and the Multiculturalism Debate of the 1980s and 90s

Johnny Cash's reference to the Vietnam War at his concert at Madison Square Garden in 1969 is an indicator that by the late 1960s the frontier myth starts to lose its naturalizing function. The Civil Rights movement as well as the protest and counter culture movements challenge the consensus about the country's self-image as the land of freedom. Minorities at this time not only claim political participation and equal opportunities but also a recognition of their cultural difference. Multiculturalism becomes a highly contested concept. In 1990, Pat Buchanan, a well-known representative of the Right, sees America in decline if the European dominance were lost:

> The question we Americans need to address, before it is answered to us, is: Does this First World nation wish to become a Third World country? Because that is our destiny if we do not build a sea wall against the waves of immigration rolling over our shores. [...] Who speaks for the Euro-Americans, who founded the USA? [...] Is it not time to take America back? (Buchanan 1990)

The most recent Conservative who promises to 'make America great again' is President Donald Trump, who founded his presidential campaign on the frustration many Americans feel with a declining economy and the loss of international reputation that the United States have suffered from since their military interventions in the Middle East. In one of his campaign speeches, Trump accused the Mexican government of "forcing their most unwanted people into the United States":

> They are, in many cases, criminals, drug dealers, rapists, etc. [...] the worst elements in Mexico are being pushed into the United States by the Mexican government. The largest suppliers of heroin, cocaine and other illicit drugs are Mexican cartels that arrange to have Mexican immigrants trying to cross the borders and smuggle in the drugs. The Border Patrol knows this. Likewise, tremendous infectious disease is pouring across the border. The United States has become a dumping ground for Mexico and, in fact, for many other parts of the world. (Walker 2015)

Trump here takes recourse to the two stereotypes that have their origin in the Alamo representations of the nineteenth century: a corrupt Mexican government that sends criminals, and people incapable of self-government across the border to bring down America. Trump's statements and his suggestion to extend and fortify the wall between the two countries seem a desperate attempt to re-establish the dominance of European Americans and the frontier myth with its inscribed racial hierarchies.

In recent decades, literary authors and filmmakers have challenged the Alamo myth and its construction of America as the embodiment of universal values. The focus has been shifted from the border and its divisive function to the borderlands. One of the most popular texts of the 90s in academic circles was Gloria Anzaldúa's *Borderlands/La Frontera*, which uses the borderlands as a metaphor for cultural diversity and hybridity. In interviews, Anzaldúa chooses phrases which foreground the role of the category "space" in the construction of individual and collective identities as in, for example, "We're becoming a geography of hybrid selves" (Anzaldúa 2000: 255) or in "I see the mestiza as a geography of selves – of different bordering countries – who stands at the threshold of two or more worlds and negotiates the cracks between the worlds" (Anzaldúa 2000: 268). Anzaldúa's reference to geography aligns her with the "spatial turn." Postmodern thinkers such as Foucault, Jameson, and Soja argue that while modernism was obsessed with the category time, the focus should be shifted to space. As a category which is perceived as concrete and tangible, it is in need of deconstruction. French philosopher Vattimo has captured the effect to which postmodern thinkers put space and spatial metaphors:

> With the demise of a central rationality of history, the world of generalized communication explodes like a multiplicity of 'local' rationalities – ethnic, sexual, religious, cultural or aesthetic minorities – that finally speak up for themselves. They are no longer repressed or cowed into silence by the idea of a single true form of humanity that must be realized irrespective of particularity and individual finitude, transience and contingency. (Vattimo 1992: 8-9)

Shaped by such a postmodern "explosion" of formerly enclosed and clearly bounded spaces, more recent retellings of the Alamo foreground the minority viewpoints which have traditionally been excluded from the mythical narrative.

6. John Sayles's *The Lone Star* (1996)

The most successful attempt at deconstructing the Alamo myth is John Sayles' 1996 film *Lone Star* which is set in a Texan border town in the present. By the use of a particular technique of flashbacks, Sayles makes the presence of the past and the ways in which the Alamo has left its marks on the border community tangible. The film parodies the Western genre by crossing over into other genres. It starts as a crime story when Sheriff Sam Deeds is confronted with a dead body in the desert. The body is identified as the town's former sheriff who had been known for his corrupt regime and for terrorizing Mexicans and African Americans. In the course of his investigation, Deeds not only identifies the man who killed the sheriff and lets him go free but he also finds out that the woman he is in love with is his half-sister. His father had an adulterous affair with Pilar's mother who had illegally immigrated from Mexico. Sam and Pilar thought that it was racism that drove their parents to break up their relation when they were teenagers. When the truth comes out and threatens their newly-found love, Pilar opts for the transgression of the incest taboo. The film ends with her words "Forget the Alamo – all that history. "Why does Pilar blame the Alamo for the situation that she and her lover/half-brother find themselves in? For over a century, the Alamo myth has constructed a racial hierarchy between Americans and Mexicans and presented it as the natural order.

Throughout the film, references to the Alamo are placed strategically to challenge the status quo. When an African American prisoner accuses the Chicano deputy sheriff of Anglo-conformity, the deputy proudly counters that time has come for the Chicanos to take over the control over the region: "Our good day has come" (Sayles 1996:1:02:58). The African American, however, is unimpressed and invokes history: "You chumps haven't had a good day since the Alamo" (Sayles 1996:1:03:00). In another scene, parents at the high school where Pilar teaches history argue vehemently about how and what Texan history is to be taught. One Anglo objects to the teacher's suggestion to represent multiple perspectives in order to capture the historical complexity. In still another scene, a barkeeper expresses his fear that the Anglos might become a minority. He views the bar as the "last stand," another allusion to the Alamo. The most impressive reference to the Alamo occurs when Sheriff Deeds crosses the American-Mexican border in order to talk to a witness. When asked about the past crime, the Mexican takes a bottle and draws a line in the sand. He then goes on to tell Sheriff Deeds that on the Mexican side of the border, he has no authority at all. The camera then pans to left and the viewer is taken into the past when Sam Deeds' interlocutor witnessed how former

Sheriff Charlie Wade murdered a man in cold blood because he helped illegal immigrants across the border. These ironic references to the Alamo and the crossing over between past and present and between genres shows how filmmakers in recent decades have retold the history of American-Mexican relations in order to foreground the racialist implications of the myth.

In her 1997 presidential address to the American Studies Association, Mary Helen Washington used *Lone Star* as one of three texts to illustrate the institutional and cultural changes that at least in the academe has led to the recognition of America's multiculturalism – both present and past. In spite of her enthusiasm for the film, which she calls "a prophetic allegory of institutional change," she is critical of the ending and Pilar's call to forget the Alamo, a "colossal failure of nerve" (Washington 1997:12) in her view. Against the backdrop of the overall theme of "Disrespected Neighbours" which draws attention to the centuries-long co-existence of Mexicans and Americans in the region, a different reading suggests itself. Pilar's statement is not meant to be taken literally as a call to forget history but rather as an expression of resistance to the racial hierarchies inscribed in earlier representations of the Alamo. *Lone Star* challenges the way in which earlier representations have performed the "making of a "Self" – or more precisely, the fashioning of a masterful Anglo Self – over a Mexican "Other" within a structured relationship of dominance" (Flores 2002: 159). The broken screen of the town's drive-in-movie theatre that Sheriff Deeds faces at the end of the film indicates the need for new representations of Anglo-Mexican relations. The incest motif is an explicit attempt to allegorically portray the nation as a dysfunctional family, as John Sayles himself suggests in an interview (Ratner 1998: 203). By portraying the characters as members of one big family and by making them transgress the taboo that society has erected around incest, the characters come into focus as individuals – rather than as members of an imagined community that abstracts from the individual. The film thus turns disrespected neighbours into neighbours, and national stereotypes into individuals who inhabit the borderlands, a site of a shared, if conflicted history.

7. A Post-9/11 Retelling of the Alamo Narrative: John Lee Hancock's *Alamo* (2004)

As the examples discussed have shown, the myth of the Alamo is evoked in particular at times of a perceived crisis: John Wayne's retelling of the Alamo during the Cold War, Johnny Cash's analogy between the Alamo and the Vietnam War, *Lone Star*'s invocation of the controversial debate over multiculturalism in the 1990s. Representations of the Alamo as a frontier narrative fulfill the function to affirm the idea of America as the land of freedom and democracy and to unite the nation against a common enemy who is depicted as a racial "Other." Despite the 1990s representations of the borderlands which "challenge the homogeneity of U.S. nationalism and popular culture" (Saldívar 1997: ix), the tradition of the Alamo myth has persisted.

In 2004, John Lee Hancock presented a new filmic version of *Alamo* which some critics read as a response to 9/11 (cf. Pérez 2003; Yilmaz 2016). Considering that after 9/11, the Southern border was increasingly perceived as "porous and a threat to U.S. national security" (Ganster 2016: xxi), it does not come as a surprise that the Alamo was once again used as analogy for the current crisis.

In Hancock's retelling, historical details that had been mentioned in earlier representations gain new significance when read against the backdrop of the War on Terror. Whereas the 1836 poem "The Fall of the Alamo" contrasted American individuals fighting for freedom with an anonymous mass of Mexican soldiers who need to be forced to fight, Hancock characterizes the "El Degüello" – Spanish for cut throat – a term that goes back to the times when Spain was under Muslim rule. The bugle call tells the enemy that they could expect no mercy if they did not surrender immediately. In case of defeat, all enemies would be killed. In his fictionalized history of Texas, James Michener in 1985 had mentioned the playing of the "Degüello" and had contrasted it with Davy Crockett playing the fiddle (Michener 1987: 461-464). According to Michener's version of the Alamo, the night before the battle, Davy Crockett played to his men and for a time made his men forget their impending death. While in Hancock's film a military dirge is played by the Mexicans to intimidate the Alamo defenders, Davy Crockett is shown to respond to the dirge with an improvisation that leaves an impression with his own men as well as the enemies. The music is here used as a universal language that works through emotional affect rather than rational reflection. *Alamo* perpetuates the mythical narrative in that it has found a new way to naturalize the superiority of American democracy over Spanish autocracy. While Hancock revives the mythical Alamo, his representation acknowledges more recent historical research. In 1975, the memoir of a Mexican participant in the battle of the Alamo, José Enrique de la Peña, was translated into English and published for the first time. In his account of the battle, de la Peña reports that Crockett did not die fighting but that he surrendered to Santa Anna who did not allow for any survivors and ordered Crockett's execution. Crockett's death has since been a highly contested issue and while Hancock acknowledges the Mexican source, he turns the execution scene into another of Davy Crockett's triumphs over Santa Anna (cf. Tucker 2010: 319-327).

8. Challenging the Alamo Myth: Revisionist Historical Novels since 2000

Two more recent historical novels make an attempt to break with the myth and instead represent the historical and cultural complexity of the borderlands. Both novels try to revise traditional mythical accounts by shifting the focus from the battle and the heroic figures to the plights of culturally diverse local characters that are all affected by the conflict. Stephen Harrigan's *Gates of the Alamo*, published in 2000, focuses on the way in which local characters that do look upon themselves as neighbours and that do not side for either cause become involved in the battle. Harrigan presents the battle from the perspectives of both Mexicans and Americans and incorporates female perspectives on both sides. Harrigan's attempt at representing multiple perspectives often gives expression to predictable inversions of the traditional hero worship and to politically correct representations of Mexicans and Indians. For example, when the protagonist tries to convince a Comanche chief to return an abducted Mexican girl to her people, his thoughts are rendered in free indirect speech:

> Why was he taking this girl? Her parents were dead, and the Comanche life, he knew, was as full of richness as any – a never-ending procession through buffalo plains and verdant hills, a dangerous and primitive life that was probably no more dangerous or primitive than the one from which the girl had just been stolen. He began to sense that this rescue was nothing more than a grand gesture whose only purpose was to satisfy his own vanity. (Harrigan 2000: 35)

The declared cultural relativism, which is meant to counteract the ethnocentrism of earlier representations, however, gives way to the affirmation of the traditional hierarchy once the battle of the Alamo is represented in the second half of the novel. In spite of its attempt to represent multiple perspectives and to relegate the traditional Alamo heroes to the margins, the novel remains bound to the mythical narrative in which the good ultimately prevail.

Emma Pérez in her 2009 novel *Forgetting the Alamo Or Blood Memory* attempts a more radical break with the myth and retells the historical conflict from the point of view of a young lesbian woman. The focus of Pérez's novel is on inverting the traditional Alamo narrative, exposing the exclusion and violence that the racism inscribed in the myth has produced and at the same time legitimized. It is told from the perspective of a young lesbian of mixed descent who cross-dresses as a cowboy. In spite of its programmatic title – *Forgetting the Alamo* – the novel paradoxically affirms the power of the mythical narrative by simply inverting the stereotypical representations of selfless heroes defending universal ideals such as freedom and equality. Micaela, the protagonist, tells a narrative of conversion. In the epilogue, she invokes the values of her indigenous forbears and sets them against the violence and oppression that she sees embodied by white men:

> [...] it's like Eagle Mother said, nobody can take away memory in our flesh and nothing can take away the spirit in our blood 'cause that spirit is guiding us to new days no matter how much men like Walker, Colonel and Rove lie and cheat and murder their way through everything they touch. (Pérez 2009: 205)

9. Conclusion

As works of art that try to reconceptualise American history as a transnational project, the two revisionist novels illustrate Paul Ganster's dictum that "[t]he U.S.-Mexican border is the best known illustration of the paradoxical continued importance of borders in our globalizing world" (Ganster 2016: xvi). Although, he argues, "boundaries between economies and cultures are weakened, borders between nations, cultures, and ethnicities appear to be strong as ever – and are perhaps growing stronger" (Ganster 2016: xv). Donald Trump's determination to render the border between Mexico and the U.S. "impenetrable," illustrates Ganster's point. The renewed efforts on part of literary authors and filmmakers since the 1990s to break with the Alamo myth need to be seen in relation to the militarization of the U.S.-Mexican border that has taken place during the same period. Whether the Alamo narrative – considering its origins in 19th-century racialist discourse and the uses to which it has been put over the last 180 years – can ever be used to envision a community in which disrespected neighbours become neighbours and citizens, only the future can tell. The revisionist turn in recent decades at least allows us, as Emma Pérez concludes in *The Decolonial Imaginary*, "to look to the past through the present always already marked by the coming of that which is still left unsaid, unthought" (Pérez 1999: 127).

References

"Album Review: At Madison Square Garden – Johnny Cash." *Raise My Glass to the B-Side*. August 19, 2013. Web. 31 March, 2016.

Anon. 1836. "Fall of the Alamo." *The Knickerbocker* 8 (September), 295-298.

Anzaldúa, Gloria. 2000. *Interviews/Entrevistas*. Ana Louise Keating, ed. New York and London: Routledge.

Assmann, Jan. 1995. "Collective Memory and Cultural Identity." Transl. John Czaplicka. *New German Critique* 65,125-133.

Bal, Mieke, 1999. "Introduction." In: Mieke Bal, Jonathan V. Crewe, Leo Spitzer (eds.). *Acts of Memory: Cultural Recall in the Present*. Hanover and London: University Press of New England, vii-xvii.

Buchanan, Pat.1990. "Editorial," *New York Post* (20 June 1990).

Cash, Johnny. 1963. "Remember the Alamo." AZLyrics.com. 2000. Web. 31 March, 2016.

Flores, Richard R. 2002. *Remembering the Alamo: Memory, Modernity, and the Master Symbol*. Austin: University of Texas Press.

Ganster, Paul. 2016. *The U.S.-Mexican Border Today: Conflict and Cooperation in Historical Perspective*. 3rd ed. Lanham: Rowman & Littlefield Publishers.

Hancock, John Lee, dir. 2004. *Alamo*. Touchstone Pictures.

Harrigan, Stephen. 2000. *The Gates of the Alamo*. New York: Penguin.

Horsman, Reginald. 1981. *Race and Manifest Destiny: The Origins of American Racial Anglo-Saxonism*. Cambridge and London: Harvard University Press.

Maddrey, Joseph. 2016. *The Quick, the Dead and the Revived. The Many Lives of the Western Film*. Jefferson: McFarland.

Michener, James. 1987. *Texas*. New York: Fawcett.

Morgan, Edward. 1972. "Slavery and Freedom: The American Paradox". *The Journal of American History* 59.1, 5-29.

Muñoz, Ed A. 2009. "Gringo Justice," In: Helen Taylor Greene and Shaun L Gabbidon, eds. *Encyclopedia of Race and Crime*. Los Angeles: Sage, 326-329.

O'Sullivan, John L. 1839. "The Great Nation of Futurity," *The United States Magazine and Democratic Review* 6 (November), 426-430.

—. 1845. "Annexation." *The United States Magazine and Democratic Review* 17 (July-August), 5-10.

Peña, Manuel. 2012. *American Mythologies: Semiological Sketches*. Farnham and Burlington: Ashgate Publishing.

Pérez, Emma. 1999. *The Decolonial Imaginary: Writing Chicanas into History.* Bloomington and Indianapolis: Indiana University Press.

—. 2009. *Forgetting the Alamo, Or Blood Memory.* Austin: University of Texas Press.

Pérez, Vincent. 2003. "Remembering the Alamo, Post-9/11." *American Quarterly* 55.4, 771-779.

Quijano, Anibal. 2000. "Coloniality of Power, Eurocentrism, and Latin America." *Nepantla: Views from South* 1.3, 533-580.

Ratner, Megan. 1998. "Borderlines." In: Diane Carson, ed. *John Sayles Interviews.* Diane Carson, ed. Jackson: University Press of Mississippi, 202-209.

Saldívar, José David. 1997. *Border Matters: Remapping American Cultural Studies.* Berkeley, Los Angeles, London: University of California Press.

Sayles, John, dir. 1996. *Lone Star.* Rio Dulce/ Castle Rock Entertainment.

Slotkin, Richard. 1973. *Regeneration through Violence: The Mythology of the American Frontier, 1600-1860.* Norman: University of Oklahoma Press.

Sturken, Marita.1997. *Tangled Memories: The Vietnam War, the AIDS Epidemic, and the Politics of Remembering.* Berkeley and Los Angeles: University of California Press. Thompson, Frank. 1991. *Alamo Movies.* Plano: Republic of Texas Press, Wordwore Publishing.

Tucker, Phillip Thomas. 2010. *Exodus from the Alamo: The Anatomy of the Last Stand Myth.* Philadelphia and Newbury: Casemate.

Vargas, Deborah. 1997. *Dissonant Divas in Chicana Music: The Limits of la Onda.* Minneapolis and London: University of Minnesota Press.

Vattimo, Gianni. 1992. *The Transparent Society.* Transl. David Webb. Baltimore: The Johns Hopkins University Press.

Wayne, John, dir. 1960. *The Alamo.* Metro-Goldwyn-Mayer Studios.

Weber, David J. 1988. *Myth and the History of the Hispanic Southwest.* Albuquerque: University of New Mexico Press.

Walker, Hunter. "Donald Trump Just Released an Epic Statement Raging against Mexican Immigrants and 'Disease,'" *Business Insider* (6 July 2015). Web. 31 March 2016.

Washington, Mary Helen. 1997. "Disturbing the Peace: What Happens to American Studies if You Put African American Studies at the Center? Presidential Address to the American Studies Association, October 29, 1997." *American Quarterly* 50.1. 1-23.

Yilmaz, Fadime. 2016. "The Construction of Collective Memory in Hollywood Movies: Review of *The Alamo.*" *Turkish Studies* 11.2, 1341-1360.

Chapter Three

Racial Stereotyping and Performing Blackness: Branden Jacobs-Jenkins's *Neighbors* as Post-Black Play

Frank Obenland

1. From "Black" to "Post-Black" in the "Age of Obama"?

In the "Age of Obama" (2008-2017), critics have witnessed the arrival of the "post-black" as a new dramatic style in theatrical performances of racial differences in African American theatre and drama. As a new mode of racial performativity, the development of the post-black play has been attributed to two socio-cultural factors. On the one hand, American theatre and drama has become more appreciative of including African American playwrights, a development which is attested to by the successes of a new generation of playwrights exemplified by Lynn Nottage or Tarell Alvin McCraney (Elam and Jones 2013: xxii). On the other hand, these post-black plays also reflect a historical moment in which commentators, publicists, and historians notice a change in "the racial climate" of the United States which "has caused some to conjecture that race no longer matters in American life" (Elam and Jones 2013: xxii). Responding to the premature celebration of a "post-racial" society, these plays reflect an increasing investment of African American (and non-black) playwrights in notions of "post-blackness," that is an attempt to move away from black nationalist, post-colonial, and multicultural agendas of staging "blackness" and to define and represent the African American experience in non-traditional ways. In the context of African American drama, "post-blackness" can thus be understood as an avant-garde aesthetic and political agenda that not only fosters "heterogeneous and heterodox renderings of blackness that are grounded in the contexts and conditions of today" (Elam and Jones 2013: xv). It also seeks to revisit the complex relationship between theatrical representations of blackness and the long-standing critical discussion of what constitutes a "black play."

With the end of the "Age of Obama," the far-reaching hopes and expectations raised by the introduction of the "post-black play" have given way to a more somber and pessimistic assessment of the state of interracial relations in the United States. Harvey Young has described this form of a "black pessimism" as "a felt sense of stalled sociopolitical progress as well as anxiety over back-treading" (2016: 856). Houston A. Baker's critique is even more pointed when he observes that "[t]he presidency of Barack Obama may have motivated declarations of the birth of post-Blackness, but the men, women, and milieu of post-Blackness have not ameliorated one whit the racial humiliation and abject confinements of the U.S. Black Majority" (2015: 251). In this sense, Stuart Hall's question "Can a dominant system of representation be effectively challenged, contested or changed?" assumes a new critical urgency (1997: 269). The openly critical comments on post-blackness by Harvey and Baker also call for a more rigorous interrogation of post-black plays as vehicles for challenging the racist ideologies which they seek to overcome. Especially with regard to the farcical, satirical, and parodical features of post-black performances, it remains questionable to what degree these plays also tackle the ideological fantasies that have traditionally driven the "signifying practices" of stereotypical, racialized performances.

In order to answer these questions, I will first turn to the critical discussion of "post-blackness" in order to show the limitations of its proponents to address its own "situatedness" in a particular historical context with its specific set of discursive practices. Secondly, I will turn to a discussion of Branden Jacobs-Jenkins's play *Neighbors* (2010/12) which, I argue, offers a critique of how "post-blackness" has been conceived in contemporary theoretical debates. As I want to suggest, *Neighbors* not only expands the evolving canon of post-black plays, but also critically reflects on the limitations of post-black performances that seek to disconnect stereotypical representations of a racial Other from the racist assumptions that have historically informed their creation. In his play, Jacobs-Jenkins stages the complex struggle for an appropriate depiction of an African American identity by juxtaposing two African American families who not only represent diametrically opposed social positions but who also embody different dramatic traditions. During the play, the interaction of both families effectively deconstructs stereotypical assumptions about "blackness" and reveals the tragicomic result of any attempt to produce stable notions of cultural and ethnic identity. The play thus offers a metatheatrical commentary and surrealistic satire on the performative construction of "post-blackness" in American popular culture and thus calls for revising the imaginary and fetishistic fantasies that have traditionally sustained racist ideologies.

2. Post-Blackness and the Ends of Racial Stereotyping

Thelma Golden famously introduced the term "post-black" to the art world in her introductory essay for the catalogue of the Freestyle exhibition at the Harlem Studio Museum in 2001. Searching for a new label for the avant-garde work of young African American artists, Golden declared that "[p]ost-black was the new black" (2001: 14). For Golden, the term "post-black" describes a new period in African American art in which artists move beyond the paradigms of the black aesthetic and the Black Arts Movement of the 1960s and 1970s as well as the multicultural identity politics of the 1980s and 1990s. Golden adopts the epithet "post-black" – "ironically and seriously" as she points out – to describe artists "who were adamant about not being labeled as 'black' artists, though their work was steeped, in fact deeply interested, in redefining complex notions of blackness" (ibid.). As Golden suggests, a common denominator for this critical reconsideration of "black" art is the joyful embrace of the creativity of the individual artist whose "overwhelming sense of individuality" allows for "a relentless and unbridled expression of the self" (2001: 14; 15).

Golden's notion of "post-black art" was readily accepted by art critics to describe an aesthetic response to the legacy of the Civil Rights movement as well as a "globalized and hyper-mediated environment" that "seems to describe effectively a new sociopolitical order that goes beyond the art world" (Byrd 2002: 39).[1] The attempt to create more open and fluid treatments of blackness, however, was also criticized as "a crisis in black artistic production" whose aim to emancipate black art from "a limited set of political concerns" creates an "aesthetics of privilege and entitlement" that basically feeds into a "voracious market demand for the black body" and effectively becomes a short-hand for "a free play where racial fetishism is a virtue and satire reigns supreme" (Murray 2014: 7; 8; 9). This more irreverent approach to stereotypical and anti-black images of

---

[1] In his discussion of the "post-black" in American visual culture, Derek C. Murray describes Golden's original formula as presenting "an aesthetic that appears very similar to former expressions, only drained of didactic political or historical content" (Murray 2014: 5-6).

racialized identities is informed by a marked skepticism about the continuing relevance of discourses of respectability and racial uplift in representations of blackness. The post-black can thus be aligned with what one critic has called "a wave of late 20th century artists who insistently [...] incorporate degrading images and narratives of black identity" to confront audiences with their historical longevity and lingering cultural impact in representations of the black experience (Worsley 2010: 1).

As a concept that connects the aesthetic and the political, Golden's notion of the "post-black" assumed particular relevance in the aftermath of Barack Obama's election to the presidency in 2008. Journalist and cultural commentator Touré adopted the notion of "post-blackness" in his collection of interviews *Who's Afraid of Post-Blackness? What It Means to Be Black Now* to rebuff the idea that Obama's victory signaled the transformation of the United States into a "post-racial" society in which racial differences have mostly lost their meaning (Touré 2011: 12). While Touré rightly suspects that established discursive practices of racialization do not vanish over-night, he turns to the public figure of Barack Obama as a cultural icon for a more individualist, creative, and less restrictive definition of "blackness." Similar to Golden's original formula, he celebrates "the dynamic hyper-creative beauty of modern individualistic Blackness" embodied by Barack Obama who is "rooted in but not restricted by Blackness" (Touré 2011: 12). In Touré's account, "post-blackness" thus moves away from an African American identity that is primarily understood in collective, political or activist terms. As its chief objective, then, the post-black seeks "to banish from the collective mind the bankrupt, fraudulent concept of 'authentic' Blackness" (Touré 2011: 11). It aims at rejecting and deconstructing "a hierarchy of authenticity" that was created to narrowly define widely shared notions of blackness (Touré 2011: 11; 153). This traditional discourse of authenticity is replaced by an unrestricted individualist and emancipatory demand for a rigorous form of cultural and artistic self-determination.

As it is popularized by Touré, the post-black also opens the relationship between aesthetics, performance, and politics to further argument and contestation. As Christian Schmidt has rightly pointed out, the critical claims for post-blackness should not be misconstrued as a complete break with African American traditions in literature and critical theory. Instead, the post-black paradoxically also continues and re-inscribes itself into the very literary and artistic traditions which it sets out to overcome. In Schmidt's account, post-black fiction appropriates and expands more traditional forms of "signifyin(g)" described by Henry Louis Gates, Jr. in that it extends its playful signification beyond a narrowly defined African

American tradition of story-telling and writing (Schmidt 2016: 114). What post-black fiction shares with previous signifyin(g) practices, however, is its parodic adaptation of literary pretexts. According to Schmidt, "parody is *the* ideal vehicle of postblack [sic] art in that it re-contextualizes 'black' art without ridiculing it" (2016: 126). Parody also offers an escape from confining notions of blackness and critical constrictions that see African American writing as prompted by and responding to racist views and ideologies.[2]

The paradoxical tension between traditional forms of literary and artistic praxis and avant-garde attempts to transform them has also influenced the staging of racialized identities in the new genre of the "post-black play." According to Harry J. Elam, African American theatre and drama has also taken its inspiration from the "rich racial paradox" of the post-black in its creation of "new racial meanings" (2013: 258-259). In this sense, the editors of an anthology of post-black plays notice a growing readiness of contemporary playwrights to "incorporate but also diverge from what have become normative dramaturgical formations of black drama" (Elam and Jones 2013: xi).[3] These post-black playwrights move consciously away from black nationalist, post-colonial, and/or multi-cultural practices of staging a unified "black" experience and insist on negotiating critical demands for a "singular artistic perspective" with the need of developing inherently collective art forms such as theatre and drama (Elam and Jones 2013: xix).

In view of the post-black plays' readiness to "manipulate dramatic, theatrical, and performance conventions" and to produce "formal complexities" (Elam and Jones 2013: xii; xxv), this new dramatic style seems to be infused with a postmodernist sensibility and an interest in formal and representational innovations.[4] In addition to a surrealistic mode of representation, the most prominent and also most controversial feature of this new dramatic style consists of its use of parody and farcical treatments of black characters. Relying on metatheatrical commentaries

---

[2] For Schmidt, "postblack [sic] art consciously claims the freedom from having to respond always – and single-mindedly – to racism" (2016: 125).

[3] For the editors, the post-black plays in the anthology share a revisionist agenda and "express dissatisfaction with the status quo and exhibit the desire to remake black theatre practices on their own terms" (Elam and Jones 2013: xix). In contrast to the black aesthetic and the performative activism of the Black Arts Movement, however, the editors emphasize that the post-black play(wright) adopts a decidedly "post-ideological" posture.

[4] For a more detailed discussion of how post-black literature uses postmodernist techniques, see Schmidt (2014).

and elements that self-consciously address the inherently performative and unstable construction of blackness in culture and society, post-black performances provocatively include blackfacing of white and black characters as well as pointed and sharp parodies of previous performances of blackness. Following an avant-garde aesthetic, the plays aim at blurring and deconstructing racial categories and racial thinking primarily by including traditionally denigrating and insulting stereotypes of black characters.[5] Elam and Jones's post-black plays thus abandon the aesthetic and organizational separatism of African American theatre and drama that can be traced back to W.E.B. Du Bois's theatrical manifesto, the agit-prop theatre of the Black Arts Movement, as well as August Wilson's defiant call for cultural and institutional self-reliance. In addition, the editors of the anthology have expanded the "canon" of the post-black play beyond African American authors and have also included a section featuring two post-black plays by non-black playwrights Young Jean Lee and Diana Son. They join the other authors in the volume in the endeavor to question and subvert existing images and notions of "authentic blackness" by emphasizing the diversity and plurality of the African American in the present (and the past).

While post-black plays thus present themselves as responding to the sensibilities and complexities of the post-civil rights generation of African Americans, it remains questionable how this post-black aesthetic can address any ostensible political concern or demand when it postulates the possibility of a celebratory and playful (re-)interpretation of "authentic blackness." Instead, post-black performances operate on the speculative premise that racist ideologies have been largely overcome and that the denigrating, racist implications of stereotypical characters have thus become either negligible, absent, or moot. As the example of Young Jean Lee's *The Shipment* (2009) and its problematic references to the tradition of minstrel performances exemplifies, however, the post-black ambiguously

---

[5] As the editors explain, the criticality of the post-black play not only extends to obviously racist representations of stereotypical African American characters. Elam and Jones have organized the anthology into four sections that offer the four main areas of critical revision of the traditional "black play." The first section on "The New Black Family" includes plays that re-conceptualize notions of home and family as sites for constructing and defining personal identities. The second section features works by two non-black, ethnic playwrights. The third and fourth sections then offer "re-imaginings" of the "distant present" of African American history as well as a renewed engagement with Africa as mythical homeland of a circum-Atlantic diaspora. The plays' attempts to revise and deconstruct such stereotypical characters also includes blackface performances by white and black actors alike.

combines the reinterpretation of the traditional minstrel performance with the stereotypical exposure of the black male character to ridicule and laughter.[6] Such uses of comedic and farcical performative routines introduce a critical ambiguity. For one, blackface performance in the twenty-first century highlights the performative and theatrical quality of staging "blackness." Relinquishing the performance's intrinsic demands for the audience's respect, however, also incurs the critical question to what extent the "post-black" critique and revision of traditional performance conventions effectively counter the racist ideologies and conventional forms of defining "authentic blackness" which it at least partially seeks to evade.

A host of critical commentators have pointed at the limitations of the post-black as an avant-garde concept that re-positions conventional views on performative and literary representations of blackness. In particular, critics have objected to abandoning the notion of "identity" as a critical cornerstone of racialized performances and representations. Acknowledging the performative dimension of identities, Nadine George-Graves has argued, however, that "[w]e need to reclaim identity" by focusing more on the intersection of different markers of identity such as "race, class, gender, sexuality, religion, etc." (2005: 612; also see: Murray 2014: 15). She criticizes the inherent openness of the idea of the post-black as symptomatic for a problematic "trend in post-civil rights African American literature toward conceiving racial identity in individualistic terms" (Leader-Picone 2015: 422). It remains questionable how this individualistic dimension of the post-black can develop a broader social significance in that it renders visible "emerging groups [...] whose voices and issues are entrenched in communities but are not a part of the social agenda, public discussion, national politics, or collective black identity" (Womack 2010: 23).

---

[6] The most problematic dimension of these post-black plays is probably best illustrated by the opening of Young Jean Lee's play *The Shipment* that begins with a routine performed by two African American dancers and a black stand-up comedian. Ostentatiously relying on the performative conventions of the minstrel show – "a flash of possible minstrel reference" (Lee 2010: 7) – the black stand-up comedian performs the caricature of an African American urban male who addresses the audience in a scatological monologue that includes obscene, profane, and sexually explicit jokes and references. The similarity to nineteenth-century minstrel routines is invoked to problematize the continuities between nineteenth-century and twenty-first-century American popular culture. Such performances of black characters are obviously intended to provoke and shock audiences into questioning their conscious and unconscious beliefs and assumptions about race as well as conventional cultural constructions of blackness.

In this context, the post-black critique of popular notions of an authentic blackness has also been criticized for missing the implications of an "overemployment" of "blackness" in a globalized American popular culture featuring "black" styles, music, and performances (Iton 2008: 4). As critics have pointed out, the post-black operates within a global economy that threatens to commodify and level heterogeneous notions of blackness by creating ever new and stereotypical images of blackness. This might in fact very well warrant a "contemporary and continuous effort to craft an authentic racial identity against these popular stereotypes and misconceptions" (Schur 213: 238).[7] Particularly noteworthy in this context is how Touré criticizes the notion of an "authentic" African American identity for what he deems a restrictive "proximity to the ghetto experience" (Touré 2011: 153). As Greta Fowler Snyder has argued, Touré's disdain for "the black lower class" and his celebration of the heterogeneity and the social achievements of an African American middle class resembles rather than supersedes a more "traditional" approach to political activism and its claims for public and political respect (Snyder 2014: 340). In addition, Touré's post-blackness also articulates a largely uncritical orientation towards the political framework of the American nation state and the institutional political framework it provides. Particularly Touré's interpretation of the election victory of Barack Obama in 2008 as signaling the unqualified symbolic inclusion of the black citizenry into the national community offers a conjunction of nationalist and civil rights orientations that are more backward-looking than progressive or emancipatory (Snyder 2014: 341). For Snyder, Touré's "popular post-blackness" is thus largely ineffective in articulating an encompassing emancipatory politics and in opening cultural avenues for resistance and self-determination (Snyder 2014: 343).

In a similar manner, K. Merinda Simmons has taken Touré to task for disregarding the discursive formations structuring claims to racial identities

---

[7] From the perspective of similar debates in England, which also underlines the transnational scope of critical discussions of blackness, Koye Oyedeji concurs that the globalization of consumerist appropriations of blackness requires a response by artists who offer an innovative and critical aesthetic vision of post-blackness "that no longer merely re-presents what black meant in the past, but one that permits the expression of what we can be in the future and what our impact in a world driven by capital and global economics may become" (Oyedeji 2007: 133). As Oyedeji suggests, the post-black thus includes a prospective dimension that moves beyond a mimetic depiction of social realities because globalization entails the risk of disseminating denigrating images and notions of blackness on an unprecedented scale.

and for underestimating the role of the complex "interests or motivations" that inform the processes of racial and cultural othering (Simmons 2015: 4). Such criticisms of political and aesthetic notions of post-blackness also illustrate the limitations of this concept to describe successful interventions in "[s]tereotyping as a signifying practice that is central to the representation of racial difference" (Hall 1997: 257). Considering its resemblance to postmodernist dramaturgical strategies, the "post-black play" can also be understood as a cultural counterstrategy that focuses on reworking "the *forms* of racial representation" and on exposing the fetishistic, erotic, and sexualized fascination that often motivates acts of racial stereotyping (Hall 1997: 274).[8] However, it remains questionable how such formal innovations translate into an effective transformation of discursive and hegemonic practices of racial stereotyping.

Considering the use of parody and satire as means of "estrangement" and subversion, cultural critic Slavoj Žižek has cautioned that a postmodern, almost cynical awareness of particular political causes or, for that matter, racist assumptions does not necessarily result in them withering away. From Žižek's point of view, the idea of a post-racial society would be an illusion in the sense that it perpetuates the "ideological fantasy" on which it is built. Even if we are consciously aware of the denigrating images of racist stereotypes, this does not signal an end to the illusory and phantasmagoric assumptions that inform them. Speaking of the illusionary quality of an allegedly post-ideological stance, Žižek remarks:

> The illusion is therefore double: it consists in overlooking the illusion which is structuring our real, effective relationship to reality. And this overlooked, unconscious illusion is what may be called the ideological fantasy. (2002a: 30)

Informed by ideological fantasies, racist and anti-racist ideological messages are so inextricably interwoven in racialized performances of post-blackness and racist ideologies that we can no longer draw a clear line of separation between the two. In this light, post-black performances

---

[8] In his search for cultural counter-strategies to hegemonic racial stereotypes, Hall identifies reversal, substitution, and "making it strange" as the three main avenues of resistance. Reversal focuses on a re-evaluation of established stereotypes while substitution aims at replacing negative with positive images. The first two strategies are delimited, however, by accepting stereotyping as a viable form of cultural meaning making and by turning the "acknowledgment and celebration of diversity" into a range of commodifiable products. Hall finds a more promising and decisive intervention into existing regimes of racial representations in the third counter-strategy of contesting the formal properties of cultural stereotyping.

also require a revision and reform of the imaginary and fetishistic fantasies that sustain racist ideologies and such social practices that work towards maintaining racialized differences between socially constructed identities.[9] As I want to argue next, such a revisionary intervention on the level of a racist ideological fantasy is offered by Branden Jacobs-Jenkins's play *Neighbors*. Even though it is not included in Elam and Jones's anthology, the play ostentatiously participates in the mode of the post-black play. At the same time, however, it also offers the most comprehensive performative exploration of the often unacknowledged "interests and motivations" that have structured performances of racialized identities.

3. Post-Blackness and Branden Jacobs-Jenkins's *Neighbors* (2010/12)

Branden Jacobs-Jenkins's *Neighbors* (N) saw a first run at New York City's Public Theatre in 2010 and at the Company One Theatre in Boston (MA) early in 2011. In 2012 it was produced as a staged reading for the HighTide Festival on 13 May 2012 in Halesworth, Suffolk in the UK (N 221). In a 2010 review for the *New York Times*, Patrick Healy pointed out how the play joins a series of similar stage productions – like David Mamet's *Race* (2009) or the Wooster's Group adaptation of Eugene O'Neill's *The Emperor Jones* (1920) – which all interrogate and challenge contemporary conceptualizations of blackness on the American stage. Following the tradition of the American family play, *Neighbors* is built around two African American families that find themselves as new neighbors in an unspecified suburb of an American college town. The African American protagonist Richard Patterson is a specialist in Aristotelian political philosophy who has just recently re-located to a new house together with his wife Jean, who is white, and their interracial daughter Melody. The play begins with a dream-like scene in which one day Richard observes how the Crow family moves into the building next door. This second family consists of a set of characters whose names denote a tradition of denigrating and openly racist popular stereotypes of African Americans: Mammy as the portly and asexual motherly figure, Zip Coon, the simpleton and buffoon, Sambo the mentally retarded, muscular field hand in need of paternal guidance and supervision, Jim Crow, the Dandy-like urban male, and Topsy, the infamous, unruly child from Harriet Beecher Stowe's *Uncle Tom's Cabin*. The play thus juxtaposes a well-to-

---

[9] For a systematic sociological and historical assessment of such practices, see Omi and Winant (2014).

do, well-educated, interracial middle-class family with a set of neighbors who impersonate the stock characters of a minstrel show. In this sense, *Neighbors* presents an intriguing and controversial attempt to parody and satirize stereotypical notions of blackness and black identity which includes the presentation of negative stereotypes and traditional, racist images of blackness. As I want to suggest in the following, however, the play's embrace of a "post-black aesthetic" and its critique of minstrel performances is subjected to a further critical examination of its juxtaposition of the two African American families, the Pattersons and the Crows.

The most controversial dimension of Jacobs-Jenkins's play, of course, is how he depicts the Crow family. Prior to its first run, one critic described the play's reliance on the American blackface minstrel show tradition as "another piece of shock theatre" (Healey 2010) while theatre historian Harry J. Elam described the unsettling and provocative treatment of race relations in *Neighbors* as an example of "artistic license and racial irreverence" (2013: 269). In fact, the Crows' appearance on stage includes behaviors and performances reminiscent of nineteenth-century minstrel show routines that depict Zip, Mammy, Sambo, and Topsy as comical darkies and oversexualized buffoons. In the play's first interlude of four, for example, Zip first loses his clothes and underwear and is then shown in a failed attempt to lift up a bugle with his clenched behind. In such scenes, *Neighbors* confronts its audiences with the racist legacy of nineteenth-century American popular culture. As Harvey Young has argued, these minstrel elements are not only "clearly bracketed within the frame of satire" but also succeed in "destabilizing blackness as a singular, essential category" (2013: 66) by undermining any notion of authentic blackness.

One of the play's climactic moments consists in a dress rehearsal in which the Crows prepare for the comeback production of their family act. In the course of the rehearsal the family members enact the Jim Crow routine as it was first developed by Thomas Dartmouth Rice in the early 1830s. Since the family's father has passed away, his place is now taken by a reluctant Jim Crow, Jr., who was chosen by Mammy to substitute for his deceased father. Jim Crow, Jr. initially refuses to join the family's staging of stereotypical minstrel characters: "Mammy, I can't do this! I am not like Sambo and Topsy!" (N 237; also see: N 264). Nevertheless, Jim Crow, Jr. temporarily acquiesces to play the part of his deceased father in the family's minstrel show performance, which also renders him complicit with his family's minstrel-style staging of racial differences. When he takes part in the rehearsal, however, Jim Crow, Jr. enters into a performative competition about manhood with his brother Sambo in which the two brothers attempt to win the attention of imaginary white females. At the climax of this surrealistic and excessive performance of "coon-ness" (N 286-289), Jim's ultimate creation of a more "authentic" Jim Crow routine performance results in the explosion of a cookie jar that is their father's urn (N 289). This explosion of the "cookie jar" clearly symbolizes a corrective intervention in the detrimental connection between American racism and blackface minstrelsy. Earlier in the play, this connection is established in the play's secondary text, when the urn is described as having "the shape of a black tramp biting into a huge slice of watermelon or maybe stealing a chicken" (N 233). By literally exploding this symbol of minstrelsy's racist depiction of blackness, Jim Crow, Jr. not only repeats the original racialized performance of T.D. Rice's impersonation of an African American character. His excessive performance effectively allows Jim Crow, Jr. to break out of the performance genealogy of the Jim Crow stereotype. In his revisionist neo-minstrel show, Jacobs-Jenkins simultaneously employs and challenges stereotypical stagings of racial difference. It not only exhibits the same ambivalence that Eric Lott has found in nineteenth-century blackface performances.[10] With its farcical and surrealistic elements, Jim Crow Jr.'s revisionist performance also resembles the individualistic ethos and aesthetic of the post-black. Furthermore, it addresses the conundrums of intra-racial biases as well as interracial desire and mixed-race identities (Elam 2013: 270-271).

In structural terms, however, the most prominent feature of the play's staging of "post-blackness" is the juxtaposition and encounter of the two neighboring families, which also aligns the play with the figure of the "neighbor" and its conceptualization in current critical theory. As I want to suggest, the play's complex investment in "post-blackness" as a critique of conventional images of racial identification can be understood according to Slavoj Žižek's recent conceptualization of the "neighbor" in the context of a Lacanian theory of alterity. In his critical consideration of a philosophical discussion of the "neighbor" in philosophy and ethics, Žižek proposes a more complex understanding of the "neighbor" as a figure of otherness. As Žižek argues, any encounter with an alien "other" can be analyzed according to Lacan's three orders of the imaginary, the symbolic, and the real (Žižek 2006: 143). According to Žižek, the recognition of the

---

[10] As Eric Lott has shown, the complexity and ambivalence of nineteenth-century blackface minstrelsy consists of a "dialectical flickering of racial insult and racial envy, moments of domination and moments of liberation, counterfeit and currency, a pattern at times amounting to no more than the two faces of racism, at others gesturing toward a specific kind of political or sexual danger, and all constituting a peculiarly American structure of racial feeling" (1996: 6).

neighbor as "imaginary other" is predicated on a mirror-like mutual understanding of the other as an extension or reflection of the self. In the context of the symbolic order, the neighbor's position is defined by the symbolic "big Other" who defines the relationship to the other according to "the impersonal set of rules that coordinate our coexistence" (ibid.). The fact that "there is no intersubjectivity (no symmetrical, shared, relation between humans) without the impersonal symbolic Order" does not preclude the existence of a third dimension in which the neighbor assumes a phantasmagoric dimension and represents the radical otherness of an impenetrable human being, the "inhuman partner," as Žižek calls it, "with whom no symmetrical dialogue, mediated by the symbolic Order, is possible" (ibid.). In this sense, the neighbor represents "the abyssal dimension of another human being" and the "unfathomable abyss of radical Otherness, of someone about whom I ultimately do not know anything" (Žižek 2010: 234). For Žižek, this monstrous dimension of the neighbor can be traced back to the Judeo-Christian tradition in which "an alien traumatic kernel forever persists in my neighbor – the neighbor remains an inert, impenetrable, enigmatic presence that hystericizes me" (ibid.). In Jacobs-Jenkins's play, this triadic structure of encountering a neighbor is played out in the complex relationship between the members of the Patterson family and their neighbors.

With regard to the Patterson family, the play tells the tragicomic story of a middle-aged interracial couple whose marriage is predicated on the assumption that "race" does not matter (N 307). Richard and Jean had met in a poetry class at Dartmouth where they fell in love. In their early years they adorned their life with poetry which provided them not only with a common ground, but made their different racial backgrounds seemingly irrelevant. Retrospectively, their early years suggest the possibility of living a life beyond the social constraints traditionally placed on interracial marriages. In the early phase of their marriage, the spouses successfully mediated their racial difference through the symbolic order of English poetry which allowed them to transcend the confines of racialized identities. However, in the course of the play, the audience learns about the estrangement between the spouses and their "post-racial" marriage. Jean now lacks the romance and the intimacy of these early days of their marriage that was informed by a shared appreciation of English poetry. Exposed to her new neighbors, Jean realizes a fundamental limitation and insecurity regarding her marriage. During a visit to her home, Jean tells Zip about her fascination with a romance novel she read in her teens (N 294-296). From the fragmented account she gives, the audience learns that Jean was intrigued by the erotic love story of an African slave and the daughter of a plantation owner. While she realizes that this fictional account conveys a thinly veiled racist image of the slave as rapist African American, Jean is troubled and fascinated by the romance's intimation that the white girl had enjoyed her nightly tryst with her father's slave. This thinly veiled racist image of interracial desire and the sexual prowess of African American men proves to be especially unsettling for Jean. As Jean confides in Zip, the memory of this episode amounts to the fundamental fetishistic fantasy that has not only motivated her interest in literature, but also her desire for Richard. As the audience realizes, Jean's entrance into an interracial marriage was predicated on the integration of Richard into the symbolic order of English literature and was driven by Jean's erotic fantasies of being with a black man. This duplicity of Jean's symbolization of interracial desire adds to her increasing alienation from her husband. As a consequence of her remembering her childhood fascination with "black" sexuality, Jean begins to press Richard to confide in her whether his love for her is equally informed by an interracial erotic desire. Alienated and repelled by Jean's discovery of a fetishistic dimension in their marriage, Richard takes offense and refuses to articulate why he loves her. This effectively prevents Jean from maintaining a mirror-like, imaginary identification with Richard that is mediated through the symbolized desire in the literary texts she has perused. Jean even articulates her frustration with the enigmatic nature of Richard's desire (N 296). It is this impenetrability of her spouse as a desiring subject that prevents her from sustaining her imaginary identification with him. Unable to maintain a mirror-like correspondence between her own desire and that of her husband, Jean starts to befriend Zip, with whom she engages in a more intimate relationship after she leaves Richard.

Another factor in the dissolution of Jean and Richard's marriage is the fact that the two spouses fundamentally disagree about their neighborly relations with the Crows. From the beginning, it is Richard who objects to the appearance of the new neighbors. Not only is he uncomfortable with his daughter Melody befriending Jim Crow. He also objects to Jean taking the initiative by inviting Zip to join her for a cup of tea. Having finally landed a position as substitute for his former classics professor in a class on Greek tragedy, Richard is afraid that his academic career might be stalled again when his family is seen consorting with his new neighbors. Throughout the play, he expresses his condescending views about the Crows. When they move in, he refers to them as "[a] bunch of . . . niggers" (N 224). Later he refers to Jim as a "predator" who lusts after his daughter (N 303). Both instances of using racial slurs can be seen as an expression of his anxiety about his social status. As he explains to Jean:

> My dissertation is finally about to go to press, I am struggling to make a good impression, and things are just finally starting to line up for us. They are just starting to pay off! And I just cannot – I will not stand to have a bunch of ... bumpkins move in and fuck up my flow, okay? I'm too old to go through this again! I'm tired! (N 250)

What becomes clear from such remarks is that Richard has internalized the racist perspective of their social environment. Richard thus not only "understands the effects of racial socialization" (Young 2013: 67), but develops a paranoiac subjectivity in which the new neighbors posit a threat to his social existence. When he becomes increasingly troubled by how Jim Crow and Zip approach his daughter and wife, Jean calls him literally "paranoid" (N 277) which seems an appropriate description for Richard's middle-class bias against the Crows whose presence contributes to his mental disintegration.

In the course of his encounters with the Crows, Richard finds himself in a struggle with his neighbors, who for him assume a more and more monstrous quality. When he finally confronts Zip with his relationship with Jean, Zip intentionally feeds into Richard's paranoia by insinuating that he had plotted on stealing Richard's wife from the very beginning. When Zip finally suggests that in their mutual desire for the same woman Richard has become like Zip, Richard physically attacks Zip and involves him in a life-and-death struggle. While Zip turns himself into a trickster-like figure, Richard remains under the influence of blatantly racist views and deep-seated fantasies about a transgressive African American sexuality. This inability to appropriately conceive of interracial desire not only limits Richard's symbolization of "blackness," but also contributes to his alienation from his wife and daughter. Their becoming more and more intimate with their neighbors for Richard constitutes an instance of the Lacanian "answer of the real," a sudden encounter with a lack in the symbolic order that assumes the form of a "nightmarish unreal spectre" (Žižek 2002b: 19). Already at the beginning of the play, the stereotypical characters of the Crows moving in next door is presented as a dream-like apparition for Richard (N 223-224). Richard's avoidance of interracial desire and sexuality makes him susceptible to racist fantasies and is one of the central reasons for them assuming an increasingly monstrous appearance. The monstrous quality of the minstrel characters does not only derive from Richard's middle-class prejudice against the itinerant Crows, but also follows from a view of the neighbor that can be understood according to Žižek's conceptualization of the neighbor qua the Lacanian Real – here the Real of interracial sexuality and African American hypermasculinity.

The third family member, Melody Patterson, is presented as a counter-example to the failings of her parents. Whereas Jean remains driven by her fetishistic, imaginary identification with black masculinity and whereas Richard's disavowal of interracial desire erupts into a violent struggle with his rival, Melody appears to be more successful in her consistent attempts to mediate her relationship with the Crows through established forms of symbolization. As the mixed-race offspring of her parents' interracial marriage, Melody is characterized by a basic insecurity about her mixed-race identity and "as suffering from the angst of trying to belong" (Elam 2013: 270). In one of their conversations Melody confides in Jim, Jr. that in early childhood she was traumatized by her realization of having a dark skin. As Harry J. Elam has rightly pointed out, in her "struggle for racial acceptance and identity" Melody engages in a sexual relationship with Jim, Jr. which soils her already brown skin with additional layers of blackness. In this sense, Melody's struggle for a racial identity also becomes a struggle for sexual self-determination for both where "sexual intimacy functions as a racializing act, bringing her closer to blackness and belonging" (Elam 2013: 271). What needs to be added here is the fact that Melody's reconciliation with blackness comes at the end of a process of symbolization in which she attempts to integrate her relationship with Jim, Jr. and the Crow family into a new symbolic order that differs from the patterns established by her parents. Melody consistently seeks appropriate appellations for Jim Crow, Jr. when she greets him as "neighbor" (N 232) or when she turns him into her boyfriend by kissing him (N 257).

In her quest for an appropriate integration of pathological images of blackness into her symbolic universe, Melody even makes herself complicit with Mammy and her schemes for a revival of the family's minstrel performance. It is Melody who finally convinces Jim, Jr. to play the role of his father and even considers becoming a part of the minstrel routine herself. These instances of identifying with the performance tradition of American minstrelsy allow Melody not only to escape from the restrictive notions of blackness embodied by her father. It could also be understood in analogy to the Lacanian notion of "traversing the fantasy." Her rebellion against her father allows her to look beyond the deceptive masks of the minstrel routine and prepares her for reaching beyond the process of racial stereotyping that have limited existing notions of blackness.[11]

---

[11] In this context, it is important to note that Melody's integration of the minstrel performance into her personal symbolic universe is preceded by her rejection of "blackness" symbolized by her father. Her rebellion against his kind of

This dynamic is fully incorporated by the complex ending of the play which combines different diegetic levels and even penetrates the fourth wall separating the audience from the stage. While Richard and Zip continue their physical altercation in the back, the family prepares and conducts its minstrel routine in which even Jim, Jr. participates. During their final preparations for their minstrel show, the characters express their awareness of the racialized dynamic of the performance when they discuss how to best feed their show to a white audience: namely by engaging in performances that affirm racialized differences and a binary distinction between black and white perspectives. In this sense, the staging of a minstrel show serves as a meta-theatrical commentary which articulates the need for a post-black performance style by highlighting the limitations of staging race. Finally, the end of the minstrel performance coincides with the end of *Neighbors* itself which introduces another meta-theatrical device. At the end of the play *and* the minstrel show, Melody is described as sitting in the first row of the audience and applauding the show. She is thus turned into a synecdochical figure that stands for the interracial audience attending the play.

The play's secondary text gives a condensed description of the performative coda to the play, which also includes the revisionary argument of the performance. It is described how Melody mingles with the audience leaving the theatre and is then joined by the actor who played Jim Crow, Jr. While he thus finally breaks the illusion of the "fourth wall" separating audience and performers, the playwright practically leaves it to chance if spectators witness the final exchange between Melody and Jim, Jr.:

> *Eventually **Jim** comes out of the stage door to greet her. They hug and kiss. Maybe she gives him a cigarette, which he smokes. Maybe people catch this, maybe they don't.*
> MELODY. How do you feel?
> *'We Are Family' is heard blasting away over the speakers back in the empty theater, as the actor playing Jim Crow starts to tell her how he really feels.* (N 319)

Here Melody's question obviously attempts to penetrate the theatricality of the minstrel performance and seeks to transform Jim from minstrel character to actor to human being. The question of "How do you feel?" even evokes a symbolic universe in which recognizing a shared human

---

"blackness" also emancipates her from the Lacanian "big Other" and allows her to realize that the "big Other does not exist."

nature suffices to move beyond race. This simplistic reduction to a universal *conditio humana* is complicated by two facts. For one, Melody is re-enacting the behavior of her mother who had also implored her father to tell his real feelings. Her question thus conjures up the danger that an articulation and understanding of these true feelings might not lead to a satisfactory outcome. In addition, the actual answer of "Jim Crow, Jr." is not included or symbolized within the performance itself. This implies that Melody's question opens up a space for acknowledging the Other/neighbor as the repository of unacknowledged needs, desires, and urges. In this sense, Melody's question eschews idealizing Jim in a particular role or as being invested with particular features. The play's end avoids a mystification of "blackness" that turns the "racial Other" into a melodramatic victim-hero who is invested with dignity and virtue only because of his/her suffering from racial oppression. Instead, Melody's question precludes a facile and preliminary form of identification between the two lovers. This denial of closure allows Jacobs-Jenkins not only to bring this new sensibility of "post-blackness" to the stage but also challenges the dominance and pervasive influence of the stereotypical images that he has created by laying open the underlying fantasies that inform them.

4. Conclusion

In contrast to the advocates of a post-black aesthetic that look to the individual artist as the source for cultural renewal, Jacobs-Jenkins's post-black minstrel tragicomedy focuses on the effect of post-black performances on audiences. Branden Jacobs-Jenkins's *Neighbors* presents exactly such a challenge to the audiences of his play who are not only confronted with racist images but who are simultaneously encouraged to move beyond them. By satirizing, challenging, and thus ironically preserving the American tradition of blackface minstrelsy, the play very effectively skewers consciously or unconsciously held beliefs and stereotypes that inform the performative construction of blackness on the American stage. However, Jacobs-Jenkins does not simply juxtapose a comedic neo-minstrel show with European tragedy as two distinct dramatic forms – one elitist, one popular. By staging "post-blackness" in the form of a struggle and interaction between two neighboring families with a tragicomic outcome, the play demonstrates the desire to push beyond the boundaries of such generic constraints. Offering an escape from overdetermined racialized performances of identity, the play's open ending, which does not include Jim, Jr.'s answer to Melody's question, allows his character to emerge as a subject whose identity is characterized by "impenetrability and opacity" (Žižek 2006: 138). Melody's openness to this conceptual void resembles an ethics of a "mutual recognition of limitation" that "opens up a space of sociality that is the solidarity of the vulnerable" (Žižek 2006: 138-9). In *Neighbors,* post-black performances thus establish a decidedly intersubjective notion of post-blackness. Spectators are not only confronted with the symbolic and structural violence inherent in the representational strategies of racialized performances, they are also provoked to question the duplicitous ideological fantasies that motivate and drive stereotyping as cultural practice of symbolizing racial differences.

References

Baker, Houston A. 2015. "Conclusion: Why the Lega Mask Has Many Mouths and Multiple Eyes." In: Houston A. Baker and K. Merinda Simmons, eds. *The Trouble with Post-Blackness*. New York: Columbia University Press, 247-256.

Byrd, Cathy. 2002. "Is There a 'Post-Black' Art? – Investigating the Legacy of the 'Freestyle' Show." *Art Papers* 26.6, 34-39.

Du Bois, William Edward Burghardt. 1926. "Krigwa Players Little Negro Theatre." *Crisis* 32 (3 July), 134-136.

Dyson, Michael Eric. 2011. "Tour(é)ing Blackness." In: Touré. *Who's Afraid of Post-Blackness? What It Means to Be Black Now*. New York: Free Press, xiii-xx.

Elam, Harry J., Jr. 2001. "The Device of Race: An Introduction." In: Harry J. Elam, Jr, ed. *African American Performance and Theater History: A Critical Reader*. Oxford: Oxford University Press, 3-16.

Elam, Harry J. 2013. "Black Theatre in the Age of Obama." In: Harvey Young, ed. *The Cambridge Companion to African American Theatre*. Cambridge: Cambridge University Press, 255-278.

Elam, Harry J., Jr., and Douglas A. Jones, Jr. 2013. "Introduction." In: Harry J. Elam, Jr. and Douglas A. Jones, Jr., eds. *The Methuen Drama Book of Post-Black Plays*. London: Bloomsbury Publishing, ix-xxxv.

George-Graves, Nadine. 2005. "Basic Black." *Theatre Journal* 57.4, 610-612.

Golden, Thelma. 2001. "Introduction: Post..." In: Thelma Golden and Hamza Walker, eds. *Freestyle*. New York: Studio Museum in Harlem, 14-15.

Hall, Stuart. 1997. "The Spectacle of the 'Other.'" In: Stuart Hall, ed. *Representation: Cultural Representations and Signifying Practices.* London: Sage, 223-290.

Healy, Patrick. 2010. "New Play Puts an Old Face on Race." *The New York Times* (2 February 2010). Web. 10 April 2016.

Iton, Richard. 2008. *In Search of the Black Fantastic: Politics and Popular Culture in the Post-Civil Rights Era.* Oxford: Oxford University Press.

Jacobs-Jenkins, Branden. 2012. "Neighbors." In: *American Next Wave: Four Contemporary Plays from HighTide Festival Theatre.* London: Methuen Drama, 219-319.

Leader-Picone, Cameron. 2015. "Post-Black Stories: Colson Whitehead's *Sag Harbor* and Racial Individualism." *Contemporary Literature* 56.3, 421-449.

Lee, Young Jean. 2010. *The Shipment and LEAR.* New York: Theatre Communications Group.

Lott, Eric. 1996. "Blackface and Blackness: The Minstrel Show in American Culture." In: Annemarie Bean, James V. Hatch, and Brooks McNamara, eds. *Inside the Minstrel Mask: Readings in Nineteenth-Century Blackface Minstrelsy.* Hanover: Wesleyan University Press, 3-32.

Maus, Derek C. 2014. "'Mommy, What Is a Post-Soul Satirist?': An Introduction." In: Derek C. Maus and James J. Donahue, eds. *Post-Soul Satire: Black Identity after Civil Rights.* University Press of Mississippi, xi-xxiii.

Murray, Derek Conrad. 2014. "Post-Black Art and the Resurrection of African American Satire." In: Derek C. Maus and James J. Donahue, eds. *Post-Soul Satire: Black Identity after Civil Rights.* Jackson: University Press of Mississippi, 3-21.

Omi, Michael, and Howard Winant. 2014. *The Theory of Racial Formation. Racial Formation in the United States.* Florence: Taylor and Francis.

Oyedeji, Koye. 2007. "In Search of … (Adequate Representations of Our Post Black Condition)." In: R. Victoria Arana, ed. *"Black" British Aesthetics Today.* Newcastle upon Tyne, England: Cambridge Scholars, 119-134.

Schur, Richard. 2013. "The Crisis of Authenticity in Contemporary African American Literature." In: Lovalerie King and Shirley Moody-Turner, eds. *Contemporary African American Literature: The Living Canon.* Bloomington: Indiana University Press, 235-254.

Schmidt, Christian. 2014. "Dissimulating Blackness: The Degenerative Satires of Paul Beatty and Percival Everett." In: Derek C. Maus and James J. Donahue, ed. *Post-Soul Satire: Black Identity after Civil Rights*. Jackson: University Press of Mississippi, 150-161.

—. 2016. "The Parody of Postblackness in *I Am Not Sidney Poitier* and the End(s) of African American Literature." *BSP: Black Studies Papers* 2.1, 113-132.

Simmons, K. Merinda. 2015. "Introduction: The Dubious Stage of Post-Blackness – Performing Otherness, Conserving Dominance." In: Houston A. Baker and K. Merinda Simmons, ed. *The Trouble with Post-Blackness*. New York: Columbia University Press, 1-20.

Snyder, Greta Fowler. 2014. "On Post-Blackness and the Black Fantastic." *Souls* 16.3-4, 330-350.

Touré. 2011. *Who's Afraid of Post-Blackness? – What It Means to Be Black Now*. New York: Free Press.

Wilson, August. 1997. "The Ground on Which I Stand." *Callaloo* 20.3, 493-503.

Womack, Ytasha L. 2010. *Post Black: How a New Generation Is Redefining African American Identity*. Chicago, Ill.: Lawrence Hill Books.

Worsley, Shawan M. 2010. *Audience, Agency and Identity in Black Popular Culture*. New York and London: Routledge.

Young, Harvey. 2013. *Theatre & Race*. Basingstoke: Palgrave Macmillan.

—. 2016. "Pessimism and the Age of Obama." *American Literary History* 28.4, 854-858.

Žižek, Slavoj. 2002a. *The Sublime Object of Ideology*. 2nd ed. London: Verso.

—. 2002b. *Welcome to the Desert of the Real! – Five Essays on September 11 and Related Dates*. London: Verso.

—. 2006. "Neighbors and Other Monsters: A Plea for Ethical Violence." In: Slavoj Žižek, Eric L. Santner, and Kenneth Reinhard, eds. *The Neighbor: Three Inquiries in Political Theology*. Chicago: University of Chicago Press, 134-190.

—. 2010. "Psychoanalysis and the Lacanian Real: 'Strange Shapes of the Unwarped Primal World.'" In: Matthew Beaumont, ed. *A Concise Companion to Realism*. Malden, MA: Blackwell, 225-241.

CHAPTER FOUR

BETWEEN THE NEED TO FIT IN AND THE DESIRE TO STAND OUT: RACE, GENDER, AND SEXUALITY IN CELESTE NG'S *EVERYTHING I NEVER TOLD YOU*

BRYGIDA GASZTOLD

1. Introduction

Celeste Ng's debut novel *Everything I Never Told You* (2014) tells the story of a mixed-race Chinese/Caucasian couple living in a small town in Ohio in the1970s, at the time when such relationships were still uncommon. This multi-layered novel explores life in an interracial family, interrogating the question whether an Asian man and a white woman should marry against the advice of the family and when they do what obstacles they might encounter on the way to marital bliss. Racial identification of their children, whom they hope to be accepted as third-generation Americans, but who instead are seen as immigrants at birth, constitutes another issue of the narrative. An omniscient, third person narrator does not adhere closely to one character's perspective but, demonstrating a degree of neutrality, gives all of them significant depth. The storyline is built on dichotomy of us – the white majority – versus them – the Asian American minority, represented in the novel by the white, middle-class, mainstream American society of the 1970's and a Chinese American family. As the Lees are portrayed as fully assimilated, the narrator provides little culture specific information, and the only examples of code-switching are an Anglicized "kowtow" and a Chinese term *char siubau* – a type of pork bun cooked for James by a Chinese American assistant, in whom he confides because she has an aspect that his Caucasian wife can never match. Otherwise, there is no information about

Chinese holidays, typical foods, customs or rites, as the Lees are shown as a successfully acculturated family. Lydia's unsuspected death pulls the Lee family into an emotional vortex, forcing its members not only to confront their individual insecurities but also to grapple with their identity as a biracial family in the 1970's Midwest. As each of them tries to make sense of what happened to the sixteen-year-old middle daughter, their inquiries reveal deep cracks in the relationships with one another. Exposing and confronting their family secrets pressures the Lees to revisit the painful memories that have contributed to the extremely tense and fragile undercurrents which have informed their family relations. In the case of Ng's novel, an overarching thread guiding the narrative is the idea of difference, communicated through the medium of race relations, gender roles, and sexuality. This paper will discuss significant social and cultural changes that took place in American society in the 1970's through three critical lenses: race/ethnicity, gender/feminism, and (homo)sexuality. The focus on the private sphere as the realm of family and home life and its potential for providing individual satisfaction and self-fulfilment provides a narrative background to explore the idea of difference. By offering a voice to the characters that represent counter-narratives to the official discourse, the author acknowledges their existence and demonstrates how they influence the nature and dynamics of identity construction.

2. The Dynamics of Racial Discrimination

Celeste Ng's novel presents American society in the 1970s as racially constructed, with upper middle-class jobs (university professors, doctors) predominantly taken by white professionals. The protagonists live in a segregated, white neighbourhood, and their children go to an all-white school, having virtually no contacts with other ethnicities. As anti-miscegenation laws were only declared to be unconstitutional by the Supreme Court in 1967, the introduction of an interracial marriage illuminates the problems that such couples faced at that time. Ng's narrative traces the actual changes that were altering the shape of American society, such as the 1967 Loving vs. Virginia case:

> a white man, a black woman, who would share a most appropriate name: Loving. In four months they would be arrested in Virginia, the law reminding them that Almighty God had never intended white, black, yellow, and red to mix, that there should be no *mongrel citizens,* no *obliteration of racial pride.* It would be four years before they protested, and four years more before the court concurred, but many more years before the people around them would, too. Some, like Marilyn's mother,

never would. (Ng 2014: 55, emphasis in the original)[1]

Or the news that "Yale admitted women, then Harvard. The nation learned new words: affirmative action; Equal Rights Amendment; Ms." (159). Set against the backdrop of a challenging time in American social history, Ng's novel provides an insight into a society on the cusp of acknowledging the growing significance of its non-white as well as female members. Having an interracial family as neighbours, a non-white colleague at work, or a non-white student in class are depicted as a big step in the direction of acknowledging diversity. Simultaneously, the narrative calls upon and reveals the points of contention that such changes may generate.

The novel signals a bodily difference as a crucial factor in racial identification, one that is easy to observe and stereotype. "To a large extent racialization relies on bodily attributes when physical differences not only signify but also provide, often visual, evidence of racial differentiation" (Gasztold 2015: 155). A sense of physical difference is expressed through language, such as the frequent references to straight ink black hair, slanted eyes, thin body, and short height. Marilyn observes her Chinese American boyfriend as if he was a different species: "How skinny he was, she thought, how wide his shoulders were, like a swimmer's, his skin the color of tea, of fall leaves toasted by the sun. She had never seen anyone like him" (35). The students wonder about their new professor: "This little man, five foot nine at most and not even *American*, was going to teach them about cowboys?" (31-32, emphasis in the original). A woman in a shop speculates about Hannah's origin: "Chinese? ... I knew by it, by the eyes. She'd tugged the corner of each eye outward with a fingertip" (3). The predominance of physical racial markers, which are stereotypically attributed to Asian origin, defines the social boundaries that are based on bodily difference. Physical othering leads to racial discrimination, which appears to be manifested in many ways:

> You saw it in the sign at the Peking Express – a cartoon man with a coolie hat, slant eyes, buckteeth, and chopsticks. You saw it in the little boys on the playground, stretching their eyes to slits with their fingers – Chinese – Japanese –a look at these –a and in the older boys who muttered *ching chong ching chong* ching as they passed you on the street, just loud enough for you to hear. (193, emphasis in the original)

On employment, James's parents get English names: "That evening, each brought home a navy-blue uniform stitched with a new English name: *Henry. Wendy*" (42, emphasis in the original). The price for being hired is

---

[1] All further quotes refer to this edition.

a partial renunciation of their Chinese identity, which later leads to their son's cultural estrangement. There seems to be no escape from the pattern of prejudice, as there is no exposure to cultural diversity, and social relations are based entirely on fixed stereotypes, such as the one that the Chinese are "quiet and hardworking and clean" (41).

Representational practices such as stereotyping demonstrate how easily the racialized body becomes the signifier of otherness and racial inferiority when one attempts to define oneself in terms other than those that are provided by one's physical appearance. To grasp the behavioural norms of American society, James has to negotiate the forms of domination imposed by the mainstream culture. Therefore, he tries to assimilate through cultural mimicry: "he trimmed his hair; he bought a blue-striped Oxford shirt" (46). James feels embarrassed because he looks different from other kids and his parents hold menial jobs: "Alone, he could pretend to be just another student. He could pretend that, in the uniform, he looked just like everyone else" (44). Sartorial imitation allows him to blend in and gives him a semblance of a desired identity but does not guarantee acceptance. That is why he immerses himself in the study of the topic that is universally considered to derive from the heart of American history:

> he studied the most quintessentially American subject he could find – cowboys –but he never spoke of his parents, or his family. He still had few acquaintances and no friends. He still found himself shifting in his seat, as if at any moment someone might notice him and ask him to leave. (45)

The figure of the cowboy, which embodies the values of traditional western rural culture and represents the struggle between the frontier and civilization, is an important element in the creation of American popular culture and the mythologization of the West. As Jennifer Moskowitz claims in her essay "The Cultural Myth of the Cowboy, or, How the West Was Won," "in the American imagination the late nineteenth/turn of the century cowboy came to be perceived as a uniquely American creation" (2006: 1).

Since language and a manner of speaking may reveal or masque one's origin, a surname such as Lee may point at someone who is not an *Oriental*, but "someone in a sand-coloured blazer, someone with a slight drawl and a Southern pedigree" (31). Similarly, an accent may be acquired: "Where had he come from, she wondered. He sounded nothing like what she'd been told Chinamen sounded like: *so solly, no washee*" (32, emphasis in the original). But the truth is James "had stopped speaking Chinese to his parents, afraid of tinting his English with an accent; long before that, he had stopped speaking to his parents at school at all" (48).

Having mastered the language and cultural mores of white Americans, James is ready to claim: "Well, I *am* American," he says when people blink, a barb of defensiveness in his tone" (19, emphasis in the original). He may have fulfilled the assimilative requirements and "acted white," but the other side is not ready to acknowledge this fact, leaving him in-between two identities:

> I don't just kowtow to the police. Bent-backed coolies in cone hats, pigtailed Chinamen with sandwiched palms. Squinty and servile. Bowing and belittled. He has long suspected that everyone sees him this way – Stanley Hewitt, the policemen, the checkout girl at the grocery store. But he had not thought that everyone included Marilyn. (116).

By refuting the stereotyped representations of a Chinese American, he validates his right to construct his own self and not to conform to the common label. At the same time, however, both father's and son's aptitude for learning – they are both admitted to Harvard – evokes and perpetuates a stereotypical image of Chinese American students as "superachievers." Henceforth, the author marks a fine line between undercutting stereotypical thinking and reiterating it. Resulting from the inability to escape the effects of social stereotyping is the crisis of self-perception, accompanied by feelings of confusion and frustration, such as can be seen in James's characterization.

Since the Chinese American protagonists are often referred to as the only Orientals to attend school or live in the neighbourhood, the practices of racial discrimination are presented as resulting from a lack of knowledge about otherness. "She had never seen one [Chinese] in person before" (31), says Marilyn, and her statement proves that the idea of racial mixing is implied as a rare phenomenon. Similarly surprised are James's new school-friends: "That first morning, James slid into his seat and the girl next to him asked, 'What's wrong with your eyes?'" (43); others stare at him because "he looked like no one they'd ever seen" (43). Louise, James's teaching assistant, is the school novelty: "Eighteen years at Middlewood College, he'd thought, and here was the first Oriental student he'd ever had" (9). A fear of the unknown, which accompanies ignorance, fosters the instinct of self-preservation. As Nelson has convincingly shown,

> a lack of intergroup contact or low levels of contact may predispose people to perceive outgroups as threatening [...] A lack of knowledge means that ingroup members are likely to have only a limited understanding of the outgroups' beliefs and values. Ignorance of the outgroup is also likely to breed uncertainty, mistrust, and suspicion. (2016: 263)

The absence of interracial mixing and a lack of the cognitive sophistication to recognize identity as racially and sexually constructed result in the development of biased attitudes. On the one hand, stereotyping and prejudging help the characters to accommodate their anxiety about the unfamiliar, but on the other such attitudes perpetuate the idea of segregation and discrimination as the mechanisms which are typically employed to cope with racial and cultural difference. Hence, lack of access to representation only maintains the dominance of white meta-narratives.

The examples of racial discrimination are presented in the novel as important elements of public interactions, which negatively affect social and economic prospects of the minorities but do not thwart them entirely. The Lees follow a typical immigrant path:

> James's father had taken the name of his neighbor's son, who had drowned in the river the year before, and come to join his "father" in San Francisco. It was the story of nearly every Chinese immigrant from Chester A. Arthur to the end of the Second World War. (40)

Then, his parents move to Iowa because it gives their son a unique opportunity: "There was a special policy, said the brother, for children of employees. If they could pass an entrance exam, they could attend the school for free" (41). That is how James becomes "the first Oriental boy to attend Lloyd" (43). Thus, a son of illiterate Chinese immigrants manages to finish high school and later graduate from Harvard. He does not, however, succeed in getting a job there and has to move to Middlewood, Ohio, "where a Saturday night out means the roller rink or the bowling alley or the drive-in, where even Middlewood Lake, at the center of town, is really just a glorified pond" (7). The maintenance of power and white privilege allow him only a limited degree of social advancement but bar his entry into the highest echelons of academia. As much as hard work and brainpower enable him to get prestigious education, the Caucasian academic majority denies him the opportunity of social advancement in a predominantly white milieu. James's story is, and at the same time is not, representative of the Chinese American diaspora: The story of arrival reflects the common traits within the diaspora, whereas his academic success is a unique example of an individual achievement. Like Mary Antin at the beginning of the twentieth century, James chooses education as the avenue through which to gain American acceptance. In fact, this strategy affords him a degree of acceptability and partially allows him to be seen first of all as a scholar, then as a Chinese American.

James exhibits what James Clifford calls a diasporic consciousness, which is characterized by "dwelling-in-displacement" (1997: 254). Being born in the U.S., he does not "desire another place" (Clifford 1997: 255), but the politics of racial bias permeates his life and prevents his full participation and integration into American society: "He had never felt he belonged here, even though he'd been born on American soil, even though he had never set foot anywhere else" (40). Since birth, he has felt insecure: "In Chinatowns, the lives of all those *paper sons* were fragile and easily torn. Everyone's name was false. Everyone hoped not to be found out and sent back. Everyone clustered together so they wouldn't stand out" (41, emphasis in the original). Educational institutions recreate the same segregated pattern and even if they provide a chance for socializing, "he'd been embarrassed to ask classmates to his house, afraid that they'd recognize his mother from the lunch line, or his father from mopping the hallway. They hadn't had a yard, anyway" (89). Even a marriage to Marilyn fails to furnish James with the feeling of self-confidence. He still considers himself not good enough to have a white girl and worries that she will realize her mistake and leave him: "After a while, the fear became a habit, too" (46). James constantly seeks reassurance that she will stay, such as the smudge on the wall after they make love, which he calls another tiny miracle – the first one being the persistence of their conjugal bond.

What he learns is that matrimony may offer an entrance to white America, but it does not necessarily secure a warm welcome. This constant feeling of uncertainty that fills him is highlighted by his affair with Louise, his Chinese American assistant, who makes him Chinese buns and reminds him of home: "This is the sort of woman, he thinks, he should have fallen in love with. A woman who looked just like this. A woman just like him" (205). James's efforts at engaging himself in Americanization through the consumption of American culture and behaviours are matched by his determination to distance himself from immigrant roots – a signal of his internalization of racist discourse. The concept of home escapes his grasp but introduces ambivalence to his life, as he neither identifies China as his home nor is allowed to feel at home in America. The author demonstrates how striving for inclusion into the white mainstream uproots the protagonist, leaving him in between "yellow peril" and "model minority" stereotypes.

James and Marilyn are attracted to each other for different reasons. He sees their liaison as a vehicle of acceptance: the white blonde who embodies America will secure his desire for recognition and belonging: "she pulled him to her again. It was as if America herself was taking him in" (45). Through marriage, James hopes to win what diligence at school, hard work, and obedience still fail to provide. What draws him to Marilyn is her easy laugh, sparkle, and chatter but most of all her unconditional inclusion into American society: "Hers had been just one of the pale, pretty faces, indistinguishable from the next, and though he would never fully realize it, this was the first reason he came to love her: because she had blended in so perfectly" (37-38). Through intermarriage, Marilyn's attention and love give him access to this segment of American society that is otherwise denied to non-whites. She is also the first American to accept him as he is, and her consent acknowledges and legitimizes his presence: "Every time she kissed him, every time he opened his arms and she crawled into them, felt like a miracle. Coming to her made him feel perfectly welcomed, perfectly at home, as he had never in his life felt before" (40). A marriage to a "true" American, through which the protagonist gains access to a desirable procedure of assimilation, is expected to be a means to transcend social isolation and battle racial prejudice. In fact, interracial marriage tests the boundaries between the two groups, indicating a low degree of integration, whereas hostile attitudes towards the Lees demonstrate the measure of social distance among groups in American society.

Marilyn, on the other hand, is urged by her mother to find a nice Harvard boy and she does so, initiating a relationship with a Chinese American professor contrary to social customs at the time that discouraged racial mixing. She is well aware of the controversy instigated by her decision–she remains silent when her mother asks if she had any "*prospects*" (47, emphasis in the original) and refuses to introduce James to her family: "Marilyn realized, suddenly, what her mother was imagining. It was 1958; in Virginia, in half the country, their wedding would break the law. Even in Boston, she sometimes saw disapproval in the eyes of the passersby" (51). Her mother's prophetic words on the wedding day: "It's not right, Marilyn. It's not right" (55) echo the widespread claim that Asians are immutably foreign in comparison to whites and anticipate the complications a mixed marriage will cause both parties. What attracts Marilyn to James is his apparent distinction: "Something inside her said, *He understands. What it's like to be different*" (36, emphasis in the original), especially considering that the other boys at school: "all looked alike, the same blend of sandy hair and ruddy skin she'd seen all through high school, all her life" (37). James's visible ethnicity presupposes his experience with racial intolerance, and she hopes that by proxy it will also help her battle social prejudice concerning working women. Contrary to the specific gender roles assigned to women by her society, Marilyn's desire is to become a doctor, not a housekeeper like her mother. James's success in academia proves his aptitude and determination in achieving what he is striving for and allows her to expect that he will also endorse her personal ambitions. Thus, the mutually perceived experience of otherness, even if differing in nature, becomes a common ground for their romantic bond. Not only does it draw them together but it also fosters a coalition building while constructing the defensive mechanism against discriminatory behaviour. The author has Marilyn reconceptualise the concept of difference by assigning to it the ability to empower individuals. A marriage to a Chinese American, as she sees it, will facilitate mutual understanding and aid her own cause by evenly distributing the burden of difference.

Once Marilyn and James start a family, it is their children who reap the negative consequences of their parents' unfulfilled ambitions. Both Lydia and Nathan become the objects of their parents' projections, with each parent transferring his and her own unsatisfied desires and failures onto the child. Thus, James dreads that the children will share his fate of a social outcast and misfit, always craving for acceptance in the eyes of others: "He was afraid to tell Marilyn these things, afraid that once he admitted them, she would see him as he had always seen himself: a scrawny outcast, feeding on scraps, reciting his lines and trying to pass. An imposter" (48). The peer approval, which James never enjoyed, has become his key to successful life: "At best, girls smiled silently at him in the hallways; at worst, they stared as he passed and he heard their snickers as he turned the corner" (44). He hopes that his children's future will be different; "He had tried to tell himself that Lydia was different, that all those friends made her just one of the crowd" (110). Similarly, he envisions his son's popularity, but "[t]he confident young man in his imagination dwindled to a nervous little boy: skinny, small, hunched so deeply that his chest was concave" (88). James applies a recipe for social popularity to his children: he

> was so concerned with what *everyone* was doing: *I'm so glad you're going to the dance, honey – everyone goes to the dance. Your hair looks so pretty that way, Lyddie everyone has long hair these days, right?* Any time she smiled: *You should smile more – everyone likes a girl who smiles.* (227, emphasis in the original).

The father's message is that a person's worth is measured by peer acceptance and reflected in other's opinions. As a matter of fact, James wants to protect his children from being perceived as fundamentally different because he knows how detrimental it might be for their self-esteem: "So part of him wanted to tell Nath that he knew: what it was like to be teased, what it was like to never fit in. The other part of him wanted to shake his son, to slap him. To shape him into something different" (92). The truth, however, is revealed in Nathan's observation: "His parents never go out or entertain; they have no dinner parties, no bridge group, no hunting buddies or luncheon pals. Like Lydia, no real friends" (59). None of the Lee's children is popular at school: "Nath was too slight for the football team, too short for the basketball team, too clumsy for the baseball team, when he seemed to prefer reading and poring over his atlas and peering through his telescope to making friends" (92). They all know that they are different and accept "the *strangeness* of [their] family" (112, emphasis in the original) as a fact, something their father is unable to do because he is obsessed with the incessant pursuit of public approval. James's fallacious beliefs about the importance of social acceptance that yields happiness result in conflicted guidance for his children, who obediently follow parental authority at the expense of their own autonomy.

As much as James wants his children to fit into American society, which in his eyes equals being well-liked and popular, Marilyn wants her daughter to break with traditional gender roles and have a professional career. The mother's failure to become a doctor is projected onto Lydia, who seems to have no say in the matter:

> She would spend the rest of her years guiding Lydia, sheltering her, the way you tended a prize rose: helping it grow, propping it with stakes, arching each stem toward perfection. Never to tell her to sit up straight, to find a husband, to keep a house. Never to suggest that there were jobs or lives or worlds not meant for her; never to let her hear doctor and think only man. To encourage her, for the rest of her life, to do more than her mother had (147).

Thus, there are science books to inspire Lydia, a real stethoscope that Marilyn had special-ordered for her thirteenth birthday, science fair ribbons, a postcard of Einstein's, a picture of Da Vinci's Vitruvian man and another one of Marie Curie. Overburdened by her mother's determination, Lydia supresses her own desires and absorbs her mother's dream, which results in her becoming estranged from her own self. Not her own desires but the fear of disappointing her mother is what motivates her. A constant feeling of failure, guilt, and shame makes her feel trapped in a situation she cannot escape from. Getting a driving license, she hopes, might give her an *ersatz* of freedom because then "she would not be trapped alone with her parents; she could escape anytime she chose" (220). When Jack confronts her: "What about you, Miss Lee? What do *you* want?" (269, emphasis in the original), she is at a loss. Having followed the prescribed path, she has forgotten what it is like to have her own voice: "Jack was right: she had been afraid so long, she had forgotten what it was like not to be – afraid that, one day, her mother would disappear again, that her father would crumble, that their whole family would collapse once more" (272). Despite good intentions, Marilyn's ambitions ruin her daughter's life and deprive her of her own will.

3. Gender Discrimination and Women's Aspirations

Ng's novel portrays American society which upholds the traditional division of gender roles of men as breadwinners and women as housekeepers. While generally women are expected to look after the home and family, the novel is set in the time when they are also presented with new opportunities to pursue an alternative path of career and professional advancement. Marilyn's mother, Doris, represents the traditional womanhood defined by domesticity. This is symbolized by a Betty Crocker Cookbook, which contains recipes and tips about how to please your husband, a guide to good housekeeping which becomes a source of satisfaction for women like Doris. Even when her marriage fails, she "insist[s] on changing clothes before dinner though there was no longer a husband to impress with her fresh face and crisp housedress" (28). The divorce is seen as a woman's personal failure and reason for shame, like the Lee's neighbour who is also divorced: "All the neighbors had whispered about it when the Wolff's had moved in, how Janet Wolff was *divorced*, how Jack ran wild while she worked late shifts at the hospital" (16-17, emphasis in the original). The fact that Mrs Wolff is a female doctor makes no difference since societal expectations have a woman choose between a professional career and being a housewife–the two seen as mutually exclusive. If she continues to juggle both, she is bound to disappoint in one of them, if not in both, public opinion holds. Therefore, when the newcomers to the school district assume that Mrs. Walker is a widow, Marilyn's mother gladly accepts this convenient explanation of her single status. "It was after [Marilyn's] father left that her mother had begun to teach" (28) home economics to young girls, "promis[ing] to teach them everything a *young lady* needed to keep a house" (26, emphasis in the original). Thus, Doris has to stretch the truth in order to face the world unashamed. The divorce has a negative impact on her material status and forces her to seek employment outside the household. The task of promoting and protecting the well-being of family members narrows her world, allowing her only limited education. That is why she is able to find employment in typical female professions–as a secretary, a nurse or a teacher, teaching the one thing that she finds most important in a woman's life–homemaking. Doris follows the socially prescribed path for young women: marry in your early twenties, start a family and devote your life to homemaking– until her divorce disturbs this pattern. Despite the trauma of rejection and social stigma she wants her daughter to follow in her footsteps. Doris's attitude reflects the patriarchal view that equals woman's happiness with domesticity and, in all her sincerity, she wishes her daughter to accept this perspective.

Marilyn, on the other hand, has an entirely different plan, as she wants to become a doctor:

> It was the furthest thing she could imagine from her mother's life, where sewing a neat hem was a laudable accomplishment and removing beet stains from a blouse was cause for celebration. Instead she would blunt pain and stanch bleeding and set bones. She would save lives. (30)

Various instances of gender discrimination accompany Marilyn's path to a professional career: "And to be honest, Miss Walker, having a girl like you in the classroom would be very distracting to the boys in the class… He meant it as a compliment, she knew" (27). When in 1955 she enrols in physics at Radcliff, she finds herself the only girl in a room of fifteen men: "By midterm, she set the curve for every exam, and the instructor had stopped smirking" (26-27). Thanks to her own hard work and determination, she overcomes obstacles and pursues her dream until marriage and motherhood begin to demand her whole attention. On the path to becoming a doctor she had to stop and surrender to a life defined by the experience of wifehood and motherhood since the narrative excludes success in professional and private aspects of female life. Even to her husband, Marilyn's ideas of becoming a research assistant are seen as an attempt to undermine his ability as a family provider: "[h]e couldn't make enough –his wife had to hire herself out" (79), that is why he talks her out of it. In his attempt to fit into an American way of life, James has maintained the patriarchal rhetoric and assumed the position of the sole provider. By accepting this responsibility, he also claims the right to make decisions that affect his wife's future.

Marilyn's escape from home is a rebellious act that reflects the time of transition, change, and confusion in American society. The spirit of revolt that encouraged American women to fight for their rights materializes in her decision to leave her husband and children and pursue her own dreams. Marilyn could have been a reader of Betty Friedan's *The Feminine Mystique* (1963), and in the author's critique of the middle-class patterns, she could have found a similar sense of discontent that haunted her own life. Examining the lives of housewives in the 1950s and early 1960s, Betty Friedan challenged the claim which insisted that fulfilment for women could be found solely in marriage and housewifery. She blamed educational system for selecting non-challenging classes for women and women's magazines and advertisers for creating and perpetuating a widespread image that narrowed women down into the domestic sphere, disregarding their individual ambitions. Friedan's book launched the second wave of the feminist movement in the United States. Marilyn does not denounce her primary responsibility as the caregiver but, at the same time, she feels that life has so much more to offer. Once she decides to search for her own personal identity rather than have it defined by male-dominated society, she becomes the voice of her generation – a wannabe feminist who tries to battle social inequality with respect to women. Her story reflects a gendered struggle for the right to make one's own choices, which in this case is access to paths of self-development other than motherhood and domesticity. At the same time, however, she fails to benefit from another gain of the women's lib movement – access to reliable oral contraception. The pill freed women from unwanted pregnancy, gave them more choices in their private lives, and opened the doors to pursue professional careers. Yet, in Marilyn's case life has written its own script and "in the end it happened just as her mother predicted" (30). She becomes pregnant with Nathan, next Lydia is born and, later, Hannah, so with three small children her dream to become a doctor slowly vanishes amidst the hustle and bustle of daily life. The decision to refuse to cook for her family is for her a way to retain a little degree of independence. The irony of Marilyn's fate reflects the complex situation of women in 1970's America and demonstrates that new opportunities may open up the world, but success or failure of one's endeavour is also subjected to external conditions.

4. Homosexuality

Racial and gender discrimination constitute the overarching guide of Ng's novel. However, there is another kind of prejudice that is signalled in the narrative, albeit only vaguely. A homoerotic infatuation of an adolescent boy runs in the background and never really surfaces or takes a definite shape. Introduced by means of stolen glances and covert actions, Jack's love for Nathan, Lydia's elder brother, is budding through high school. It is Hannah, the neglected family observer, who sees the truth behind the secure façade: Jack catches a drop of water running from Nath's shoulder,

> [t]hen, without looking at any of them, he raised his hand to his mouth and touched his tongue to it, as if it were honey… She recognized it at once: love, one-way deep adoration that bounced off and did not bounce back; careful, quiet love that didn't care and went on anyway. (211).

Jack is an adolescent boy who is discovering his sexuality, but who is afraid to openly admit what he feels. He only meets with Lydia because he cannot approach Nath directly, his sister becoming a proxy for Jack's secret affection. Lydia and Jack's friendship is based on reciprocity rather than sentimental attachment: as long as she is willing to talk about her brother, Jack is eager to spend time with her, giving her a semblance of social life which she lacks desperately. It is also Lydia who is allowed to recognize the truth about Jack's real interest in her. Confronting her about living a life tailored by others, Jack proudly declares: "At least I know who I am. What I want" (269). Even though publicly unarticulated and outlawed, Jack's unrequited love to his school friend is not presented as ephemeral but as unswerving.

The conflict between Jack and Nath is resolved in a typical western style: two men stand opposite each other and begin a fist-fight. Nath blames Jack for his sister's suicide and Jack accepts the blame for Nath's sake, reciprocating the brute force with tenderness. Not until blood is spilled can they return home: "they will be strangely aglow, all of them, as if they've been scoured" (290). The physical confrontation has a cleansing effect, allowing Nath to let off steam and Jack to demonstrate his sensitivity. The validity of this encounter will be confirmed in the future, "when, one day, [Nath] looks at the small bump that will always mar the bridge of Jack's nose and wants to trace it, gently, with his finger" (291). Thus, the future brings hope that they will finally be able to come to terms with Lydia's suicide and their own anxieties.

The issue of homosexuality is presented in an elusive way because at the time it was treated as social stigma and taboo. For that reason, Jack's homoerotic feelings are a well-guarded secret, which is kept away from the public view. The only person in whom Jack confides commits suicide, securing Jack's privacy forever. Jack is not ready yet to "come out," but societal norms will have shifted by the time he becomes an adult and he will no longer have to go out every weekend with a different girl in order to confirm his masculinity. Jack's character is a harbinger of change–a sign that in the 1970's the issue of homosexuality is getting more attention so that in the future it may gradually be recognized and decriminalized.

5. Conclusion

Celeste Ng's novel shows how unsatisfied desires may frustrate the protagonists' capacity to lead successful lives: James wants to fit in, not to be perceived as an outsider; Marilyn wants to be a doctor, not a housewife; Lydia wants to be herself, not the embodiment of her parents' desires, and

Jack tries both to communicate and suppress his homosexual desires. The narrative key to their failure is the word "different," which reveals its many meanings:

> [t]o James, years of unabashed stares prickling his spine, as if he were an animal in the zoo, years of mutters in the street – *chink, gook, go home* – stinging his ears, *different* has always been a brand on his forehead, blazoned there between the eyes. It has tinted his entire life, this word; it has left its smudgy fingerprints on everything. But *different* had been different for Marilyn. (251, emphasis in original)

Marilyn remains trapped in the world she has not chosen: "Triply sequestered by house and dead-end street and tiny college town" (251). Marilyn's disappointment is the reason for her frustration, which taints the family ties. By highlighting the complexity of difference with respect to social and family relations, the author signals its many aspects: an individual desire to be unique and the need to be communally accepted, the right to fashion one's own life and the necessity for compromise, the creative power of diversity and its destructive effect on the validity of human relations, the need to define a collective identity and the inclusion of various forms of difference - ethnic, religious, cultural, and sexual. As sociologist Richard Jenkins claims: "the notion of identity simultaneously establishes two possible relations of comparison between persons or things: *similarity*, on the one hand, and *difference*, on the other" (1996: 3-4, emphasis in original). The dialectic of identity/difference comes to the fore in the societal belief that identities can be maintained only when difference is eliminated through, for example, the process of assimilation. The notion of difference helps to acknowledge the existence of biased behaviour in respect to race, gender, and sexuality, and resulting from this observation is the need to address this issue. By contesting the boundaries of difference, Ng's narrative identifies and explores the dilemma of how to stay diverse in a relevant way.

The challenges of a marital strife, especially in the context of an interracial couple, introduce a bevy of problems that its members have to deal with, such as one's own aim in life, parenting, extramarital affairs, sexism, and the death of a child. Seen from the point of national narratives, the question of mixed marriages may be read as a cautionary tale. The author shows the intergenerational effects of Asian American assimilation and the inherent struggles of fitting in and standing out at the same time. Since an interracial marriage is depicted as highly politicized, the novel interrogates the question of how much ethnic difference is responsible for the Lee's troubles. What emerges from my discussion is the conclusion that ethnic differences may trigger more points of contention than in the case of same-race couples, but they are not depicted as the main liability that stands against marital and family happiness. Interracial relations are one of many variables that shape our lives: "Sometimes people are just too different. He did not say mixed, or interracial, or mismatched" (125). But at the same time, the readers are informed about the importance of visual signifiers of appearance, which may decide about communal acceptance or rejection: "*White* and *not white* [...] makes all the difference in the world" (202, emphasis in original). Difference is thus presented both as an empowering force that helps to break barriers and as a hindrance to one's development. Ng's novel questions the dominant, mainstream meta-narratives that use polarized white and non-white labels because they fail to reflect the real fabric of American society.

Everything I Never Told You captures the insidious nature of race-based discrimination and demonstrates that Asian Americans are not in any way exempt, despite the pervasive label of a model minority. The bias is reflected in the Lee family with Lydia, who appears more Caucasian, being the favourite child, while Nathan and Hannah appear more Chinese and feel being overlooked and even forgotten. Even though the novel draws on the Chinese American experience, it also explores how different it is between male and female experiences when the scrutiny and disapproval they have faced has taken a toll on their marriage. James and Marilyn get married because they love each other deeply, and that is what keeps them together all these years. The problem arises when they pretend that there are no cultural differences between them. The fact that they try to ignore the ways in which other people react to their relationship does not ease the pain those reactions cause; in fact, the lack of acknowledgement itself ends up being hurtful. The author maintains that racial and ethnic differences should not be overlooked but considered and addressed, as their denial would likely result in a crisis.

Ng's novel transcends racial and ethnic confines and offers an insight into a family drama, which demonstrates what happens when parents are determined that one of their children will fulfil the dreams they were unable to pursue: "'Do what everyone else is doing. That's all you ever said to Lydia. Make friends. Fit in. But I didn't want her to be just like everyone else.' The rims of her eyes ignite. 'I wanted her to be exceptional'" (243). Marilyn is a "helicopter parent," (18) to use Haim Ginott's terminology, who hovers over a child believing that her constant control will ensure the child's educational success. Born out of good intentions gone awry and the parental fears of failure, this overprotective and overbearing parenting style may cause confusion for their offspring. It is interesting to observe how the author subverts the "tiger mother" stereotype generally linked to Asian mothers by making her a white woman. James, on the other hand, feels too insecure himself to allow his children a substantial degree of autonomy, as he can only see their future through the prism of his own limitations. Caught in the maze of conflicting demands and expectations, the Lees' children find it hard to share their feelings. Therefore, they communicate with one another by means of a set of conventions, putting thoughts in a form that the listener expects and is comfortable with, unless they choose silence: "Later – and for the rest of his life – James will struggle to piece words to this feeling, and he will never quite manage to say, even just to himself, what he really means" (252). Each member of the family is shown as a solitary being that is powerless in the face of decisions that result from the need to take responsibility for one's own life, even if the motives behind one's actions will forever remain obscure to others. Put another way, Ng's novel explores the danger of silence and repression, demonstrating the repercussions of never voicing how one really feels.

References

Clifford, James. 1997. "Diasporas." In: *Routes: Travel and Translation in the Late TwentiethCentury*. Cambridge: Harvard UP, 244-278.
Friedan, Betty. 1963. *The Feminine Mystique*. New York: W.W. Norton & Company.
Gasztold, Brygida. 2015. *Stereotyped, Spirited, and Embodied: Representations of Women in American Jewish Fiction*. Koszalin: Wydawnictwo Uczelniane Politechniki Koszalińskiej.
Ginott, Haim. 1967. *Between Parent and Teenager*. New York: Macmillan.
Jenkins, Richard. 1996. *Social Identity.* New York: Routledge.
Moskowitz, Jennifer. 2006. "The Cultural Myth of the Cowboy, or, How the West Was Won." *Americana: The Journal of Popular Culture (1900-Present)* 5.1. Web.12 June 2017.
Nelson, Todd D., ed. 2016. *Handbook of Prejudice, Stereotyping, and Discrimination.* 2nd Edition. New York: Psychology Press.
Ng, Celeste. 2014. *Everything I Never Told You*. New York: Penguin Books.

CANADA

CHAPTER FIVE

THE PALESTINIANS AND THE JEWS:
"DISRESPECTED" NEIGHBO(U)RS
IN JASON SHERMAN'S *NATHANS PLAYS*

ALBERT RAU

"The twin pitfalls of writing about Israel and Palestine are: 1) nobody cares, and 2) everyone is offended." (Hartmann 2016: xix)

1. Writing from the Diaspora

Reactions to plays that deal with the Israeli-Palestinian conflict have often been as diverse as the people they are concerned with. Especially in large western theatres, this controversial topic was, for a long time, only marginally considered and at times even regarded as taboo. Only in recent years has the situation started to change globally and plays dealing with this topic have become more recognized with theatres. Still, when the playwrights Stephen Orlov and Samah Sabawi looked for plays to include in their anthology *Double Exposure: Plays of the Jewish and Palestinian Diasporas*, published in 2016, they had to experience that not many playwrights had "tackled the conflict onstage" (Orlov and Sabawi 2016: xiv). Nevertheless, Orlov, a Jewish Canadian and Sabawi, who is of Palestinian-Australian-Canadian decent, were able to put together a collection of seven plays, written in the new millennium and representing different genres, settings and views. Three plays are by Arab playwrights, three by Jewish playwrights and one is a collaboration of both.

Ten years earlier, in 2006, the Jewish-Canadian playwright Jason Sherman edited an anthology, called *Modern Jewish plays*, although he had been skeptical right from the beginning, well aware of the difficult situation for Jewish plays at theatres in Canada. He wanted to include plays in his collection that had something in common. To his surprise, the playwrights he could find seemed to have "a shared interest in writing politically-charged plays about a tiny piece of land in a part of the world that has been, for the last half-century, the source of much misery for the people who live in it, and the source of much commentary from those who don't" (Sherman 2006: 363). The plays had hardly made it to a mainstream theatre and Sherman's experience was that large theatres were afraid of losing their subscribers if they produced "imagined controversies," especially about the Israeli-Palestinian conflict. When he was asked how, from his point of view, plays on Jewish issues had been received in Canada, he could still only say: "They tend to excite a mixed bag of emotions, including anger, which upsets artistic directors and theatre boards terribly, which is why the plays tend not to be produced much, and certainly never by large theatres" (quoted in Glaap 2008: 127).

Jason Sherman's own "Jewish" plays have experienced similar controversial reactions. His "Nathans" trilogy, which spans the period of about forty years, is concerned with the protagonist's relationship to Israel and its politics, but, in particular, follows his search for an identity as a Jew, who is living in the Diaspora. Moreover, how should he, as a Canadian Jew, react to atrocities and injustice happening in the Middle East? This article attempts to analyse Sherman's views on these issues.

2. Jason Sherman – A Jewish View from the Diaspora

Jason Sherman was born in Montréal in 1962, but he grew up in Toronto and belongs to one of the most important Jewish Diaspora communities in the world. He is certainly one of the country's renowned contemporary theatre voices and he has won a number of awards, for example, the Governor General's Award for the Drama *Three in the Back, Two in the Head* and the Chalmers Canadian Play Award for *The League of Nathans*, a play that, in particular, marked him as an emerging artist of merit.

Although Jason Sherman's plays have been produced throughout Canada, the US and Great Britain, he himself is also quite familiar with controversial responses to his plays and productions, especially to *The League of Nathans* and *Reading Hebron*, the first two of the "Nathans plays," already written in the 1990s and dealing with the Palestinian-Israeli conflict. The plays are about prejudices and stereotypes, about land claims and about a seemingly irreconcilable hatred. Sherman stated, for example, about *The League of Nathans* that on "the surface it was a very political piece and there was a wide range of opinion about it in the Jewish press, because it seemed to attack the very underpinnings of Zionism" (Gladstone 2011). Despite high acclaim and positive reviews, these plays have only occasionally been produced and staged by large theatres.

Sherman stopped writing plays for the stage around 2007 and focused more on screenwriting for film and television, because the "indifference to my work was one thing, the hostility another, but the inability to make a living at it finally forced me into another area, namely television" (quoted in Glaap 2008: 127).

Fortunately, Sherman returned to the stage six years later and has had new productions. In May 2013, for example, an adaptation of Arthur Schnitzler's *La Ronde* was produced by Soulpepper Theatre in Toronto. Just recently, on the occasion of Canada's 150th anniversary, he created *The Complete 150*, a satirical podcast also produced at Soulpepper Theater. It premiered May 9th, 2017, with new parts released each Tuesday and Friday, until Canada Day. Moreover, after twenty years, he has finally also started to write *United Nathans*, the third and final part of his "Nathans Trilogy."

In the introduction to *Jason Sherman – Six Plays*, an anthology published by Playwrights Canada Press in 2001, Urjo Kareda, Tarragon's former Artistic Director, says that "The theatrical vitality of Jason Sherman's plays starts from the sheer size of his central characters: the size of their desires, the size of their imagination, the size of their intelligence." These characters are "transfixed in critical dilemmas, personal, political, ethical, religious, artistic — and sometimes combinations of them all" (Kareda 2001: ii). Nathan Abramowitz, a Canadian Jew from Toronto, is one of these characters and he is the central character in all of Sherman's "Nathans Plays." Nathan Abramowitz looks for an answer to the question of what is a good Jew and wants to find out whether there is a difference between Jews who live in Israel and Jews who live in the Diaspora and, in particular, whether a Jew from the Diaspora has a right to comment on or even criticize Israeli politics.

The "Nathans Plays" are very personal plays and Nathan Abramowitz is in many ways the playwright's alter ego, who was, as a young boy, troubled by the same concerns, "things in my head, this writhing mass of conflicted thoughts and emotions about who I was, what I believed" (Sherman 1998: 32). Sherman wants to show the emotional side of his characters, how they cope with difficult situations and what determines their actions.

3. *The League of Nathans* – "the Bar Mitzvah"

The League of Nathans, the first of Jason Sherman's "Nathans plays," premiered in Toronto in 1992. In this play the audience meets three young Jews from Toronto, Nathan Abramowitz, Nathan Glass and Nathan Isaacs, who are close friends and have formed a secret society. In an interview, conducted on November 28, 2015, Sherman said about Nathan Abramowitz:

> When I set up to write League of Nathans I was absolutely writing about my own [...] not the events, certainly, not my upbringing, my indoctrination into a way of thinking, but the way of thinking itself and then I put that into the lives of invented characters. So that it's autobiographical in that everything that Nathan Abramowitz feels and is confused by and wonders about and wants to do something about are things that I feel and think about and want to do something about and the words and actions of the other characters in the play are invented, but they are invented based on what I believe to be possible and plausible, words and actions. (Sherman, Interview 2015)

The League of Nathans takes place in 1993, and all three Nathans are already 33 years old. However, the play spans 20 years and works with multiple flashbacks, a narrative technique that can be found in many of Jason Sherman's plays. The play switches back and forth within the confines of the twenty years, constantly mixing past and present. *The League of Nathans* assumes Abramowitz's perspective and in the course of the play the audience learns how he meets the other two Nathans at a Hebrew school, where they all study for their bar mitzvah. As best friends, they form a boyhood league for life, with secret meetings, chants and rituals. Nathan is afraid of having to sing from the Torah in front of the whole congregation and he asks his grandfather, his Zaydie, who prepares him for his important day, again and again, whether he really has to have his bar mitzvah. Yet, it is the most important event for a young Jew, since it is supposed to make him a man and, above all, a good Jew. Moreover, Nathan is told that, without a bar mitzvah, he is only a weak person.

The play opens with a scene set in Nathan Abramowitz's bedroom in Toronto in 1973. He is thirteen years old and already in bed. It is the night before his bar mitzvah and Zaydie, his 70-year-old grandfather tells him as a bedtime story how Abraham tried to bargain with God in order to save some righteous people in Sodom, in particular, Abraham's favorite nephew Lot. Nathan's grandfather does not tell the story to the end, but, as the story goes, Sodom was destroyed and only Lot was saved. Nathan wants to know whether Abraham, whom the Jews regard as the founder of Judaism and their forefather, was a good Jew since he tried to save people's lives and therefore even dared to argue with God. Zaydie only evasively answers that Abraham was a good man and the question remains insufficiently answered. At the end of the story "Yahweh" asks Abraham: "Tell me, Abe: do you really care about the people of Sodom – or do you just have a Lot on your mind?" (Sherman, *League* 1996: 17). Nathan's grandfather uses this play on words to question Abraham's true intentions, whether he is really pleading for the welfare of the many or whether he is just trying to save his own kin. "Yahweh's" question goes, as Sherman explains, "to the heart of the Nathans plays. Where does one's loyalty reside? Is it only to one's own people or is it to the community and the greater good?" (Sherman, Interview 2017). "Yahweh's" question is closely connected with the central question of the play that is already raised in this first scene and that will determine Nathan's whole life and dominates all three "Nathans Plays": What is a good Jew and is a good Jew also a righteous Jew? Nathan, however, is too young to understand that Zaydie is trying to make him think about the importance of communal well-being, nor is the advice his grandfather and confidant gives him before his bar mitzvah of any help. Abramowitz remains confused, left alone with his unanswered questions that are fundamental for his identity as a Jew:

> What I'm saying to you Nathan is this: the day you become like your enemy is the day you become worse than your enemy. You got to figure out the rest yourself. You understand? (Sherman, *League* 1996: 26)

The most decisive event of the play that challenges Abramowitz's idea of a good Jew happens when one night in 1980, seven years after the bar mitzvah, his closest friend Glass turns up at his home and tells him about the murder of an Arab kid and confesses that he has had a complicity in this murder. He was only an onlooker, but he did not help the victim:

> GLASS.They killed him Nathan, they cracked his head open.
> ABRAMOWITZ.Why didn't you – why didn't you get out of the car?
> GLASS.It was so fast, Nathan. I didn't know what to do.
> ABRAMOWITZ.Why didn't you get out of the car?
> GLASS. I couldn't. I couldn't get out of the car. I just watched it, through the windshield.
> ABRAMOWITZ.Why didn't you get out of the car, Glass?
> (Sherman, *League* 1996: 52-53)

Glass, who is completely terrified, demands from his friend to keep quiet and not to talk about this to anybody. Although Abramowitz now knows about the murder of this Arab boy he remains loyal to his friend and does not tell anybody, not even their friend Isaacs. Nevertheless, from that moment on he feels constantly troubled. What should he have done? What would a good Jew, a righteous Jew, have done? Is he a good Jew because he stays loyal to his friend and fellow Jew or should he as a righteous Jew not rather call for justice?

After this incident the group splits up. Glass escapes to Israel and Abramowitz does not hear from his friend until thirteen years later in 1993, when Isaacs calls to tell him that their friend Glass has asked him to organize a reunion of their boyhood league in Toledo, Spain. In the final scene of the play the three Nathans, who are now 33 years old, meet in a Synagogue in Toledo and the two friends learn that it was actually Isaacs who had planned and organized this reunion because he had wanted to revive the secret boyhood league to recall happy memories. Isaacs, however, still, does not seem to know anything about the murder and the importance this meeting has for the two friends. Abramowitz demands an apology from Glass and wants him to show remorse and to come back home. But Glass, now a Zionist settler in Kiryat Arba on the West Bank, defends what he did and even justifies the murder of the Arab kid: "My home is Judea. My conscience is clear. And you are still as hopeless as you always were. All we did was rid the world of one more terrorist" (Sherman, *League* 1996: 77-78). Glass has developed a deep-rooted hatred towards the Palestinians and he has decided for himself that a good Jew goes to Israel, becomes a settler and defends the Jewish state and the land taken from the Palestinians. Glass has adopted the Zionists' ideology, who believe that Moses led the Israelites out of Egypt to the Holy Land and that the Palestinians do not have any right to be there. His attitude is clear-cut and there is no room for a more objective or even conciliatory view:

> GLASS. Come on, Nathan. You sit around, you talk about "the oppression of the Palestinians," the the the "occupation"...
> ABRAMOWITZ. Yeah?
> GLASS. All you do is criticize, criticize, criti—you never talk about the achievements.
> ABRAMOWITZ. Like bombing Beirut back to the middle ages?
> GLASS. See, that's what I'm talking about. We try to clear the PLO out of Lebanon and...
> ABRAMOWITZ. This isn't about clearing the PLO out of Lebanon, Glass, it's about innocent people being murdered.
> GLASS. Don't talk to me about "innocent people," alright? these Arabs, they're terrorists, every one of them (Sherman, *League* 1996: 28)

Abramowitz, however, remembers Zaydie's lesson not to be worse than one's enemy and reminds Glass of the plight of the Palestinians and of the responsibility the Jewish people have:

> I was brought up to believe that because we suffered, because of the terrible things that were done to us, we had a duty, a responsibility to alleviate suffering, not to cause it but remove it, because we know what it

is to suffer, and if we forget that, if we forget that most basic part of ourselves, Glass then we stop being who we are, we stop being Jews. (Sherman, *League* 1996: 80)

Instead of showing some guilt or remorse, Glass completely ignores his friend's loyalty and even reproaches him of being a weak person and of having silently and hypocritically "condoned" the murder, because "in your heart, Nathan that what we did was something you only wish you had the courage to do. You only wish you had the strength" (Sherman, *League* 1996: 78**)**. Glass does not question what is happening in the Middle East. He rather urges his friend to come to Israel to understand:

> [...] you'll touch the land and feel like a Jew for the first time in your life. You'll understand what it means to be a Jew, because you'll be in the land that was given to us, the land that was stolen from us, the land we took back once we'd found the courage to be who we really are (Sherman, *League* 1996: 81).

Abramowitz's dilemma, however, is that on the one hand he has learned that Jews have to alleviate suffering, but on the other he is told that he has to be loyal to Israel and remain uncritical of what is happening there. He has also learned that asking questions is fundamentally Jewish: "Questioning is the root of it: not being defensive about questions, not being afraid to ask the questions, and being open to the answers even if they're not your own" (Greenberg 2013: 53). So, why should he not be allowed to ask critical questions. Yet, he recalls in his mind that already before his bar mitzvah, his Grandfather had warned him not to ask too many questions because it would cause trouble:

> ABRAMOWITZ. So I can ask questions about being Jewish and I can still be a good Jew?
> ZAYDIE.Of course. That's what makes us different, Nathan: we don't take a yes for an answer.
> ABRAMOWITZ.Is asking questions the most important thing about being Jewish?
> ZAYDIE.You hear that, your daddy's calling me. You probably got me in trouble now with all your questions (Sherman, *League* 1996: 56-57).

The play has an open ending and when, finally, Glass challenges Abramowitz to name at least one thing that he has ever done to qualify himself as "good," his mind stays blank and he can only admit that he has "not done anything," yet, simply because he still does not know what a good Jew is:

ABRAMOWITZ. Oh, Glass. I'm not saying I'm a good Jew. I don't even know what that means. My whole life I've been trying to figure it out and I don't think I ever will. (Sherman, *League* 1996: 80)

4. *Reading Hebron* – "Mutual Sorrow, Mutual Gain"

Sherman's second "Nathans play", premiered in Toronto in 1995. The audience meets only Nathan Abramowitz again, who is now 35 years old. He still has not gone to Israel and he still has not talked about Glass's crime. In *Reading Hebron*, Abramowitz finally wants to take action and the play is his next attempt to come to terms with his Jewish identity. He starts an inquiry into what happened in Hebron in 1994 when the Jewish settler Dr. Baruch Goldstein shot dead 29 Palestinians who were praying in the Isaac Hall, a part of the Mausoleum of the Patriarch in Hebron, a holy site for both Muslims and Jews. Abramowitz does intensive research and collects all the information he can get because he wants to find out how the massacre was possible, how Goldstein, as a Jew, "who is essentially a good person" (Sherman, *Hebron* 1996: 29), could commit such a crime. The title of the play is ambiguous and suggests more than only the reading of a book or a report about the events; it can also be understood as "understanding" or "explaining" this massacre. Moreover, in the Palestinians' "reading" the massacre is a horrible crime, whereas in Israel's "reading" the massacre appears as a justified act to get rid of a few more terrorists.

The play is not a mere documentary about the events. Abramowitz is in his room and he leads an inquiry into himself and the conflicting thoughts and ideas troubling him. The play is a fantasy and everything is taking place in his head, although some scenes appear entirely realistic. *Reading Hebron* is even more challenging for the audience than *The League of Nathans*. In addition to its non-linear structure, the play has 59 characters. One actor plays Nathan Abramowitz, the other 58 characters, however, are played by only four other actors, two males and two females. Since the play is happening in Abramowitz's mind, even the idea of a one-man show seemed possible. However, Sherman explains:

> […] it's true, economically you could do the play with one actor, but also, it's just more theatrical to have four actors playing all those different roles; in a way the audience is on the joke and it is a kind of a joke, but you just accept it. That's what theatre is. (Sherman, Interview 2015)

Staging the play with such few actors also has the effect that what the 59 voices say and the opinions they express seem interchangeable. Sherman demands from his audience to use their imagination and to listen to the spoken word to unravel the various views they hear. Abramowitz imagines all the dialogues, court inquiries and telephone calls and his confusion and inner turmoil are enacted in front of the audience.

The play opens with a court scene, where witnesses are questioned, who were there when the massacre happened. The inquiries, however, are interrupted by Nathan himself questioning various people, ranging from librarians to government officials and even a number of celebrities, for example, Noam Chomsky, Edward Said, but also the Palestinian legislator, activist and scholar Hanan Ashwari. He looks for diverse opinions of people who are either critical or non-critical, either living in Israel or looking at it from the outside and he gets both, voices that are supportive of the Palestinian's desperate situation and opinions that confirm the Israeli point of view. Abramowitz reads books, newspaper articles, testimonies and the reports of the court inquiry. However, as Jason Sherman says in the interview: "The more you read the less you know" (Sherman, Interview 2015). And the more insight Abramowitz gets into the massacre, the less he understands.

In the final scene he even becomes a witness in the trial himself, where he is questioned by the judge and where he tries to formulate his serious concerns about what is happening in the Middle East and that he believes that the state of Israel will disappear if it does not change its politics. However, Abramowitz's attempt to convince the judge of his concerns is in vain because, again, he is only considered a "Visitor from Toronto," who is denied any right to criticize what is going on in Israel:

> Well,
> Mr. Abramowitz [..]
> We appreciate your comments
> and your observations
> But they are of no concern
> to those of us who live here (Sherman, *Hebron* 1996: 103)

Has a liberal Jew from the Diaspora no right to criticize Israel's politics? Are there "outsider Jews" and "insider Jews"? Is a good Jew only somebody who lives in Israel? In his fantasy, he imagines a telephone conversation with an Israeli consulate, who irrationally accuses him of being an "anti-Semite, self-hating Jew...Betrayer of your race... ASSIMILATIONIST!" (Sherman, *Hebron* 1996: 18). Abramowitz has always been told to be loyal to Israel but he questions whether this also implies turning a blind eye to the atrocities that are happening in the Middle East. Jason Sherman's "Nathans Plays" revolve around these questions and Abramowitz asks himself these questions again and again, but never gets sufficient answers. Sherman comments here:

> Our opinions matter when they are in line with theirs and so we support everything Israel does, of course they want your opinion because it bolsters their argument, but when we say: wait a second, that's wrong what's going on, then our opinion isn't of interest and we're traitors and so it very much becomes about loyalty, about brand loyalty, brand Israel. (Sherman, Interview 2015)

The whole inquiry shows how unsure Abramowitz still is of his real intentions and positions. He even imagines that the Palestinians at the Palestine House tell him that he has no right to "point fingers in the direction of a land to which you have never been, and you say "That's no way to act" (Sherman, *Hebron* 1996: 30) and reproach him of only indulging in "an intellectual pursuit" (Sherman, *Hebron* 1996: 29) rather than having a real interest in the Palestinian cause.

However, among the celebrities Abramowitz questions is Cynthia Ozick, an American writer, critic and playwright, who expresses what he sees as the only way out of the conflict: "Mutual Sorrow, Mutual Gain" (Sherman, *Hebron* 1996: 63). Only when the two parties acknowledge that both sides kill and both sides suffer and that there is a shared guilt and only when they stop to follow the "mathematics of atrocity" and to take "an eye for an eye," can there be a chance to listen to each other instead of turning a deaf ear to their neighbours.

5. "United Nathans" – Making Aliyah

> [T]he day you make aliyah is the day you'll be a Jew, and not before. (Sherman, *League* 1996: 24)

Sherman started to write *United Nathans* almost twenty years after he had written *Reading Hebron*. At present, the play has reached the stage of a "2nd workshop draft" and has not been produced and staged yet. It takes place 25 years after the reunion in Toledo in *The League of Nathans*. The three Nathans are now 58 years old and they meet again, however, this time in Israel itself:

> The narrative of the third play is that Nathan [Abramowitz] is going to confront Glass and condemn him for his actions and make it very clear where he, Nathan [Abramowitz], stands on all these issues. [Reading Hebron] is a fantasy and it's finally in this [third] play that Nathan is acting on his moral conscience. He's found some kind of courage, not the

courage to just go to Israel, not [... as] a tourist, but to go there [...] to make a documentary which will be a public statement of his thoughts on the subject of Israel and to condemn Glass. It's for the Israeli authorities to act on this information. So, it feels that there is some kind of completion there. (Sherman, Interview 2015)

The play opens in a law office board room with Abramowitz telling two lawyers about Glass's crime about forty years ago that has haunted him since. At the end of *The League of Nathans* he only says to Glass "I don't condone with what you did" (Sherman 1996: 80) and in *Reading Hebron* he just tries to understand why Jewish people can think and behave that way. In this third and final play, however, he finally wants to ease his conscience and he stands up to his beliefs and convictions and what he believes are his responsibilities as a Jew. He takes action and finally names the wrongs, regardless of whether he might even be punished himself for having covered up a crime:

> [...] it's been inside me all these years and – I've never spoken a word of it, not to anyone – well, except for him. And I can't anymore. And if it means I'll face punishment, even possible going to jail, I'm – oh God. I don't know. (Sherman 2017: 5)

Abramowitz wants Glass to be held liable for his complicity in the murder, but the two lawyers inform him that he has waited too long to come forward with his confession and that after that many years there is hardly any chance to hold Glass accountable for what he did. In addition, they are of the opinion that he must have had helpers to escape to Israel, who will probably still back him today. The only chance to have him punished is to go to Israel and to get his confession.

The next scene shows Abramowitz together with Isaacs on the plane to his first visit ever to Israel and to meet their friend again after twenty years. Glass expects Abramowitz to "make aliyah" to come home to Israel to finally join him and to accept the country's views and politics. However, Abramowitz is still only a visitor and does not want to follow Glass's example. The official reason for his visit is that he wants to find the forest where the tree[1] was planted that was given to him at his bar mitzvah, forty-

---

[1] The project of planting trees was already started in 1908 by the Jewish National Fund, an organization that was founded in 1901 to buy and develop land in Palestine, today Israel, and the Palestine territories for Jewish settlement. Until today, the JNF has planted over 250 million trees in Israel and established numerous parks.

five years ago, and that he now wants to make a documentary movie about it:

> When I was 13 years old, someone gave me a tree for my bar mitzvah. Not the actual tree, of course. No, it was a present, a donation, to be planted – in my name – in Israel. (Sherman 2017: 25)

Isaacs and Glass accompany him on the search for his tree and in the course of their "journey" the audience learns that there are three places where trees by mainly Canadian donors were planted. They travel to the various parks until they finally arrive at Canada Park, close to Tel Aviv, which seems the most likely location for Abramowitz's tree, because the park was opened the year of his bar mitzvah. Trees have a variety of symbolic meanings in Jewish culture and one of them is that trees have been planted whenever the Jews "redeemed the land" that was taken from them (Sherman 2017: 47). Jason Sherman, however, is rather critical and explains that

> [...] for all the spiritual, religious, environmental, symbolic purposes ascribed to trees there are other less lofty ones – using them to grab land, to cover up destroyed Arab villages, and to bind diasporic Jews to Israel through donations and emotional connection. (Sherman, Interview 2017)

In Canada Park, the three Nathans learn that they are standing on the ground where there used to be old Arab villages. When the land was "redeemed" by the Jews, the Arab villages were erased and trees were planted.

In *United Nathans* everything falls into place and becomes understandable for Abramowitz. He is shocked and feels utterly betrayed when he learns that his lawyers were right and that actually Isaacs and his family were the accomplices in Glass's escape and that Isaacs had known about the murder all the way. Isaacs had also organized the reunion in Toledo, to reconcile Abramowitz and Glass and to give them a chance to plainly and honestly talk things over on neutral ground.

The audience does not need to know the first two plays because Sherman again uses the technique of flashbacks and memories to inform the audience about the background to this final play. However, the facts are not simply summarized. Instead, the audience gains even more information of what happened when the three Nathans were young. For example, the audience takes part in lessons at Hebrew school and in the boys' preparation for the bar mitzvah. A flashback even shows the actual ceremony where Nathan feels utterly embarrassed, almost humiliated when he has to sing from the Torah and fails. The audience also learns how the young Jews are indoctrinated at school in believing that Arabs do not want peace, but rather attack Israel "to throw the Jews into the sea: There'll be another Holocaust!!!" (Sherman 2017: 17). Therefore, the only chance for the Jews is to fight the Palestinians. However, Glass admits that he was, just like Abramowitz, also an angry and confused young man and it becomes, at least partly, understandable why he went to Israel and adopted the Zionists' position. "I was a confused young man, full of anger. No Nathan, I didn't take part. I watched, as I told you. I watched them kill that boy. Are you satisfied now?" (Sherman 2017: 89). At their reunion in Israel, Glass tries to avoid talking politics and when his friend provokes him and wants to know whether he considers Goldstein a hero, he only stays silent. However, when Abramowitz films how Jewish soldiers mistreat Palestinians, Glass sarcastically asks: "what are you going to do with it? Post it online? Show the world your one-sided view of Israel?" (Sherman 2017: 54).

Nathans United is also about "tikkun olam," an important issue and concept in Jewish thinking which reflects the Jewish commitment to social justice. Jews do not only feel responsible for creating a model society in their own communities but also consider themselves responsible for the welfare of society at large. Since they know what suffering and oppression mean, they see it as their ultimate duty and task to heal the world from sadness. In an interview in 2013, Joel Greenberg, the director of the Toronto-based theatre Studio 80, a company founded in 2002 focusing on socially relevant theatre that wants to provoke public discourse, said: "Socially relevant theatre is about taking moral and ethical responsibility for the world. It's probably a little Hallmarkian to say it's like *tikkun olam*, our way of repairing the world. But that's what it is" (Greenberg 2013: 51). Nathan Abramowitz's dilemma is that what happens in Israel is not compatible with his idea of "tikkun olam," of alleviating suffering and of responsible behavior. At the end of the play, Glass defends Abramowitz against the attack of a settler when he joins a group of activists and symbolically plants a tree for the Palestinians. He has taken action and "[p]lanting this tree is his *tikkun olam*" (Sherman, Interview 2017).

United Nathans is the resolution to Abramowitz's search for identity. He knows that he cannot right the wrongs, but now he has named them, he has expressed his opinion publicly and he has taken action. The Nathans are reunited, but the play has an open ending. Abramowitz has got Glass's confession, but what will he eventually do with it? What will Glass do? Will he change his attitude and will both of them respect each other's views? Will Abramowitz's action change anything?

6. *Tikkun Olam*

The issue of the Israeli-Palestinian conflict is as topical today as it has been at any moment in the past 70 years. In November 2015, Jason Sherman expressed his conviction that from a bird's eye view things hadn't really changed in the Middle East. However, when looking down closer, it was even worse, with only some glimmers of hope.

Jason Sherman has returned to the stage, although he expects his plays to still get diverse reactions. When he was asked whether he felt like a disrespected writer, he said:

> I can't say I'm disrespected; I just think I'm not appreciated. For me, it's not a question of respect. I think, in fact, I'm told that I'm quite respected, it's just that the people are afraid to do the plays. They're afraid of offending people. They're actually afraid of stirring up real emotion. (Sherman, Interview 2015)

Sherman wants to write plays about the real world, about the world he lives in, about human beings, about "people confronting the ugly, bitter reality of who they are." He is of the opinion that "Tough Times ask for tough plays" (Sherman 2001: 363). In the "Nathans plays" he uses the possibilities of the theatre and the stage to give both, Arabs and Jews, a voice, asking for a more balanced and objective view (see Sherman 1998: 30). No doubt, the plays deal with political issues, but Sherman explains: "I don't think of myself as a political playwright any more than I do a Jewish playwright" (Sherman, Interview 2015). This is also a reason why he prefers to call the trilogy "Nathans Plays" instead of "Jewish Plays" because he wants to stress that, although the plays deal with Jewish issues, they are rather about the three Jewish-Canadians, who "talk about life and Israel." Nevertheless, he is convinced that his plays "can ask people to think about their world and, maybe, can stimulate change, maybe?" (Sherman, Interview 2015). Sherman looks at this conflict from a very personal position and puts forward that both sides suffer and that there has to be a dialogue. Betty Shamieh, who wrote one of the two introductions to *Double Exposure*, also demands that there is the urgent need to "insist on the ability to listen," stressing that the most difficult step "is to give dignity to both of our stories" (Shamieh 2016: xxvii). In fact, when the two editors of *Double Exposure* started to look for plays, not all playwrights, Jewish as well as Palestinian, were ready to be published in the same anthology, although all playwrights lived in their respective Canadian and Australian diasporas in large distances from the conflict area. They obviously all felt and still feel culturally and emotionally too closely connected to the land of their parents and families and to what is happening in the Middle East. However, when even artists in the diaspora are not ready to share their views, how should the people who are actually involved be ready for a dialogue?

A positive example are two Montréal poets, Endre Farkas and Carolyn Marie Souaid, who stress that "Artists have an important role to play in the discussion of what unfolds on the international stage" (Farkas and Souaid 2010: 8). In 2010, they published and performed *Blood is Blood*, a video poem, which thematises the Jewish-Palestinian conflict in the Middle East as part of their collaborative work to recite poetry on stage. The layout of the text in the booklet visualizes the two voices facing each other and suggests the notion that "the so-called enemies are, in some ways, mirror images of each other" (Farkas and Souaid 2010: 9). Souaid is of Lebanese-Christian descent, with her family still living in the Lebanon, but she was born and raised in Montréal. Farkas was born in Hungary of Jewish Holocaust survivors, but the family emigrated to Montréal in 1956. The two poets value each other's work and have decided to work together and to write poems, using this medium to formulate their "dark prejudices and deal with them, rather than sweep them under the carpet" (Farkas and Souaid 2010: 8).

Jason Sherman's "Nathans trilogy" is an appeal to speak up, but also to listen to the other side. The plays are about loyalty, about righteousness and about "tikkun olam." They delineate Nathan Abramowitz's mental and physical journey to Israel where he finally stands up to his beliefs and the audience accompanies him on "the road he's on, which is to go from observer to participant, putting himself in the way of physical danger rather than 'merely' talking about the situation that so offends his sensibilities" (Sherman, Interview 2015).

When Rick Salutin, another well-known Jewish-Canadian playwright was asked whether his Jewishness influenced his writing and what his plays were about, he said: "I'm told that all my plays end Jewishly. They end with a question" (Salutin 2007: 374). Jason Sherman's plays are full of questions and the first of the "Nathans plays" even starts with a question that dominates the whole trilogy.

The "Nathans plays" are political in so far as Sherman critically points his finger to what is happening in the Middle East. However, the plays' main protagonist Abramowitz is not simply siding with the Palestinians against the Jews or vice versa, he rather pleads for mutual respect. He wants justice and not "an eye for an eye" and he wants these neighbours to *not* disrespect each other any longer. Although the question remains whether plays like the "Nathans Trilogy" can ultimately initiate a change, they definitely force people to listen.

In his interview, Joel Greenberg also said: "[W]hen you look at theatre programs, there is no preponderance of Jews: on stage, writing plays, directing, producing. There isn't a Jewish voice in the arts in Canada" (Greenberg 2013: 50). Greenberg obviously intended to sound provocative because there is a number of active Jewish playwrights in Canada who are raising their voice. However, he said this shortly before Jason Sherman returned to the stage. Today, he would have, at least, mentioned Jason Sherman.

References

Farkas, Endre and Carolyn Marie Souaid. 2010. *Blood is Blood*. Winnipeg: Signature Editions.

Glaap, Albert-R. 2008. *Jewish Facets of Contemporary Canadian Drama*. Trier: Wissenschaftlicher Verlag Trier.

Gladstone, Bill. 2011. "Interview with playwright Jason Sherman." *Billgladstone.ca*. (10 October 2011). Web. 31 October 2017.

Greenberg, Joel. 2013. "Studio 180's Political Engagement: Finding the Jewish Soul in Canadian Theatre". Interview by Laura Levin und Belarie Zatzmann. *Canadian Theatre Revue* 153, 50-55.

Hartman, Karen. 2016. "Introduction". *Double Exposure: Plays of Jewish and Palestinian Diasporas*. Stephen Orlov and Samah Sabawi, eds. Toronto: Playwrights Canada Press, xix-xxiv.

Kareda, Urjo. 2001. "Introduction." *Jason Sherman - Six Plays*. Jason Sherman. Toronto: Playwrights Canada Press, ii-iii.

Orlov, Stephen, Samah Sabawi, eds. 2016. *Double Exposure: Plays of Jewish and Palestinian Diasporas*. 2016. Toronto: Playwrights Canada Press.

Salutin, Rick. 2007. "The Meaning of It All." In: Don Rubin, ed. *Canadian Theatre History. Selected Readings*. Toronto: Copp Clark, 368-375.

Shamieh, Betty. 2016. "Introduction." In: Stephen Orlov and Samah Sabawi, eds. *Double Exposure: Plays of Jewish and Palestinian Diasporas*. Toronto: Playwrights Canada Press, xxv-xxvii.

Sherman, Jason. 1996. *The League of Nathans*. Winnipeg: Scirocco Drama - Gordon Shillingford Publishing.

—. 1996. *Reading Hebron*. Toronto: Playwrights Canada Press.

—. 1998. "Life Among the Puritans, and Other Matters." *Zeitschrift für Kanada-Studien* 34/18.2, 27-41.

—. 2001. *Jason Sherman – Six Plays*. Toronto: Playwrights Canada Press.

Sherman, Jason, ed. 2006. *Modern Jewish Plays*. Toronto: Playwrights Canada Press.
Sherman, Jason. 2007. "Scenes from My Last Play." *This Magazine* November/December, 22-26.
—. 2015. Unpublished Interview. Brühl: November. 2015.
—. 2017. Unpublished Interview. Brühl: August. 2017.
—. 2017. *United Nathans*. Unpublished 2nd Workshop Draft: Courtesy of the playwright.

CHAPTER SIX

GOLD MOUNTAIN AND THE YELLOW PERIL: LITERARY REPRESENTATIONS OF CHINESE CANADIAN RELATIONS

EVA GRUBER

In the larger context of stereotyping among spatially adjacent yet otherwise diverging groups this contribution focuses on the relations between Asian Canadians and Eurocanadians as represented in Asian Canadian writing. The discussion will be framed by an analysis of a short story by Canadian First Nations author Lee Maracle, as it provides valuable insights into the nature and processes of stereotyping and prejudice in an Asian North American context. This literary perspective will be supplemented by historical and sociological information on the Asian presence in North America,[1] giving particular attention to the role of Chinatowns as the loci of racialization and segregation. Building on these observations, the final part offers an analysis of literary representations of historical moments in which stereotypes and prejudice tip over into violence.

1. Lee Maracle's "Yin Chin": Reflections on the Process of Stereotyping

In Lee Maracle's autobiographically inspired short story "Yin Chin,"[2] a First Nations writer reflects upon her encounters with and conceptions of

---

[1] While there are many important differences between the Asian American and Asian Canadian experiences, the racial stereotypes and prejudice the Asian population of North America was faced with also exhibit enough similarities and parallels to justify a joint North American, rather than a narrower national perspective.

[2] "Yin Chin" is how Chinese Canadians refer to Native people, i.e. an Asianized pronunciation and spelling of "Indian."

Vancouver's Chinese population at various stages in her life: as a child, a college student, and as a mature writer. The most poignant of those memories centres on her childhood experience of going grocery shopping in Vancouver's Chinatown with her mother. Once a month, the family shops at "Mad Sam's" because he offers bargain prices for foodstuffs slightly beyond their prime. While her mother gets the groceries, the girl is "watchin' ol' Chinamen, makin' sure they don't grab little kids" (Maracle 1990, 69). As she explains, "Ol' Chinamen are not funny. They are serious, and the words of the world echo violently in my ears: 'Don't wander off or the ol' Chinamen will get you and eat you'" (Maracle 1990: 70). While for the longest time no one seems to be aware of the little girl's ideas, on one occasion they come to the fore:

> I can see the little old man still shuffling his way across the street. Funny, all the cars stop for him. Odd, the little Chinee boy talks to him, unafraid.
> Shuffle, shuffle, plunk of his cane, shuffle, shuffle, plunk; on he trudges. The breath from the corner near my window comes out in shorter and louder gasps. It punctuates the window with an on-again, off-again choo-choo rhythm of clarity. Breath and fog, shuffle, shuffle, plunk, breath and fog. BOOM! And the old man's face is right on mine. My scream is indelicate. Mad Sam and mama come running.
> "Whatsa matter?" ... "Wahiss it?" from Sam and mama respectively.
> Half hesitating, I point out the window. "The Chinaman was looking at me." I can see that that is not the right answer. Mama's eyes yell for pete's sake and her cheeks shine red with shame – not embarrassment, shame. Sam's face is clearly, definably hurt. Not the kind of hurt that shows when adults burn themselves or something, but the kind of hurt you can sometimes see in the eyes of people who have been cheated. The total picture spells something I cannot define. (Maracle 1990: 71)

What can this story tell us about prejudice against and stereotyping[3] of Asian Canadians? First of all, that stereotypes – at least in this narrative – are not, as one strand of psychological theorizing argues, acquired through first-hand experience which is then abstracted into patterns of expectation about all members of a group (see Stangor and Schaller 2000: 65-66). Rather, when viewed "as cultural representations then they exist beyond our own personal experiences of others, in the shared culture that we learn from other members of our cultural group" (Hinton 2000: 151). The

---

[3] As Stangor (2000: 8) points out, "in contrast to stereotypes, which involve thoughts or beliefs about a group, prejudice has an emotional component as well. Prejudice involves negative feelings toward group members, including likes and dislikes, anger, fear, disgust, discomfort, and even hatred."

sources of this form of "common knowledge" are parents and peers, teachers, religious leaders, media etc., and it enters our minds almost unwittingly, early in life (see Stangor 2000: 10). The story's protagonist is a prime example. Wondering what created her ideas about Asian Canadians, she recalls:

> "Cun-a-muck-ah-you-da-puppy-shaw, that's Chinee for how are you," and the old Pa'pa-y-ah [grandfather] would laugh. "Don't wander around town or the old Chinamen will get you, steal you, . . . Chinkee, chinkee Chinamen went down town, turned around the corner and his pants fell down," and other such truck is buried somewhere in the useless information file tucked in the basement of my mind." (Maracle 1990: 66)

Interestingly, it is not her own mother whom her behaviour is modelled on – "mama has never warned me about them" (Maracle 1990: 70) – which explains why the mother is so terribly embarrassed by her daughter's outcry in front of Sam. Rather, the source of the stereotype remains disconcertingly vague, and the protagonist's last utterance in the story underlines this: "How unkind of *the world* to school us in ignorance," she tells an old Chinese woman (Maracle 1990: 72, emphasis added). Stereotypes, that is, "do not simply exist in individuals' heads. They are socially and discursively constructed in the course of everyday communication, and, once objectified, assume an independent and sometimes prescriptive reality" (Augoustinos and Walker, quoted in Hinton 2000: 158).

The second characteristic of stereotypes the story reveals is that they are based on lack of familiarity and assume generic characteristics about the unfamiliar Other. As the protagonist admits at one point: "I have lived in this city in the same neighbourhood as Chinese people for twenty-two years now and don't know a single Chinese person" (Maracle 1990: 66). Assumptions are held about "the Chinese" in general, and upon categorizing an individual as a member of that group these generic assumptions and prejudices are readily activated (see Stangor 2000: 2). Conversely, individuation works against stereotyping. While Sam is also Chinese, the protagonist knows him[4] and consequently his Chineseness fades into the background; he is not perceived as a possible incarnation of "the old Chinaman" out to get her. In the context of stereotyping, race is an especially salient since immediately visible marker for categorization (see Stangor 2000: 5): All the little girl has to do is "watch," as she can

---

[4] She says that much in the story: "In the fifties, there were still storeowners who concerned themselves with their customers, established relationships with them, exchanged gossip and shared a few laughs. Sam was good to us" (Maracle 1990: 69).

recognize an "old Chinaman" immediately. What is more, stereotyping seems to happen almost subconsciously, and it is only late in life that the protagonist reflects upon the ways in which stereotypes have influenced her relation with Chinese Canadians.

Thirdly, the story highlights the fact that stereotypes are considered an illegitimate assessment or attribution, seen as unjustified at the very least by the group itself, but partly also by outsiders. While there are approaches in psychological research that argue that there is a "kernel of truth" to stereotypes (see Stangor 2000, 7) and emphasize that they are in fact indispensable for processing the mass of information the individual is confronted with,[5] the story through the mother's embarrassment showcases her awareness that the stereotype of the child-stealing Chinaman lacks a referent and is thus distorting and morally wrong.

A fourth point the story makes obvious is that stereotypes hurt. They are not harmless tools that simplify information processing, but rather are ideological weapons wielded in social power struggles. Clearly Sam's emotions are hurt by the girl's stereotypical conceptualization of "the Chinaman," which he cannot but apply to himself as well. I will come back to the emotional and at times even physical impact of stereotyping at the end of this contribution.

Last but not least, the story shows both the stability and mutability of stereotypes and prejudice over time. As a grown-up woman, her childhood fears appear absurd to the protagonist, and in fact it is very unlikely that a child in Vancouver today would hold the same prejudice, thanks to Canada's educational investment in managing diversity. Yet as a young adult she still hesitates to sit with a group of Chinese students in the cafeteria. Stereotypes, the story thus demonstrates, are both historically contingent, the product of particular social, cultural, and political

---

[5] In this context it is interesting to consider the term's "etymological origin [as] denoting an innovation in the technology of printing: a stereotype is a one piece printing plate cast in metal and made from a mold which, in turn, is made from a body of single types that make up a page. Rather than printing from the body of types themselves one can now use the stereotype as a printing surface for thousands of impressions. Thus the term is associates with the efficiency, the repetitiveness, and the uniformity of mass production. During the course of the 19th century the word turned into a metaphor and applied to any unvarying pattern or action [...], then also to preconceived and oversimplified ideas and notions which were, as the examples given by the Oxford English Dictionary show, often collocated with 'common' or 'commonness' and associated with the people or, more precisely, the masses" (Franke 1999: 19).

circumstances (see Hinton 2000: 158) *and* stable in the sense that they cannot be easily shifted or erased from people's minds.

This last point begs the question of representation and intervention: How can stereotypes be brought to attention, how can they be changed, can they be changed at all? Much later in life, the protagonist of Maracle's story attends a cross-cultural Asian Canadian and First Nations writers' conference.[6] To her delight, discussions there no longer centre on white discrimination and stereotyping, but instead on the progress of the attending writers' work: "We ran on and on about our growth and development, and not once did the white man enter the room. [...] We could laugh because we were no longer a joke." In an afterthought she adds, though: "But somewhere along the line we forgot to tell the others, the thousands of our folks who still tell their kids about old Chinamen" (Maracle 1990: 68). But did they really – or do their books tell the story for them? Arguably texts by authors such as Sky Lee, Wayson Choy, Paul Yee, or Jen Sookfong Lee *do* tell their readers about the ways in which the relations between Eurocanadians and Chinese Canadians were and to some extent still are determined by stereotypes and prejudice. The format they use is frequently the historical novel (such as Paul Yee's *A Superior Man* and *The Bone Collector's Son* and Wayson Choy's *The Jade Peony* and *All That Matters*) or texts which in a diachronic approach blend a historical narrative with a contemporary narrative strand (such as Sky Lee's *Disappearing Moon Café*, Jen Sookfong Lee's *The End of East*, or David Wong's graphic novel *Escape to Gold Mountain*, to name but some examples). They thus engage in the cultural negotiation of stereotypes and prejudice over time, through their writing chronicling and describing, but at the same time intervening in the practice of stereotyping and by implication in the relations between Chinese Canadians and Eurocanadians. Before I move on to examples from some of these texts, I very briefly want to review the prejudices held against the Chinese in Canada as well as at the patterns of spatial segregation and legislation they are enmeshed in.

2. Stereotypes and the Chinese Presence in North America

Stereotypes and prejudices against Chinese Canadians formed early on in the history of Chinese immigration to Canada, as shown by the following

---

[6] She refers to "Telling It: Women and Language across Cultures" (1988), organized by Daphne Marlatt, which brought together First Nations and Asian Canadian writers.

quote from the 1902 "Report of the Royal Commission on Chinese and Japanese Immigration":

> They come from southern China [...] with customs, habits and modes of life fixed and unalterable, resulting from an ancient and effete civilization. They form, on their arrival, *a community within a community, separate and apart, a foreign substance within but not of our body politic*, with no love for our laws or institutions; a people that cannot assimilate and become an integral part of our race and nation. With their habits of overcrowding, and an utter disregard for all sanitary laws, they are a continual menace to health. From a moral and social point of view, living as they do without home life, schools or churches, and so nearly approaching a servile class, their effect upon the rest of the community is bad. (quoted in Anderson 1987: 580, emphasis added)

While direct neighbours, somehow "within the community," the Chinese in Canada from the beginning were seen as the unassimilable Other, the epitome of the foreign in their looks, practices, and beliefs. Spatial segregation in a complex dynamic was created by and in turn reinforced this presumed and actual Otherness, since the very conditions early Chinese Canadians were faced with like a self-fulfilling prophecy almost forced them to live up to their stereotype: Chinese Canadians were usually given little land in undesirable areas at the edges of settlements (such as the swampy region of Vancouver's Chinatown) and possessed few means to erect solid housing, adequate sewage systems, etc. Not only did this breed the unsanitary conditions and overcrowding subsequently deplored;[7] the social ghettoization and hostility they were faced with reinforced the understandable tendency among Chinese Canadians to cling to their "imported" identity and customs (which were considered "heathen practices" by Eurocanadians). After the completion of the Canadian Pacific Railway in 1885, Canada introduced a Head Tax on Chinese immigration and eventually prohibited immigration from China altogether through the so-called Chinese Immigration Act of 1923 (also called the Chinese Exclusion Act, in effect until 1947). By thus preventing the immigration of eligible women and the reunion of families, a mere bachelors' society was created. The diversions sought by its members –

---

[7] Anderson quotes Secretary of State Chapleau commenting on Vancouver's Chinatown in the 1885 Report of the Royal Commission on Chinese Immigration: "Their custom of living in quarters of their own – in Chinatowns – is attended with evils, such as the depreciation of property, and owing to their habits of lodging crowded quarters and accumulating filth, is offensive if not likely to breed disease" (1987: 585-586).

gambling, prostitution, drug abuse – only served to heighten already existing stereotypes and fixed the Chinese immigrants as deeply amoral in the Euro Canadian mind (see Anderson 1987: 589ff.), with Chinatown construed as an abominable vice district ruled by organized crime in the form of tong societies. What is more, after work on the railway – the main reason Canada allowed Chinese workers into the country in the first place – was completed, jobs for Chinese immigrants became scarce. There was a ban on most qualified jobs and professions, leaving them only low-paid manual work and housework with little to no chance for economic advancement. Without money, even the way back to China was barred, as the CPR did not honour its promise to pay the workers' passage home when Chinese labour was no longer needed.

As work by social geographer Kay Anderson has shown, relations between Canada's white European and Chinese population cannot be thought of without considering the issue of Chinatowns. While the Chinese did bring and tried to maintain their own traditions, alien to the European population surrounding them, it was also Europeans' imaginaries, their ideas about Chinatown that defined the place (both literally and figuratively) of the Chinese in Canadian society:

> As a Western idea and a concrete form Chinatown has been a critical nexus through which a system of racial classification has been continuously constructed. Racial ideology has been materially embedded in space [...] and it is through 'place' that it has been given a local referent, become a social fact, and aided its own reproduction. (Anderson 1987: 584)

As in Maracle's story, historically, stereotypes about the Chinese in North America relied on unfamiliarity and generalization. Spatial segregation prevented actual contact, and it was not first-hand experience but information transmitted through other outlets – "popular periodicals, government documents, and labour union pamphlets of the late-nineteenth and early-twentieth centuries" (K. Scott Wong 1995: 4) – that formed the basis of the stereotype of "the Chinaman."[8] This process was catalysed by the civic authorities, for whom

> 'Chinatown' signified no less than the encounter between 'West' and 'East'; it distinguished and testified to the vast asymmetry between two 'races.' As such, Chinatown was not a benign cultural abstraction but a

---

[8] As Perry R. Hinton (2000: 155) points out, "we should not underestimate the importance of the mass media in the formation of and communication of social representations through the rapid communication of ideas and images."

political projection, through which a divisive system of racial classification was being structured and institutionalized. (Anderson 1987: 589)

Not least of all, the Chinatown imaginary served as a foil to define Euro Canadian identity as Christian, clean and healthy, law-abiding, diligent, and productive (see also K. Scott Wong 1995: 4) – in a word, "superior." Indeed, one explanation for the use of stereotypes is that they provide self-enhancement: "accentuating or magnifying differences on relevant dimensions may serve to underscore the positive features of some in-group with respect to outgroup members, thereby contributing to a positive social identity" (McGarty, Yzerbyt, and Spears 2002: 7). This aspect of stereotypes also helps us understand why, according to psychological research, stereotypes figure more prominently in times of crisis, often strategically wielded by leaders in order to "reduce potential ambiguity, stifle dissent, and to provide a clear set of behavioural norms" (Stangor and Schaller 2000: 75). This in turn can be applied to the context at hand: Shortly after the turn of the century, immigration from Asian countries, especially Japan, increased drastically, particularly in 1907 as compared to 1906 – a development clearly perceived as a threat by the population of British Columbia. Accordingly, 1907 saw the founding of the Canadian Asiatic Exclusion League, aiming "to keep Oriental immigrants out of British Columbia." While the League lost members and influence again in the following years, it resurfaced with an increasing membership in the years immediately preceding the Chinese Exclusion Act of 1923. It was the Trade and Labour Council that in 1907 was behind the founding of the Asiatic Exclusion League in Vancouver,[9] and the immediate backdrop for its foundation, and for the riots that erupted after an anti-Asian parade it organized, was formed by the scarcity of jobs at the time. Eurocanadians feared large-scale unemployment due to economic recession and were afraid that the growing number of Asian immigrants, willing to work for lower wages and do more dangerous jobs than white workers, would take their jobs. Similarly, after WW I, with returning soldiers looking for work and a decrease in economic conditions in the early 1920s, Asian immigrants served as scapegoats. So just as the protagonist in Maracle's story resorts to stereotypes in moments when she herself is out of her comfort zone – in the frighteningly alien world of Chinatown, or the sole Native student in the college cafeteria – the Euro Canadian public seems to resort to anti-Asian stereotyping most readily

---

[9] The League soon broke all ties with the Trade and Labour Council, though (see Knowles 2000).

when it feels threatened in terms of cultural integrity and "purity" as well as job security.

3. Representing Anti-Chinese Prejudice and Violence in Recent Chinese Canadian Writing

In view of the historical realities just discussed, it comes as no surprise that Chinese Canadian writers through their texts engage with these stereotypes and frequently showcase the racial bias and prejudice characterizing the relations between Eurocanadians and Chinese Canadians. Rather than looking at textual depictions of these stereotypes in general (a task too large to tackle within the limited scope of this essay), I will focus on literary representations of those moments in which the "merely disrespected" Chinese neighbours seem to turn into enemies within. What can fictional texts tell us about the point when smouldering aversion and prejudice turn into open conflict, what can they tell us about the role stereotypes play in the eruption of anti-Chinese violence? I will briefly look at three rather disparate examples which depict the 1907 and 1923 anti-Asian riots in Vancouver: David H.T. Wong's graphic novel *Escape to Gold Mountain* (2012), Paul Yee's juvenile fiction book *The Bone Collector's Son* (2003), and Jen Sookfong Lee's novel *End of East* (2007).

Escape to Gold Mountain – Gam Saan, as the Chinese referred to North America –tells the story of the Wong family after their emigration from China to North America. While otherwise epic in scope, it touches upon the Vancouver riots only briefly: Just three of the graphic novel's panels are dedicated to the events of September 7, 1907, and these do not show the violence itself but rather the gathering of the Anti-Asiatic League which precedes it [Fig. 1] and the aftermath of the destruction [Fig. 2]. Held in shades of dark grey, the text illustrates the moment in which the stereotype-based anti-Asian sentiment of the rally turns into armed racist aggression. It shows white faces distorted by anger and men carrying clubs in two small close-ups and then, larger, a destroyed building complex in Chinatown.

While the text previously deals with racist stereotypes and anti-Asian discrimination, it does not show what in particular sparks the violence that day (though tellingly the panels immediately follow the departure of two of the Wong family's sons for Vancouver in order to look for jobs – jobs that the white population fears will be taken away from them). It also does not show direct contact between the Chinese and the rioters, instead focusing on how sinophobic sentiment is stoked and how verbal fury leads to the radicalization of the mob.

106   Chapter Six

Fig. 1: David H. Wong, *Escape to Gold Mountain*, 173

Fig.2: David H. Wong, *Escape to Gold Mountain*, 174

Paul Yee's novel *The Bone Collector's Son* describes the same events from a different vantage point. Bing, the novel's young protagonist, finds himself stuck in the middle of the masses heading for the parade organized by the Anti-Asiatic League and subsequently experiences the several thousand rioters as an anonymous, aggressive sea of people that threatens to sweep him away on their way to Chinatown: "Just as he reached the corner of Chinatown, he heard a roar explode behind him. He turned to see the crowd change direction and charge at him in a massive wave. Hundreds of men were shouting, screaming, hooting and jeering. They brandished sticks and bats and thrust their fists into the air" (Yee 2004: 169). Yee's text, which was commissioned by Tradewind Books as "a novel for young readers about Vancouver's anti-Chinese riot of 1907"[10] is first and foremost a ghost story. Its finale, however, closely chronicles the historical event of the riot from adolescent Bing's innocent point of view. As he witnesses the preceding parade, readers can piece together various factors contributing to anti-Asian agitation at the time: misguided patriotism (a marching band plays "a patriotic tune, as if this were a day of celebration," Yee 2004: 167[11]), the trade unions' fears about losing jobs to the Chinese, and last but not least, racist stereotypes. In the novel's historical afterword, Yee points out that in contrast to the actual riot, "the description of the parade in this book is fictional. But the riot really happened. It started out as a parade, but soon turned violent" (Yee 2004: 174). It is therefore interesting to look at the way in which Yee chooses to depict the events which immediately precede the eruption of violence:

> Behind the bakers, a pair of horses pulled a large wooden frame with a banner. A man's boot labelled British Columbia was kicking a pigtailed Chinese man off a high cliff into the ocean. *Keep Our Province White*, the caption said. The audience cheered and whistled, as the men with the banner smiled and waved. [...] Two horses pulled a wagon carrying a hangman's scaffold. From it hung pants and a shirt stuffed with straw, a crude representation of a Chinese man, a pigtail hanging from its head. The straw figure dangled upside-down, suspended by its foot. Three boys took turns swinging baseball bats at the head. Bing recognized one of the boys as Freddie Cox. He heard loud applause and repeated shouts "Bravo! Well done, boys! Hit him again!" (Yee 2004: 167-168)

---

[10] "Author's Note" on http://paulyee.ca/resourcesDetail.php?The-Bone-Collector-s-Son-9 (accessed April 28, 2017)
[11] Historical accounts list "Rule Britannia" and "The Maple Leaf Forever" (see Museum of Vancouver).

As the quote illustrates, in Yee's text habitualized disrespect and anonymized stereotypical thinking pave the road to violent aggression. A particular style of shirt and pants plus a pigtail suffice to visually evoke "the Chinaman," who then is unquestioningly accepted as the legitimate victim of assault fuelled by righteous anger – first symbolically and subsequently for real as the spectators head for Chinatown and Japantown to vent their hatred and anger.

End of East, finally, like *Escape to Gold Mountain*, is a family novel which spans three generations: from Seid Quan, who emigrates to Vancouver in 1913, to his granddaughter Samantha, who still walks present day Montreal, her home of six years, "convinced that [the well-dressed Montrealers] could still smell the stink of Vancouver's Chinatown – durian and rain-soaked cardboard boxes – leaking out of [her] pores" (J. S. Lee 2007: 11). It is Samantha's discovery of her grandfather's head tax certificate which launches the novel's historical exploration. Furthermore, it does not appear as a coincidence that Seid Quan, upon his arrival, similarly fears being defined as the unassimilable Other in olfactory terms. Stepping off the boat, dirty and smelly from the long voyage, "he fears that the stink will be mistaken for the smell of China, but he does not know how to say that there would be no smell if Canada never was, if the boats were not so full of desperation, men trading one kind of poverty for another" (J. S. Lee 2007: 14). Seid Quan is confronted with racist stereotypes from the start. The first time he dares venture out of Chinatown, he is met with hostile glances and whispers: "Another one, did you see, Robert? I wonder if they simply cut off their fingers to grow more Chinamen and breed themselves that way" (J. S. Lee 2007: 18). In the course of his life in Canada, Seid Quan witnesses everyday racism[12] and is faced with such milestones of immigration policy as the 1923 Chinese Exclusion Act which has severe repercussions within Vancouver's Chinese community. He chronicles their fears, frustration, and devastation as well as their struggle, and he also experiences anti-Chinese rioting twice: once soon after his arrival and once in 1923.

Early on in his time in Vancouver, while cleaning a dressmaker's shop in Chinatown, Seid Quan

> hears footsteps, several of them, running. [...] A man is shouting in English, "There, over there! All these places are owned by them!"

---

[12] For instance, upon applying at the sawmill, Seid Quan's best friend Lim is abducted and beaten up by angry mill workers fearing for their jobs (J.S. Lee 2007: 26).

Just as Seid Quan begins to understand what it is that they're shouting, the front window of the shop shatters. Seid Quan ducks, covering his head and face with his arms. Someone outside laughs and the running footsteps continue. He can hear other windows breaking in the distance.

He walks to the front, glass cracking under his feet. A brick lies on the floor, and he sees that there are English words written on it. Just then, Mr. Yip, who lives upstairs, comes down in his nightshirt. He […] takes a look at the writing and drops the brick on the floor. "It says, 'Die Chinaman, die.'" […] "Such anger," he says, shaking his head again. "They are only afraid of us, you know. Afraid that we will take jobs they think are theirs, afraid that we will one day be their next-door neighbours and turn their children into lazy opium addicts." (J. S. Lee 2007: 21)

This experience teaches Seid Quan to expect violence anytime. Yet here he also encounters a tamely resigned and surprisingly differentiated response to this violence, in that the shop owner Mr. Yip considers the rioters' underlying fears and spells out what motivates – if not justifies – the violence in the first place.

By 1923 Seid Quan has become a shop owner himself and – curiously after being warned by a white man – is forced to witness another attack on Chinatown. The text establishes a connection to the earlier riot by having Seid Quan "wonder if this could be something just as destructive […as the] 1907 riot" (J. S. Lee 2007: 40), but it also clearly references the historical wave of anti-Chinese riots preceding the Chinese Exclusion Act in Western Canada.[13] Shocked, Seid Quan watches destruction sweep through Chinatown:

> a dozen white men are throwing bricks and stones through windows of all the shops, dragging boxes of produce and bags of laundry out onto the sidewalk, where they overturn them into the mud. Seid Quan can see Chinese men running away, ducking into the alleys only they know so well, disappearing into skinny gaps between buildings. Some of the white men chase them, but the Chinese always manage to slip away from the crowd and vanish. […] Seid Quan has never seen such violence first-hand and is afraid that Chinatown will fall, be flattened to its very foundations. The windows are all broken, and the white men have started to laugh and pound each other on the backs. (J.S. Lee 2007: 41)

Like Mr. Yip in the earlier event, Seid Quan has become accustomed to a measure of disrespect as a constant in his Canadian life. Unlike his former employer, though, after the riot he does not reflect upon the perpetrators'

---

[13] See https://www.uoguelph.ca/diversity-human-rights/book/export/html/283 (accessed April 28, 2017).

motivations, but rather experiences anger at his own resignation, at his own accommodating first response. Assessing the damage done to his shop, he thinks: *"It could have been worse,"* just to follow it up with: *"But why should I be grateful for that?"* (J. S. Lee 2007: 42, emphasis in the original). The aftermath of the riot consequently finds him in the middle of the Chinese community's efforts to get through to the city council, the mayor, the government and even the prime minister to lobby for support and reparations – just to be faced with the news of the Chinese Exclusion Act from the papers, a slap in Chinese Canadians' faces (J. S. Lee 2007: 42-43).[14]

Let me, by way of synopsis, briefly present some ideas on how particular modes of representing events might influence our understanding of stereotyping in the eruption of violence. In *Escape to Gold Mountain*, which uses external focalization, a camera-like take on things, the riot itself at that particular point in the graphic novel appears almost unmotivated –although the text previously depicts the tensions and racism inherent in the relations between white North Americans and Chinese immigrants. The graphic novel is able to visualize the emotional dimension of racism far better than a conventional novel. By showing us but a glimpse of the preceding white anger and then jumping straight to the aftermath of the destruction, though, it leaves the riot and its underlying causes strangely unreal. By contrast, Bing in *The Bone Collector's Son* acts as an internal focalizer, and through his observations the text offers distinctly more information. Yet by using an adolescent's point of view marked by a lack of understanding of what exactly is happening around him, Yee's text leaves it to the reader to piece together this information for arriving at a larger picture, as Bing records rather than interprets. *End of East*'s Seid Quan, acting as a focalizer for large parts of the text as well, demonstrates far more insight into the workings and politics of racism and Chinese Canadian relations. His experiences of being the "disrespected neighbour" grow over a lifetime and their legacy still marks the life of his granddaughter. By having us experience the riots along with Seid Quan, Lee's novel thus manages to provide readers with a differentiated and nuanced portrayal of these instances of racially motivated violence.

What unites all of these fictional texts is that they depict stereotypical representations of the Asian Other as the breeding ground for violence.

---

[14] The Act went into effect on July 1, 1923, and thus coincided with Victoria Day. Chinese Canadians subsequently refused to participate in the festivities of Dominion Day (July 1st, celebrating the anniversary of confederation), referring to it instead as "Humiliation Day."

They differ, however, in how strongly they establish this link, and it appears to me that this correlates with the experiential dimension of these texts – a dimension hinging on factors such as narrative situation, character development, level of mimesis, and historical depth. Texts employing a homodiegetic narrative situation using internal focalization and well-fleshed out characters situated in realistically depicted, detailed historical scenarios seem to be able to portray this link more plausibly and comprehensibly, at least in the examples discussed here.[15]

In Maracle's short story discussed at the beginning, the protagonist admits that "the shape of [her] social life is frighteningly influenced by those absurd sounds" (Maracle 1990: 66), i.e. the racist nursery rhymes about Asian Canadians buried somewhere in her mind. Still one could ask provocatively: even if they are distorting, do stereotypes really "hurt" anyone? As Charles Stangor points out, "There would be no particular reason to be concerned about social categorization if it did not have such important outcomes for the individuals we categorize and stereotype, and who are the targets of our prejudice" (Stangor 2000: 11). In the textual examples discussed here stereotypes do hurt, not just in the figurative sense of limiting the characters' opportunities or affecting their emotional and psychological well-being; they hurt in the most literal of senses: physical violence. Open disrespect, partly sanctioned by public institutions and authorities, is shown to prepare the ground for anti-Asian violence, to lower the threshold for picking up that brick and shattering windows – along with Chinese Canadian relations.

References

Anderson, Kay. 1987. "The Idea of Chinatown: The Power of Place and Institutional Practice in the Making of a Racial Category." *Annals of the Association of American Geographers* 77.4, 580-598.

Franke, Astrid. 1999. *Keys to Controversies: Stereotypes in Modern American Novels*. Frankfurt/New York: Campus/St. Martin's Press.

Hinton, Perry R. 2000. *Stereotypes, Cognition, and Culture*. Philadelphia, PA: Taylor & Francis.

---

[15] A further case in point here would be Sky Lee's novel *Disappearing Moon Café*, which references the 1924 Janet Smith murder case, in which a Chinese houseboy was accused of having killed a white nanny working in the same household. The entire Chinese community depicted in the novel panics, as it knows how stereotypes – based as they are on generalization, i.e. one murdering "Chinaman" turns all Chinese Canadians into potential killers – lead to violence. Bearing in mind the previous riots, they consequently fear being attacked again.

Knowles, Valerie. 2000. *Forging Our Legacy: Canadian Citizenship and Immigration, 1900–1977.* Public Works and Government Services Canada.

Lee, Jenn Sookfong. 2007. *End of East.* New York: Thomas Dunne.

Maracle, Lee. 1990. *Sojourner's Truth and Other Stories.* Vancouver: Press Gang.

McGarty, Craig, Vincent Y. Yzerbyt, and Russell Spears. 2002. "Social, Cultural, and Cognitive Factors in Stereotype Formation." In: Craig McGarty, Vincent Y. Yzerbyt, and Russell Spears, eds. *Stereotypes as Explanations: The Formation of Meaningful Beliefs about Social Groups.* Cambridge: Cambridge University Press, 1-15.

Museum of Vancouver. "1907 Anti-Asian Riots Teacher Notes." Web. 28 April 2017.

Stangor, Charles. 2000. "Volume Overview." In: Charles Stangor, ed. *Stereotypes and Prejudice: Essential Readings.* Philadelphia, PA: Taylor & Francis, 1-16.

Stangor, Charles and Mark Schaller. 2000. "Stereotypes as Individual and Collective Responses." In: Charles Stangor, ed. *Stereotypes and Prejudice: Essential Readings.* Philadelphia, PA: Taylor & Francis, 64-82.

Wong, David H.T. 2012. *Escape to Gold Mountain: A Graphic History of the Chinese in North America.* Vancouver: Arsenal Pulp.

Wong, K. Scott. 1995. "Chinatown: Conflicting Images, Contested Terrain." *MELUS* 20.1, 3-15.

Yee, Paul. 2004. *The Bone Collector's Son.* Vancouver: Tradewind.

GREAT BRITAIN

CHAPTER SEVEN

ANTI-IRISH, WELSH AND SCOTTISH
PROPAGANDA IN ELEVENTH- AND TWELFTH-
CENTURY ANGLO-NORMAN WRITINGS

KATARZYNA JAWORSKA-BISKUP

1. Introduction

The Norman conquest of the British Isles was a pivotal moment when the seizure of England by William the Conqueror (1028-1087) in 1066 revolutionised all aspects of life. The changes pertained specifically to law, language, culture and architecture, to mention but a few areas. Once they had conquered England, the Anglo-Norman usurpers pursued a continued aggressive invasion of the neighbouring countries, such as Ireland, Wales and Scotland, with the view of forcing them to subordinate to Anglo-Norman law, economy and politics (Davies 1990, Davies 2002, Carr 1995, Frame 1981, Dickinson and Duncan 1977, Otway-Ruthven 1968).

The epitome of the Anglo-Norman conquest was the extermination of distinctive markers of the Irish, Welsh and Scottish nations, which stood in sharp contrast to the Anglo-Norman cultural, social and legal notions. Military achievements of the Anglo-Norman kings provided solid ground for the development of an imperial anti-Irish, Welsh and Scottish rhetoric as voiced in colonial literature produced during those times of transition. Anglo-Norman writers denounced the Irish, Welsh and Scottish as peoples of low moral, legal and social standards in comparison to those who wielded power at the Anglo-Norman court (Bartlett 2006: 21-22, 36-44, Davies 2002: 18-19, 113-141; also see Martin 1969, Snyder 1920).

2. Major Literary Sources of Anti-Irish, Welsh, and Scottish Propaganda

An analysis of Anglo-Norman xenophobic views cannot be made without insight into the works of Girladus de Barri (Giraldus Cambrensis – hereinafter referred to as Gerald of Wales). Gerald of Wales's (1146-1223) critical examination of the Irish people was presented in *Topographia Hibernica (The Topography of Ireland)*, which was first published in 1188 and *Expugnatio Hibernica (The Conquest of Ireland)* which was a pro-Anglo-Norman account of the conquest of Ireland of 1169.

Though born in Wales and of mixed Norman and Welsh blood himself, he focused on another "target group" for his negative attacks – the Welsh, dedicating two of his books to Wales and its inhabitants. The first was *Itinerarium Kambriae (The Journey through Wales)* published in 1191, which documented his and Baldwin's, the Archbishop of Canterbury, journey through Wales in 1188 to recruit volunteers for The Third Crusade.[1] This was followed by *Descriptio Kambriae (The Description of Wales)* in 1194, which featured his detailed profile of the Welsh nation (Richter 1976: 6-7, Bartlett 2006, Pryce 1989, Martin 1969).

Gerald of Wales's travels and ethnographic literature will be compared with the following works: a) William of Malmesbury, *Gesta Regum Anglorum (Deeds of the Kings of England)* of 1125, b) William of Newburgh, *Historia Rerum Anglicarum (History of English Affairs)* of 1196-1198, c) John of Hexham, *The History of the Church of Hexham*, of unknown dating, d) Henry of Huntingdon, *Historia Anglorum (History of the English)* from the second half of the twelfth century, and e) *Gesta Stephani (The Acts of King Stephen)*, which was written by an anonymous writer most likely in the middle of the twelfth century.[2]

What all these sources have in common is that not only that they record the primary events of the eleventh- and twelfth-century Anglo-

---

[1] The Third Crusade was an English-sponsored expedition to Jerusalem against Saladin (1137-1193), the sultan of Egypt and Syria in the period between 1189-1192. The military mission commanded by Richard the Lionheart (1157-1197) was launched to oust Saladin from power in Jerusalem and recapture the Holy Land from the Islamic hands.

[2] Anglo-Norman twelfth-century historical and pseudo-historical literature abounds in many examples. Chief representatives of this genre are the following: a) William of Malmesbury (c. 1095-1143), the monk of Malmesbury Abbey, b) William of Newburgh (c. 1135-1198), an Austin canon at Newburgh, c) Henry of Huntingdon (c. 1088-1157), the archdeacon of Huntingdon, and d) John of Hexham (died in c. 1209), the prior of the church of Hexham.

Norman era, but also contain commentaries about the protagonists who shaped the political and social landscape of those times. These commentaries echo the Anglo-Norman anti-Irish, Welsh and Scottish propaganda disseminated by the Anglo-Normans to substantiate their imperial claims. In the first place, the sources selected for the ensuing analysis document how the Anglo-Normans exploited literature to impose their own power structures on the neighbouring Irish, Welsh, and Scottish cultures. The corpus of selected Anglo-Norman literature serves also as a vivid illustration of how anti-Irish, Welsh and, Scottish propaganda contributed to creating a separate concept of "Englishness" as opposed to marginalised and discredited concepts of "Irishness," "Welshness," and "Scottishness."

3. The Pillars of Anglo-Norman Propaganda

3.1 Savages versus the Civilised

From the descriptions of the Irish, Welsh, and Scottish which emanate from the afore-listed sources, it is clearly understood that the Anglo-Norman writers perceived their neighbours as a savage and primitive people, who led crude and simple lives, totally isolated from the more "civilised" Anglo-Norman world. The Anglo-Normans construed their biased ideas of "savage" Irish, Welsh, and Scottish from their supposedly in-depth observations of the appearance, warfare, lifestyle and language of the inhabitants of Ireland, Wales, and Scotland.[3]

Regarding the Irish people's appearance, Gerald of Wales commented that it did not resemble the fashion of "civilized men." As far as the production of their clothes, he remarked that the Irish did not use much wool and they were not in the habit of wearing hoods and cloaks as other societies such as the Anglo-Normans were. When riding on a horse, Gerald of Wales continued, they did not use saddles or spurs, nor did they wear leggings; on the battlefield they would fight naked, resisting the opponents with "primitive weapons," such as spears, darts and axes (O'Meara 1982: 101).

In the *Descriptio Kambriae*, Gerald of Wales convinced his readers that the military tactics employed by the Irish bore similarities to the ones

---

[3] As Bartlett aptly demonstrated, the concept of "barbarity" was not solely ascribed to the Celts, but was also attached to the Scandinavians, Slavs and Magyars. Based on this, it can be conlcuded that "barbarity" was a universal negative marker accrued to tribal societies. More on this point in Bartlett (2006: 131-146). See also the extensive study of Davies (2002: 113-141).

adopted by the Welsh. According to his descriptions, the Welsh would approach their enemy equipped only with light weaponry, preferably arrows, spears, and shields (Thorpe 1978: 234). By uttering high-pitched sounds with their trumpets, they would attempt to arouse fear in their adversaries, but as soon as they were surrounded by men of better skill, their bravado would fade and they would escape (Thorpe 1978: 259-260). In a chapter entitled "How the Welsh can be Conquered," Gerald of Wales implied that Welsh soldiers were not only devoid of military prowess, but also had no respect for ethics. When giving advice on how to successfully subdue the Welsh, he recommended bribing the soldiers (Thorpe 1978: 267).

Gerald of Wales's portrayal of the Irish and the Welsh resonates with Henry of Huntingdon's depictions. In one of the fragments of *Historia Anglorum*, he cast aspersions on the Welsh by indicating their poor warfare. Through his eyes, the Welsh were "ill-armed and recklessly rash; and being unskilled and unpractised in the art of war, they are ready to fall like wild beasts into the toils" (Forester 1853: 278).

The alleged "savagery" of the Irish and Welsh did not only pertain to their outward appearance and conduct on the battlefield, but also to their everyday manners. For example, Gerald of Wales commented that the Irish devoted little attention to their children's proper upbringing, often leaving their offspring unattended. According to him, in the Irish households, infants were not put in cradles, neither were they bathed nor swathed and when midwives nurtured newly born children, they did not use hot water (O'Meara 1982: 100).

Gerald of Wales concluded his judgements of the Irish people based on the characteristics ascribed to them with the following words: "But although they are fully endowed with natural gifts, their external characteristics of beard and dress, and internal cultivation of the mind, are so barbarous that they cannot be said to have any culture" (O'Meara 1982: 101). This short passage is a clear illustration of a device commonly used in Anglo-Norman literature – that of comparing the culture-specific meanings of certain Welsh and Irish concepts to the imperial ideology propagated by those colonising the Celtic peoples. For Gerald of Wales and the other Anglo-Norman propagandists, "culture" was a term related exclusively to Anglo-Norman customs and traditions. Since the Welsh and Irish did not adhere to what were considered proper Anglo-Norman social models, they were reputed to be "cultureless." From a broader standpoint, according to this line of reasoning, the "barbaric societies" did not possess a "culture" since they rejected all inventions of the Anglo-Norman "modern world" for the sake of preserving their old indigenous customs. The Anglo-

Norman elite thus defined "culture" through the prism of Anglo-Norman social structures, lifestyles, manners and laws and in a marked opposition to the norms of tribal Irish and Welsh societies.

In the corpus of the collected Anglo-Norman literature, the Irish, Welsh, and Scottish were persistently presented, or rather misrepresented, as impulsive and violent. They were portrayed as having quarrelsome natures, and they would instigate constant conflicts with other people, which always ended in brutal and bloody confrontations. The Anglo-Norman writings abound in vivid images of ferocious, bloodthirsty and revenge-seeking Irish, Welsh, and Scottish military groups that were renowned for invading the lands of their neighbours, pillaging sacred places and murdering civilians.

In relation to that, William of Newburgh (1136-1198) in his *Historia Rerum Anglicarum* called the Welsh "a restless and barbarous people," more specifically, "men of savage manners, bold and faithless, greedy of the blood of others, and prodigal of their own; ever on the watch for rapine, and hostile to the English" (Stevenson 1856: 447). Likewise, the author of *Gesta Stephani* portrayed the Welsh as "half-savage, swift of foot, accustomed to war, always ready to shift both their habitations and their allegiance" (Forester 1853: 329).

According to Gerald of Wales's narratives on the invasion of Ireland, which he described in his *Expugnatio Hibernica*, the Anglo-Normans witnessed many acts of uncontrolled rage, brutality and even cannibalism in that country. The savage, unpredictable nature of the Irish was seen as being reflected in the behaviour of the Irish King Dermitius. Gerald of Wales reported that after a successful battle against Duvenald, the king of Ossory, which was won by an army commanded by Robert Fitz-Stephen, all dead men's heads were collected and brought to Dermitius. When Dermitius recognised the head of his enemy, Duvenald, in a frenzy-like state he picked it up by the ears and hair and tore the nostrils and lips with his teeth (Wright 1894: 193).

The descriptions of the Scottish from the chronicles of Henry of Huntingdon, Jordan Fantosme (died c. 1185), and John of Hexham, can serve as parallels. In the passage of his *Historia Anglorum* depicting an account of King Stephen's arrival to Scotland, Henry of Huntingdon highlighted the "barbarous" welcome the English received from the Scottish soldiers. He commented that "[w]herever the Scots came, there was the same scene of horror and cruelty; women shrieking, old men lamenting, amid the groans of the dying and the despair of the living" (Forester 1853: 266-267).

Analogous to Henry of Huntingdon, another commentator of the English/Scottish twelfth-century conflict, Jordan Fantosme, drew an image of violent hordes of Scottish bandits who slaughtered non-combatants, ransacked properties and kidnapped women. As to their conduct, Jordan Fantosme in his chronicle asserted that the Scottish imitated the Welsh, whose greediness for wealth spurred them to perpetrate robberies on the lands of their neighbours (Stevenson 1856: 259).

The most vivid portrayal of the supposed "barbarity" of the Scottish army is presented by John of Hexham in the *History of the Church of Hexham*. When narrating the campaign of David I in Northumberland in 1138, the author depicted the Scottish army in the following way:

> These barbarians have no mercy on the infant or the orphan, the aged or the poor; they spared neither sex, age, or rank, nor any degree or profession; they cut to pieces women with child; and, having slain all the males, they next drove off in gangs to Scotland, under the yoke of slavery, the virgins and widows, naked and bound with cords. (Stevenson 1856: 7-8)

The lifestyles and manners of the Irish, Welsh, and Scottish were not the only exclusive themes of Anglo-Norman propaganda. The Celtic peoples were also stigmatised because of their languages, which for the Anglo-Normans represented an inferior form of communication compared to Latin, the medieval lingua franca, and French, which were the languages spoken by the Anglo-Norman colonisers. Of particular significance for the present study is Gerald of Wales's attitude to the Welsh language. For him, Welsh was a form of "crooked Greek" rather than a language in its own right (Thorpe 1978: 232). Although he did not deny his ancestral connection with the Welsh, Gerald of Wales refused to use the language of his maternal relatives when traversing through the territory of Wales with archbishop Baldwin.

3.2 Trustworthy versus Untrustworthy

The frequent stereotype of the Irish and Welsh which emerges from the corpus of the sources scrutinized in the present paper is a stereotype of the Irish and Welsh as being untrustworthy and unreliable. The Anglo-Norman writers, such as the afore-mentioned Gerald of Wales and Henry of Huntingdon promoted the opinion that the second nature of the Irish and Welsh was that of disclosing confidential information and breaking with their allies. Likewise, when characterising the Irish, Gerald of Wales purported:

When they give their word to anyone, they do not keep it. They do not blush or fear to violate every day the bond of their pledge and oath given to others – although they are very keen that it should be observed with regard to themselves. (O'Meara 1982: 106)

Gerald of Wales complained further that the only regard they showed was for their foster-brothers (O'Meara 1982: 108-109).

Similarly, according to Gerald of Wales, the Welsh "rarely keep their promises, for their minds are as fickle as their bodies are agile" (Thorpe 1978: 256). In the same vein, the author of *Gesta Stephani* reported that the Welsh were "always ready to shift both their habitations and their allegiance" (Forester 1853: 329). After the death of Henry II, Gerald of Wales noted, the Welsh withdrew from the previously signed treaties and returned to their savage habits of invading and plundering (Forester 1853: 329-330).

3.3 Pastoral versus Urban Society

A major result of the Anglo-Norman colonisation of the Isles was its urbanisation, which was visible in their establishment of towns and cities in lieu of Celtic rural communities. The newly established urban centres, dotted with ornate brick-made castles, attracted the Anglo-Norman newcomers who introduced their own modes of life to the subjugated lands. Towns and cities did not only propel an influx of alien elements, but were used as a focal point for the Anglo-Norman administration (Davies 2002: 142-171, Jenkins 2007: 68-70). It is no wonder that the Anglo-Norman writers vigorously contrasted the pastoral lifestyles of the Irish and Welsh with the urban settlements of the Anglo-Normans.

From the sources selected here for analysis, we learn that the Welsh and Irish led primitive and pastoral lives in the woods, contrary to the supposedly "more enlightened" nations who built towns and cities. In *Topographia Hibernica*, Gerald of Wales accused the Irish of neglecting their lands. As he presented it, the Irish deliberately abstained from cultivating their fertile fields and pastures. "Little is cultivated, and even less sown," he complained in one of the paragraphs of his book (O'Meara 1982: 102). He described the pastoral character of the Irish society as being also marked by their refusal to earn and multiply profit from producing and merchandising goods, as well as from the mining of minerals, a plethora of which was supposedly hidden in the ground (O'Meara 1982: 102).

Likewise, Gerald of Wales depicted the Welsh as farmers and hunters who lived a solitary existence in wattle huts, far from the hubbub of towns and cities (Thorpe 1978: 251-252). It was reported that as a society of warriors they spent most of their time on exercising their military skills (Thorpe 1978: 233). Neither did the interior of their houses resemble the Anglo-Norman style. A guest who was invited to a dinner in a Welsh home was not welcomed with a dish served on a carefully laid table. Rather, food was consumed from a large wooden platter by all those who gathered around it with no regard for etiquette. At the end of the day, they would retire to makeshift beds in which they stayed until the morning. The discomfort caused by such harsh conditions was only compensated by the warmth of a fire burning from dawn to dusk (Thorpe 1978: 237).

The same tone reverberates in *Gesta Stephani*, which described Wales as "a woody and pastoral country" (Forester 1853: 329). In contrast, the Anglo-Normans were presented as the reformers of rural corners of the British Isles, who introduced law and order to a primitive people and reconstructed their lands with the intention of generating more income.

3.4 Pagans versus Christians

For the Anglo-Normans, a direct result of the "barbarity" of the minority cultures of Ireland, Wales, and Scotland was paganism. Gerald of Wales maintained that the Irish and Welsh violated the Christian faith by their continuation of pagan laws, specifically adultery, incest and concubinage. The Welsh and Irish, like all tribal societies, did not develop a concept of a sacramental one-to-one male/female union. In Ireland, Wales and in some regions of Scotland (primarily in the Highlands and Islands of Scotland), people would pair in various types of relationships, not necessarily those sanctioned by the Church. For them, the very will of the partners was enough prerequisite to preserve a bond between two individuals, as well as terminate a relationship if both or one partner wished to do so (Ó Cróinín 1995: 125-132, Jenkins 2007: 47).

In Gerald of Wales's *Topographia Hibernica* he maintained that although Christianised, the Irish persistently abused the principles of the Holy Bible by, among other things, refusing to pay tithes, evading attendance of mass and last, but not least, practicing pagan laws. What Gerald of Wales considered particularly obnoxious was their custom of levirate marriages, which were contracted between the widow and the brother of her deceased husband. To quote Gerald:

> Moreover, and this is surely a detestable thing, and contrary not only to the Faith but to any feeling of honour – men in many places in Ireland, I shall not say marry, but rather debauch, the wives of their dead brothers. They abuse them in having such evil and incestuous relations with them. (O'Meara 1982: 106)

It is apparent by this that Gerald of Wales disregarded the protective function of the afore-mentioned levirate laws, which for these tribal societies served as an instrument of safeguarding personal and proprietary interests of a surviving female spouse and her children.

Gerald of Wales also critically addressed the Welsh custom of testing the suitability of a woman for the function of a wife by cohabitation with her under the same roof without sanctioning the union in a church. He also protested that the Welsh, contrary to canon law, approved of illegitimate birth and by so doing equipped their offspring born out of wedlock with inheritance rights (Thorpe 1978: 262-263, 273).

In reference to the principle of honour, Gerald of Wales maintained when observing pagan family and marriage laws that the Irish and Welsh acted contrary to honour (Wright 1894: 316, Thorpe 1978: 271). However, his conjecture did not resonate with the true character of the Irish and Welsh societies, which, since their earliest times, had been construed on the principle of honour. As honour-bound, warrior societies, the Irish and the Welsh obeyed the laws which enforced payment of a status-dependent compensation for the violation of a person's honour. In other words, physical injury or insult which resulted in a breach of honour were redressed by the wrongdoer and his kinsmen (Ó Cróinín 1995: 136-141, Charles-Edwards 1989: 76-77, Jenkins 2007: 47). Thus, Gerald of Wales's ill-founded insinuation that the Irish and Welsh had no sense of honour exhibits his discriminatory attitude and, more so, his superficial knowledge of Ireland and Wales. To recapitulate, the afore-cited passages indicate that the Anglo-Norman writers tended to reconstruct the meaning of honour of the Celtic societies. What was perceived as a reflection of honour by the Celts was deemed by the Anglo-Normans as its contravention. In the context of what has been said so far, it should be clear that the Anglo-Norman policy of reinventing Celtic tribal notions, including the commented notion of honour, was grounded in their large-scale project of disempowering neighbouring Welsh, Scottish , Irish nations.

3.5 Land versus People

Prejudice against the Welsh and the Irish was repeatedly expressed in the Anglo-Norman writings by juxtaposing the land with its inhabitants. For example, Gerald of Wales devoted a considerable part of *Topographia Hibernica* to the description of Ireland's climate, geography, fauna and flora. He meticulously depicted the specific weather conditions thereof, the species of animals that were not present in other parts of the world, as well as the position of Ireland in relation to Wales, Scotland, and England. From these depictions one could learn that Ireland was a mountainous country full of woods and marshes (O'Meara 1982: 53). The land, owing to its fertility, lack of earthquakes and abundance of wild animals, produced a large amount of food. In Ireland, there was a myriad of pastures, meadows and soils that were rich in crops, fruit and honey. Ireland also seemed immune to poisons, which is why poisonous animals such as serpents, snakes, toads, frogs, tortoises, scorpions and dragons could not be found (O'Meara 1982: 50-51).

Based on his descriptions, one can see that Gerald of Wales portrayed Ireland as an idyllic, almost paradise-like place. This image was in marked contrast to his description of the Irish people who, he said, led hedonistic, pleasure-oriented lifestyles and wasted the fertility of the land: "The wealth of the soil is lost, not through the fault of the soil, but because there are no farmers to cultivate even the best land: the fields demand, but there are no hands" (O'Meara 1982: 102).

In another passage of *Topographia Hibernica*, Gerald of Wales stated that some nations, due to their corrupt natures, did not deserve to be the rightful owners of the lands they occupied. Using Gerald of Wales's reasoning, the "depravity of the Irish" necessitated the relinquishment of the land which remained in their custody to the Anglo-Normans: "It looked as if the author of nature had judged that a land which had known such filthy crimes against nature was unworthy not only of its first inhabitants but of any others in the future" (O'Meara 1982: 65).

When reading Gerald of Wales's comments on Ireland and the Irish one can find analogies to another advocate of pro-Anglo-Norman imperialism – William of Newburgh. In precisely the same manner, William of Newburgh contrasted the fertile and poison-free lands with its inhabitants. William of Newburgh proposed the eviction of the Irish from their homeland and the assignment of Irish territory to the hands of the Anglo-Normans:

> [Ireland] abounds wonderfully in pasturage and fish, and possesses a soil sufficiently fruitful, when aided by the industry of a skilful cultivator; but its natives are uncivilised, and barbarous in their manners, almost totally ignorant of laws and order; slothful in agriculture, and, consequently, subsisting more on milk than corn. (Stevenson 1856: 481)

From the sources analysed it can be inferred that the Anglo-Norman writers entertained the assumption that, owing to the poor cultivation of the land and indolence of its inhabitants, Wales and Ireland were economically dependent on England. By asserting the economic and intellectual superiority of the Anglo-Normans, the afore-cited authors substantiated and propagated the claim of the needful symbiosis of the Celtic nations with the Anglo-Normans.

In the concluding passages of the *Descriptio Kambriae*, Gerald of Wales suggested that the most effective way to place the Welsh under Anglo-Norman servitude was by cutting the supplies of food imported from England into Wales (Thorpe 1978: 267). The same ideas concerning Wales were expressed by William of Newburgh in the following passage:

> [Wales,] having little level ground, and being barren of corn is incapable of supplying its inhabitants with food without importation from the adjacent counties of England; and since it cannot command this, except by the liberality or permission of the king of England, it is necessarily subject to his power. (Stevenson 1856: 447)

Identical views were voiced in William of Malmesbury's chronicle *Gesta Regum Anglorum* in reference to Ireland. When reporting on the conquest of Ireland, in like fashion as his Anglo-Norman contemporaries, William of Malmesbury emphasised the unbreakable economic ties that linked Ireland with England:

> For what value could Ireland be if deprived of the merchandize of England? From poverty, or rather from the ignorance of the cultivators, the soil, unproductive of every good, engenders, without the cities, a rustic, filthy swarm of natives. (Giles 1847: 443)

Like other Anglo-Norman writers, William of Malmesbury idealised the Anglo-Normans: "but the English and French inhabit the cities in a greater degree of civilisation through their mercantile traffic" (Giles 1847: 443).

4. Summary

Based on the above-mentioned examples, several conclusions of the major facets of the Anglo-Norman anti-Irish, Welsh, and Scottish propaganda can be drawn. The recurring motifs of the texts analysed are as follows: a) promoting the "savageness" of the Irish, Welsh, and Scottish, b) demanding urbanization of the Irish and Welsh tribal, pastoral societies, c) asking for annihilation of the tribal, "pagan" laws which constituted the core of Irish, Welsh and Scottish legal codifications, d) re-defining tribal concepts, such as their concept of honour, as being heretical, and e) arguing in favour of distancing the people from the land which they inhabited.

From the sources studied, Wales, Ireland and, Scotland emerge as peripheral lands occupied by savage inhabitants who had not advanced from a tribal stage in their social evolution. Three major features dominate the Anglo-Norman descriptions of the Irish, Welsh, and Scottish – namely that they were savage, primitive and pagan in everyday manners, their outward appearance and personality and their warfare, agriculture, laws and language.

This paper demonstrates that Anglo-Norman anti-Irish, Welsh, and Scottish literature is one of juxtapositions. The authors under discussion forged an irreconcilable cleavage between the Anglo-Norman and the Irish, Welsh, and Scottish nations which without doubt served as a justification for the conquest of Wales, Ireland, and Scotland. This validation of the conquest was but one aspect of the Anglo-Norman rhetoric. Another point was the Anglo-Norman authors' sheer ignorance and misunderstanding of these societies.

The anti-Welsh, Irish, and Scottish propaganda survived the period of the Anglo-Norman skirmishes and left a deep, ineffable mark on the consciousness of the colonisers as well as those colonised (e.g. Snyder 1920, Gillingham 1987). The influence of the Anglo-Norman rhetoric could still be felt in the eighteenth-century poem "Taffy was a Welshman" (c. 1780), popularising the image of a Welshman as a thief. It was also echoed in the eighteenth- and nineteenth-century travel literature of such writers as Samuel Johnson (1709-1784) and James Boswell (1740-1795), who documented the "wild Highlands of Scotland" and the related "wild Highlander." Finally, the Anglo-Norman stereotype-charged discourse carried on as was illuminated by nineteenth-century American posters and cartoons portraying the Irish immigrants as drunkards and rioters.

References

Bartlett, Robert. 2006. *Gerald of Wales: A Voice of the Middle Ages*. Stroud, Gloucestershire: Tempus Publishing Limited.

Carr, Anthony, D. 1995. *Medieval Wales*. Houndmills, Basingstoke, Hampshire: Macmillan.

Charles-Edwards, T. M. 1989. *The Welsh Laws*. Cardiff: University of Wales Press on behalf of the Welsh Arts Council.

Davies, R.R. 1990. *Domination and Conquest: The Experience of Ireland, Scotland and Wales 1100-1300*. Cambridge: Cambridge University Press.

—. 2002. *The First English Empire: Power and Identities in the British Isles 1093-1343*. Oxford: Oxford University Press.

Dickinson, Croft. W and Archibald A.M. Duncan. 1977. *Scotland from the Earliest Times to 1603*. Oxford: Clarendon Press.

Forester, Thomas, trans. and ed. 1853. *The Chronicle of Henry of Huntingdon Comprising the History of England, from the Invasion of Julius Caesar to the Accession of Henry II. Also, the Acts of Stephen, King of England and Duke of Normandy.* London: Henry G. Bohn.

Frame, Robin. 1981. *Colonial Ireland, 1169-1369.* Dublin: Helicon Limited.

Giles, J.A., ed. 1847. *William of Malmesbury's Chronicle of the Kings of England: From the Earliest Period to the Reign of King Stephen, with Notes and Illustrations.* London: Henry G. Bohn.

Gillingham, John. 1987. "Images of Ireland 1170-1600: The Origins of English Imperialism." *History Today* 37.2, 16-22.

Jenkins, Geraint, H. 2007. *A Concise History of Wales.* Cambridge: Cambridge University Press.

Martin, F.X. 1969. "Gerald of Wales, Norman Reporter on Ireland." *Studies: An Irish Quarterly Review* 58.231, 279-292.

Ó Cróinín, Dáibhí. 1995. *Early Medieval Ireland, 400-1200.* London and New York: Routledge.

O'Meara, John, trans. 1982. *Gerald of Wales. The History and Topography of Ireland.* London: Penguin Books.

Otway-Ruthven, A.J. 1968. *A History of Medieval Ireland.* London: Ernest Benn Limited.

Pryce, Huw. 1989. "Gerald's Journey through Wales." *Journal of Welsh Ecclesiastical History* 6, 17-34.

Richter, Michael. 1976. *Giraldus Cambrensis: The Growth of the Welsh Nation.* Aberystwyth: The National Library of Wales.

Snyder, Edward. 1920. "The Wild Irish: A Study of Some English Satires against the Irish, Scots, and Welsh." *Modern Philology* 17.12, 687-725.

Stevenson, Joseph, trans. 1856. *The Church Historians of England. Vol. IV. Part I. Containing the Chronicles of John and Richard of Hexham. The Chronicle of Holyrood. The Chronicle of Melrose. Jordan Fantosme's Chronicle. Documents Respecting Canterbury and Winchester.* London: Seeleys.

Stevenson, Joseph, trans. 1856. *The Church Historians of England. Vol. IV. Part II. Containing the History of William of Newburgh. The Chronicles of Robert de Monte.* London: Seeleys.

Thorpe, Lewis, trans. 1978. *The Journey through Wales. The Description of Wales.* Harmondsworth: Penguin Books.

Wright, Thomas, rev. and ed. 1894. *The Historical Works of Giraldus Cambrensis. Containing the Topography of Ireland and the History of the Conquest of Ireland translated by T. Forester.* London: George Bell and Sons.

CHAPTER EIGHT

"GRAND THOUGH IT MIGHT SEEM IN ONE WAY,
ALL OF IT WAS PETTY":
SECTARIAN CONFLICT AND NEIGHBOURLY
RELATIONS IN SHORT FICTION
ABOUT THE IRISH TROUBLES

EVA-MARIA ORTH

1. Introduction

The thirty years of political violence in Northern Ireland from the late 1960s to the Good Friday agreement of April 1998 known as the "Troubles" have since their beginning been the subject of plays, narrative fiction, and poetry. They have been a frequent topic for popular fiction writers, who have exploited them "to cater for a mass market which feeds voraciously on thrillers and romances" (Kennedy-Andrews 2003: 7). In 2005, Aaron Kelly estimated that about four hundred thrillers had been written in the preceding thirty-five years in reaction to the political violence in Northern Ireland, making the genre the "dominant fictional mode of representing the North" (Kelly 2005: 1). The preferred narrative form also of the less sensational and more serious literary responses to Northern Irish sectarian violence has been the novel rather than the short story. Yet, as Michael Storey has shown, "no issue has been treated so extensively and so probingly in the modern Irish story as the Troubles" (Storey 2004: 1). In his book length study on the subject he insists on an exceptional role of short fiction, claiming that "a reader could gain no better insight into the human aspects of the Irish Troubles than to read the many Irish stories that deal with that phenomenon" (ibid.). A focus on "the human aspects" is indeed characteristic of the depiction of sectarian division in Troubles short stories both by Irish and British authors. In a 1989 *Paris Review* interview, the Anglo-Irish novelist and short story writer William Trevor explains that for him as a writer the private and individual takes precedence over the political: "Human reasons, for me, are more interesting than political ones" (Stout 1989: 130). And quoting Frank O'Connor, he insists that "[s]hort stories are about little people" (ibid.). As a closer analysis of two representative short stories will show, such an ordinary, often marginal, perspective is, in fact, typical of Troubles stories. Mary Beckett's "A Belfast Woman" and William Trevor's "The Distant Past" look at the conflict from different perspectives while sharing a number of similarities. They represent Northern Ireland's recent violent history from the point of view of private lives, from within the domestic sphere and with a focus on personal experience. Sectarian conflict is examined in its effects on individual lives rather than subjected to an explicitly political analysis. The people on the two sides of this conflict – in simplified terms Catholic Nationalists and Protestant Unionists – are not shown as ideological antagonists but as individuals who, although unaware of their complicity and suffering from the circumstances, help to perpetuate sectarian division.

This concentration on the private and individual is characteristic of Troubles stories in general. It relies on particular character constellations and spatial configurations. The conflicting parties are frequently portrayed as neighbours in the literal sense of the word, as people living next to each other, or as living in one street, one neighbourhood, one town, and the Troubles are depicted as a conflict between and a division of neighbours, as a disruption of neighbourly relations. Such representations evoke a biblical symbolism of neighbourliness that gains a new significance in the context of sectarian violence. Benedict Kiely refers to this when speaking about his Troubles fiction in an interview in *The Irish Literary Supplement* in 1987: "[…] I do believe in my neighborhood. I say if you don't believe in your neighborhood and that your neighbor's life is sacred, there is no point in shouting about believing in God […]" (Clarke 1999: 84). Metaphors of neighbours and neighbourhoods do not only serve as ironic references to a Christian ideal of neighbourliness. Corresponding character constellations and settings illustrate that the "social is spatially constructed" (Massey 1992: 70). The metaphorical field of neighbourliness invoked here highlights that the order of things is established, represented, and contested in spatial terms. Troubles stories speak of actual and symbolic forms of control over territory. They illustrate how "space is constituted through social relations and material social practices." (Massey 1992: 70) When in Benedict Kiely's short story "Bluebell Meadow" the narrator explains Protestant and Catholic preferences for seaside holidays, an age-old political antagonism has inscribed itself into the island's geography.

Even the sea is testament to division; its waves echo sectarian "nursery rhymes":

> As a rule Protestants didn't go west to Bundoran but north to Portrush. The sea was sectarian. What were the wild waves saying: At Portrush: Slewter, slaughter, holy water, harry the papishes every one, drive them under and bate them asunder, the Protestant boys will carry the drum. Or at Bundoran: On St. Patrick's day, jolly and gay, we'll kick all the Protestants out of the way, and if that won't do we'll cut them in two and send them to hell with their red, white and blue. (Kiely 1980: 278)

Eamonn McCann remembers a childhood in which such "songs of cheerful hatred" were sung by children playing in the streets (McCann 1993: 81). Hilary Mantel also quotes from this tradition that perpetuates sectarianism in her Troubles story "King Billy is a Gentleman." While the story is set in a village near Manchester, the songs here, too, serve as symbolic markers of territory. In her story, Mantel has English and Irish children, next door neighbours, sing chants "you might have heard on Belfast streets." The children remember a sectarian history that the adults – "tolerant, or perhaps contemptuous of religion" – pay little heed to:

> King Billy is a gentleman
> He wears a watch and chain
> The dirty Pope's a beggar
> And he begs down our lane. (Mantel 2013: 13)

With their songs, the village children bridge the spatial distance not only to the North of Ireland; as they "drop time and tense altogether from their sense of this event" (Isaacs 1989: 228), the temporal distance to the Williamite Wars vanishes, too. The choice of characters is obviously symbolic. Mantel underlines the significance of history with the children's reenactment of a violent past even before the Troubles have begun. In the narrator's 1950s childhood a tribal knowledge survives in the children that determines their identities, irrespective of where they actually are. Lacking clear markers of territory, they create imaginary spaces in which they articulate their rivalry in the tradition of Irish sectarianism.

2. Mary Beckett, "A Belfast Woman"

A less symbolic fight over territory is the topic of Mary Beckett's short story "A Belfast Woman," which was first published in 1979 and reprinted in 1980 as part of her short story collection of the same name. In this story, Beckett, a Catholic writer, who was born and grew up in Belfast, where she worked as a teacher until 1956 before moving to Dublin, deals with religious or ethnic residential segregation in her home town at the beginning of the Troubles. Like William Trevor, Beckett insisted on the significance of the private for her fiction. In a 1995 interview with *The Irish Literary Supplement*, she characterized her writing as "family stuff" rather than "political stuff," well aware of the fact that this meant being taken less seriously by the critics (Sullivan 1995: 10). "A Belfast Woman," although characteristic in its "focus on domestic relations" (D'hoker 2016: 128), is more obviously concerned with the politics of Northern Ireland than most of her other stories.

The first-person narrator, an elderly Catholic working-class woman living in a Protestant neighbourhood of Belfast, remembers how she received a threatening letter:

> I mind well the day the threatening letter came. It was a bright morning, and warm, and I remember thinking while I was dressing myself that it would be nice if the Troubles were over so that a body could just enjoy the feel of a good day. When I came down the stairs the hall was dark but I could see the letter lying face down. I lifted it and just my name was on the envelope, "Mrs. Harrison" in red felt pen. I knew what it was. There was a page of an exercise book inside with "Get out or we'll burn you out" all in red with bad printing and smeared. (Beckett 1980: 84, all further references are to this edition)

While the warm and sunny morning that marks the beginning of the short story at first might just seem an ironic backdrop to the dreadful threat, it in fact evokes actual events (which, however, precede those of the story). These are the riots of August 1969 – the beginning of the Troubles – when thousands were displaced in Belfast. A *Times* headline from August 7, 1969 reads "City fears Ghetto future. Belfast families tell of terror by evictions" (Chartres and Clare 1969: 6). It was in this summer that the British government received the request that troops be deployed to Northern Ireland. In the early 1970s people in Belfast continued to be forced out of their neighbourhoods and Beckett's contemporary readers would have been aware of the continuing conflicts. A *Times* article of Tuesday, March 27, 1973 summarizes the events of the preceding years:

> In four years Belfast has seen the largest population movement in any western country since the Second World War [...]. [...] [U]p to 40,000 people have been forced out of their homes by threats, shooting and the petrol bombing. In Greater Belfast, one out of every three Roman Catholic families has had to move. [...] In the bleak, working-class areas, the movement to the safety of the ghettos has become a flood over the past 12 months. (Sweeney 1973: 16)

One of the headlines of this year reads "A Feeling of Berlin in Belfast" (Fisk 1973: 16), a reference to the "peace lines," which have survived until today, built to separate Catholic and Protestant neighbourhoods and to keep the two communities apart. The threatening letter in Beckett's story belongs to this period. While it does not become clear when exactly the narrator receives it, it must be after her son and his family are forced to leave their home, for which a date is given:

> He got married to a nice girl from the Bone and they got a house up in one of the nice streets in Ardoyne – up the far end in what they call now a mixed area. It's all gone now, poor Liam's good way of living. When that street of houses up there was put on fire in 1972 his wife Gemma insisted on coming back to the Bone and squatting in an empty house. (92-93)

The evictions of the 1970s, when people are forced out of so-called "mixed areas," are not the only times that members of the family have been displaced. The narrator remembers another "'Get out or we'll burn you out' note" (85) from her youth and an even earlier instance when her home had actually been burnt out in her childhood. Her memories go back to the years 1935 and finally to 1921, the period of unrest for which the name "the (Irish) Troubles" was first used:

> In 1935 when we got the letter threatening to burn us out I said to my mother "We'll gather our things and we'll go." So we did and like all the rest of them in our street we went up to Glenard to the new houses. When we showed our "Get out or we'll burn you out" note they gave us a house […]. (85)

> One of the first things I remember in my life was wakening up with my mother screaming downstairs when we were burnt out in 1921. I ran down in my nightgown and my mother was standing in the middle of the kitchen with her hands up to her face screaming and screaming and the curtains were on fire […]. (84)

The narrator's life story is a story of continuous displacements modeled on the city's actual sectarian history. When readers reconstruct the facts of her life from her discontinuous narrative, they reconstruct major population movements of the people of Belfast in the 20th century. Beckett emphasizes the realism of her story not only through the temporal references to the major periods of disturbances in the North of Ireland in the 20th century – 1920-1922, 1935, 1969 and the early 1970s – but also through frequent and specific references to places: Ardoyne, the Bone, Glenard Estate, North Queen Street are all Belfast place names and the places she refers to here are all neighbourhoods severely affected by the Troubles. When the narrator recalls how her mother regretted all her life that she had to leave her "home down near the docks" (89) it places the family at the center of Belfast's sectarian strife. Dockside Belfast was "a continual hotbed of conflict," a site of disturbances already in the 19th century and then again in 1920-22 and 1935 (O'Connell 2014: 738). From their first home near Belfast's shipyards, the family moves to nearby North Queen Street to the narrator's grandmother's house and then to the newly built Glenard Estate in 1935. A.C. Hepburn gives a detailed account of the forced movements in Belfast's dockside during the riots of 1935 and in this context also speaks of Glenard Estate: "Glenard probably housed about 200 families (1100 people), or half the total number of Catholic refugees in 1935" (Hepburn 1990: 87).

Beckett's story tells of the separation of the city's population into two neighbouring but distinct communities. Drawing on parts of an actual history of "segregated 'ethnic zones'" (Neil 2004: 175) in Belfast which dates back to the 19th century, it shows how the sectarian conflict determines the city's topography. Where identity is "firmly linked to locality and its defence" (ibid.) the presumed difference of the city's two communities is turned into a material reality. Beckett's characters understand themselves in terms of space and in relation to places; they know where they belong. When she moves into a Protestant neighbourhood with her husband, a Catholic from a 'mixed' marriage, brought up by a Protestant family, a young Mrs. Harrison is warned by her mother in words that turn out to be prophetic:

> But when I was getting married to William, and his aunt who was a Protestant gave him the key of her house in this street, my mother was in a terrible state – "Don't go into that Protestant street, Mary, or you'll be a sorry girl." […] (85)

For mother and daughter Protestants are different people, they live differently, and the Protestant streets are not like the Catholic streets:

> There was not a soul in the street but there was nothing odd about that. You'll always know you're in a Protestant street if it's deserted. When I went across the road to get to Liam's house there were children playing and men at the corner and women standing at the doors in the sun and a squad of nervous-looking soldiers down at the other end. (94-95)

The new Protestant neighbours do not "come into the house for a chat or a loan of tea or milk or sugar like the neighbours in Glenard or North Queen Street […]" (86). The narrator's identity construction is firmly based on stereotypical conceptions of what it means to be Protestant and what it means to be Catholic; and for her, the two communities are culturally and ethnically different. To which group a person belongs cannot only be determined through their behaviour; Beckett's narrator is convinced that there is a physical difference between Catholics and Protestants. Ironically, this becomes obvious for the narrator in her own children, who do not look alike. Her son looks like a Catholic, and she recalls how her neighbours made remarks when he was born about his "mottled skin," which they regard as "a sign of a very strong baby." The narrator herself has "never seen a baby with any other colour of skin – [*she says*] I suppose Catholic babies had to be strong to get by" (86). When her daughter is born, she is unlike her brother: "She had beautiful creamy skin. She was plump and perfect and I loved her more than Liam" (86). The perception of cultural and ethnic differences here is connected to conceptions of class. Social and cultural prejudice is internalized by Beckett's Catholic narrator who accepts the superiority of her Protestant neighbours. She follows their example and she envies them: she wants to have few children, like the Protestant women, not many, like the Catholics. And when she is proud of her children, she remarks that "[t]here was no Protestant child better fed or better dressed than those two […]" (88). Beckett's story explores identity formation along sectarian lines and at the same time exposes its absurdities when her narrator insists on visible physical differences between members of the two communities although her own family is proof of the fact that these two communities have never been so clearly kept apart, and contact and mixing "have been features of Irish society for centuries" (Kennedy 2016: 51).

Although the narrator sees herself in strong contrast to her Protestant neighbours and insists on a fundamental difference between Catholics and Protestants, she also emphasizes the good neighbourly relations. She claims that her neighbours are decent people: "[…] my new neighbours […]. I couldn't complain about them, they were good decent people" (86), "they were ready to help at any time" (86), "[…] better kinder decenter neighbours you could not get" (89). Yet, in spite of the attestations of neighbourliness these nameless neighbours remain strangely absent from the story, which focusses on the family's history of evictions, the narrator's marriage and the fate of her children. When her house is vandalized after she receives the threatening letter, her neighbours do not help and support her. And when, in a final ironic turn of the story, her Protestant neighbours are forced out, the narrator refuses to acknowledge that this happens in consequence of intimidations that her own son is involved in. She prefers not to know what exactly happened:

> Then a queer thing happened. My neighbours began moving out. The woman next door told me out of the side of her mouth that they had all been threatened. I didn't understand how a whole Protestant area could be threatened but out they all went. Of course I know they can always get newer better houses when they ask for them and indeed there is a lot of shooting and wrecking on the front of the road, but I still often wondered what was the truth of it. May be I am better off not knowing. (97-98)

Beckett's narrator delivers a tale so convincing that it has been taken at face value. Her stereotypical long-suffering Catholic working-class woman from North Belfast has been praised for her "decency and resilience," "her unwavering and moving loyalty to her family" and her "neighbourliness" (McDonald 2005: 255). While the narrator would certainly like to appear in such a light, her narration with its many contradictions, omissions, and half-truths tells a different tale. It represents a denial of responsibility and an attempt to come to terms with an unacknowledged guilt. Beckett masterfully exploits the potential of unreliable narration in this fictional eye witness account of the Troubles. The story, although it never becomes obvious who the narrator is talking to, reminds of an oral history interview. Its form and style lend authority and authenticity to the narrator's testimony, while, ironically, its faithfulness results from the lack of truthfulness of her account. The story displays her shame and her inability to understand and admit her involvement in the perpetuation of sectarian division which is passed on also in her family although she insists: "[…] we never taught our children to hate the others nor filled their heads with their wrongs the way it's said we did." (98) Trapped in her tribal loyalties, both victim and complicit, she can only offer feeble excuses and justifications: "It's not right to put the blame on poor powerless people. The most of us never did anything but stay quiet and put up with things the way they were." (98)

3. William Trevor, "The Distant Past"

William Trevor looks at the early years of the Troubles from a different point of view and in a more overtly symbolic mode in his short story "The Distant Past," which is part of his short story collection *Angels at the Ritz* from 1975. Trevor characterized himself as "a small-town Irish Protestant," belonging neither "to the new post-1923 Catholic society" nor to the Irish Ascendancy (Stout 1989: 131). He grew up in Mitchelstown, County Cork, not far from Elizabeth Bowen's home, Bowen's Court, and in an interview characterized his family's social position by comparing himself to boys employed by the Bowens as ball boys on their tennis court: "I would have been one of those little Protestant boys, had I been the right age" (ibid.). In his short story, Trevor puts his focus on the fate of Ascendancy Protestants in post-independence Ireland. As in Beckett's story, neighbourly relations and their disruption are used in illustration of a wider conflict. Trevor also shows the destructive effects of a violent past that gains new significance with the beginning of the Troubles. His story, however, presents both sides of the conflict, to which the impartial narrator keeps an ironic distance. The Protestant characters are introduced as follows:

> In the town and beyond it they were regarded as harmlessly peculiar. Odd, people said, and in time this reference took on a burnish of affection. [...] The Middletons of Carraveagh the family had once been known as, but now the brother and sister were just the Middletons, for Carraveagh didn't count anymore, except to them.
> They owned four Herefords, a number of hens, and the house itself, three miles outside the town. It was a large house, built in the reign of George II, a monument that reflected in its glory and later decay the fortunes of a family. (Trevor 1992: 348, all further references are to this edition)

The story is set in a nameless prosperous provincial town in the Irish Republic, about sixty miles from the border. The two main characters are the last descendants of an Anglo-Irish family, of whose wealth only the decaying country house remains, which dates back to the 18th century as the golden age of the Protestant Ascendancy. In "The Distant Past" the big house is a symbol of an old order that the two main characters – now reduced to "shabby genteel relics of the Ascendancy Big House tradition" (Rhodes 1983: 98) – still cling to while it has become insignificant for the townspeople. In obvious symbolism, the town prospers while the house falls into disrepair, water leaking through the roof, gutters rusting, wallpaper and furniture fading. The decay of the house, like the elderly siblings' childlessness, stands for the end of the formerly dominant class and the distance between the house and the town – and the implied lack of immediate neighbours – shows the isolation of the now impoverished Middletons, who seek comfort in the townspeople's "warm companionship" (325). But there is not only a spatial distance between the Middletons and the Catholic townspeople; there is a significant difference in attitudes, which achieves a new and terrible relevance with the outbreak of disturbances in the North. Carraveagh, the Middleton's house, like the Middletons of Carraveagh themselves, is a symbol of the past. They preserve a pre-independence Ireland within its walls; the Cross of St George hangs in their hall together with the family crest and a portrait of their father, who had believed in "God and Empire and Queen," in British uniform (352). That the Middletons remain unshaken in their loyalty to England is tolerated as an eccentricity, the subject of friendly banter. In the decades of postwar progress and economic success for the town all seems well; in spite of the past and their continuing resentment of the Republic they enjoy "convivial relationships" (350) with the townspeople that surprise foreign visitors:

> The visitors who came to the town heard about the Middletons and were impressed. It was a pleasant wonder, more than one of them remarked, that old wounds could heal so completely, that the Middletons continued in their loyalty to the past and that, in spite of that, they were respected in the town. (352)

It turns out that the friendly coexistence of the Middletons and their neighbours will not last. With the Troubles the prosperity of the town comes to an end. It is too close to the border and now fails to attract tourists. After initial mutual reassurances that what happens in the North "has nothing to do with the South" (354), old differences and allegiances come to light; "a whole history of division and sectarian hatred surfaces" (Schirmer 1990: 138). Like Mary Beckett, Trevor links the present to the past. His story draws on occurrences during the Anglo-Irish War and the Irish Civil War, when the Protestant country houses were attacked and many destroyed: "In total over 300 big houses were burned from the beginning of the War of Independence in 1920 to the end of the Civil War in 1923" (Dooley and Noack 2013: 4). Even if this is not the fate of the house in Trevor's story, it is explicitly linked to that past:

> Fat Cranley, with a farmer called Maguire and another called Breen, had stood in the hall of Carraveagh, each of them in charge of a shot-gun. The Middletons, children then, had been locked with their mother and father and an aunt in an upstairs room. Nothing else had happened: the expected British soldiers had not, after all, arrived and the men in the hall had eventually relaxed their vigil. 'A massacre they wanted,' the Middletons' father said after they'd gone. 'Damn bloody ruffians.' (350)

During the years of prosperity this incident, in which the Middletons and the Catholic townspeople found each other on different sides, was the subject of good-humoured jokes, but with the Troubles the stories about the past change. As the fighting in the North reminds people of an earlier period of violence, the Middletons' home is remembered by their neighbours as "the enemy's house" and their eccentricities are not "something to laugh at anymore" (354). The formerly friendly townspeople stop talking to them.

What had been regarded as odd and harmless is now downright dangerous: "Had they driven with a Union Jack now" in their Ford Anglia, as they had done for the coronation of Elizabeth II, "they might, astoundingly, have been shot" (355). While genuinely longing for their Catholic neighbours' friendship and increasingly dependent on their good will, brother and sister preserve attitudes and behaviours that are out of place in post-independence Ireland. They are not only physically isolated in their house outside the town. With the conflict in the North, the distance from the town, once a sign of the family's superior position as landowners, turns into a symbol of their ostracism. There is no place for them and they realize: "Because of the distant past they would die friendless. It was worse than being murdered in their beds" (356). The story portrays them as unable to understand their own motivations for refusing to assimilate to the postwar society, and, at the same time, portrays that society's unwillingness to truly confront its past and achieve reconciliation.

4. Conclusion

In William Trevor's and Mary Beckett's short stories the past is retold by the characters "so as to confirm the views and convictions of the present" (Massey 1995: 186). The two communities cannot share a common space and a common story. To identify with different sides of the conflict in Northern Ireland means to read history and the politics of the (fictional) present differently. With the outbreak of the Troubles, people find themselves again separated through old allegiances that they – as Trevor puts it – instinctively adhere to. In spite of their endeavors to keep up neighbourly relations, the characters are trapped in a history of violence and "ethnic" loyalties. Both authors use stereotypical representatives of the respective communities to examine the social dynamics of sectarian strife, exposing their characters' insistence on their distinct cultural identities as destructive. Home and neighbourhood serve as central signifiers as division and social exclusion are expressed through the symbolism of space. Both stories present their main characters as isolated figures in a hostile environment and use them as symbols of segregation. The metaphorical power of neighbourhood and the symbolism of the breakdown of neighbourly relationships and the hostility of neighbours reside in the blending of private and social spheres. The political is represented through the perspective of individual experience, and, in spite of the characters' helplessness, the responsibility of the individual is affirmed. As Trevor has one of his characters say: "[g]rand though it might seem in one way, all of it was petty" (Trevor 1992: 521).

References

Beckett, Mary. 1980. "A Belfast Woman." In: Mary Beckett. *A Belfast Woman and Other Stories*. Dublin: Poolbeg, 84-99.

Chartres, John and John Clare. 1969. "City Fears Ghetto Future." *Times* (7 August 1969): 6. *The Times Digital Archive*. Web. 29 August 2017.

Clarke, Jennifer. 1999. "Benedict Kiely Interviewed by Jennifer Clarke." In: James P. Myers, ed. *Writing Irish: Selected Interviews with Irish Writers from the* Irish Literary Supplement. Syracuse: Syracuse University Press, 73-87.

D'hoker, Elke. 2016. *Irish Women Writers and the Modern Short Story*. Basingstoke: Palgrave Macmillan.

Doherty, Paul and Michael A. Poole. 1997. "Ethnic Residential Segregation in Belfast, Northern Ireland, 1971-1991." *Geographical Review* 87.4, 520-536.

Dooley, Terence and Christian Noack. [2013] "From Aristocratic Past to Public Heritage: A Comparative Case Study of Russian and Irish Country Houses since the Revolutions." *Allard Pierson Museum.nl*. Web. 29 August 2017.

Fisk, Robert. 1973. "A Feeling of Berlin in Belfast." *Times* (21 September 1973): 16. *The Times Digital Archive*. Web. 29 August 2017.

Hepburn, A.C. 1990. "The Belfast Riots of 1935." *Social History* 15.1, 75-96.

Isaacs, Harold R. 1989. *Idols of the Tribe: Group Identity and Political Change*. Cambridge, Mass: Harvard University Press.

Kelly, Aaron. 2005. *The Thriller and Northern Ireland since 1996: Utterly Resigned Terror*. Aldershot: Ashgate.

Kennedy, Liam. 2016. *Unhappy the Land: The Most Oppressed People Ever, the Irish?* Newbridge: Merrion.

Kennedy-Andrews, Elmer. 2003. *Fiction and the Northern Ireland Troubles since 1969: (De)constructing the North*, Dublin: Four Courts.

—. 2013. "'The battlefield has never quietened': Political Violence in the Fiction of William Trevor." In: Paul Delaney and Michael Parker, eds. *William Trevor: Revaluations*. Manchester: Manchester University Press, 55-75.

Kiely, Benedict. 1980. "Bluebell Meadow." In: Benedict Kiely. *The State of Ireland*. Boston: David R Godine, 274-293.

Mantel, Hilary. 2013. "King Billy is a Gentleman". In: Hilary Mantel, ed. *Learning to Talk: Short Stories*. London: Fourth Estate, 1-20.

Massey, Doreen. 1992. "Politics and Space/Time." *New Left Review* I.196, 65-84.

—. 1995. "Places and Their Pasts." *History Workshop Journal* 39, 182-192.
McCann, Eamonn. 1993. *War and an Irish Town.* London: Pluto Press.
McDonald, Ronan. 2005. "Strategies of Silence: Colonial Strains in Short Stories of the Troubles." *Yearbook of English Studies* 35, 249-263.
Neill, William J. V. 2004. *Urban Planning and Cultural Identity.* London/New York: Routledge.
O'Connell, Sean. 2014. "Violence and Social Memory in Twentieth-Century Belfast: Stories of Buck Alec Robinson." *Journal of British Studies* 53.3, 734-756.
Rhodes, Robert E. 1983. "William Trevor's Stories of the Troubles." In: James D. Brophy and Raymond Porter, eds. *Contemporary Irish Writing*. Boston: Twayne, 95-114.
Schirmer, Gregory A. 1990. *William Trevor: A Study of the Short Fiction.* London/New York: Routledge.
Storey, Michael. 2004. *Representing the Troubles in Irish Short Fiction.* Washington: The Catholic University of America Press.
Sullivan, Megan. 1995. "Mary Beckett: An Interview." *Irish Literary Supplement* 11.2, 10-12.
Stout, Mira. 1989. "William Trevor: The Art of Fiction 108." *Paris Review* 110, 118-151.
Sweeney, Christopher. 1973. "Enclaves of Fear in a City of Intimidation." *Times* (27 March 1973): 16. *The Times Digital Archive*. Web. 29 August 2017.
Trevor, William. 1992. "Another Christmas." In: William Trevor. *The Collected Stories*. New York: Viking, 514-521.
—. 1992. "The Distant Past." In: William Trevor. *The Collected Stories*. New York: Viking, 349-356.

CHAPTER NINE

OF FOREIGNERS AND FRIENDS: MUSIC, ART AND MILITARISM
AN ENQUIRY INTO THE RELATIONS BETWEEN THE PRACTICES OF THE ARTS, ESPECIALLY LITERATURE AND MUSIC, AND THE PRIORITIES OF ECONOMICS WHICH BEAR UPON MILITARY AUTHORITY, NATIONAL IDENTITY AND SCOTLAND

ALAN RIACH

1. Clichés and Caricatures

Disrespected neighbours is a familiar idea in Scotland. The cliché of caricature is the currency of diminishment, and unavoidable: tartan, kilts, haggis, heather, bagpipes, "industrial" Glasgow, "remote" islands (remote from what?). We are well aware that clichés and caricatures are political weapons, since humour can serve any political purpose. Hamlet reminds us that you can smile and be a villain, and surely, in stories and films, most villains do smile. Yet the clichés are not fiction. They are at work in society. They inform social prejudice and can in themselves be acts of cruelty and disdain. In New Zealand in the late 1980s, there was a TV advertisement regularly shown in which a train pulled up at a railway station, dozens of kilted Scots poured out and ran into the town, to the "Robbie Burns" off-licence liquor store, to buy up cheap booze in whatever special offer was on that week. I got a bit tired of this so I wrote to the TV weekly magazine *The Listener*, and said that although I wasn't entirely bereft of a sense of humour, I did think this was a bit much. Question: would this even be broadcast, if instead of Scots the people represented were of a different ethnic, racial, religious or national group? Maori people, for example? Or Jews? Nobody replied but the advert disappeared soon after.

National identities have their purpose. The formula that negates their significance is defined by the mantra "think global act local," yet this is a false balance, a utopian dichotomy of benevolent world and friendly village. Yet globalisation is not utopian and some villages are not friendly. However you do it, you're going to need some social organisation, especially if egalitarianism is an ideal. After all, there are only two reasons for the state to make laws. One is to protect the vulnerable. The other is to enhance human potential. Everything else, all legal structures and formalities, all the jargon of legislation and the state, all government, in any purpose of self-conscious moral responsibility and social authority, must serve these imperatives. They must not be fudged.

They are balanced against each other for good reason. Keep them both in mind and at best, they complement each other. All good laws rise from them. Take them to extremes and they start to break each other down. Protecting the vulnerable and enhancing human potential is to be friendly to the best in humanity, but there is a cost. Protection from some potentially inimical force may mean creating "others" whose priorities are different: "foreigners" or "enemies"; enhancing potential may mean the sacrifice or denial of some other potential, those different priorities, the preferences of those very "foreigners." For freedom, you need regulation. The question is, what sort of regulation would you like?

2. Culture and Militarism: Hugh MacDiarmid and Tobias Hume

"Foreigners and Friends" – I take it as given that in the company of scholars, we are among friends, and that, in the civilised context of reasonable academic enquiry, we can be confident that if we err in our practice it will be understood that such error comes not from malice but from a willingness to push the enquiry in an academic way. And yet, I travelled to the conference at which this essay was presented in an earlier form in April 2016, from Scotland, from Glasgow, first through what we might call the air-space of England, to land in Berlin before getting a train to Jena, where the conference was to take place. I first visited Berlin in 1986, and experienced both sides of its internal demarcation. On the journey in 2016, I could not but be aware of the experience of being among foreigners.

The journey through foreign lands and languages, mores and habits of perception and priorities of cultural climate, always brings news that can help, one way or another. It has been a pleasant and profitable experience for me, travelling professionally to various quarters of the globe, and for long periods of my life, working in England, New Zealand, and since 2001, back in Scotland again. Such work practice sensitises, hopefully, one's experience of other histories, other cultures, how these overlap or touch on a history and culture I feel identified as mind, so the world of the mind becomes an open enquiry: how might such differences best be expressed, how can the music be communicated, the stories be told, the culture be shared in sympathetic understanding, and in critical assessment?

In the very terms themselves – "foreigners" and "friends" – there is an implicit and general autobiographical or biographical aspect. From the beginning, any human being is surrounded by foreigners. From conception to birth, one might hope, parental care promises friendship to come, but the unborn have no articulate knowledge of what they will find. From birth through childhood, foreigners among family will become known and some (most, one hopes) develop friendliness, and from childhood through to maturity, friendships will come, in the way of things, if we are fortunate. So far, it might seem, so obvious.

But the unborn of the future have still to discover the foreignness of friends they might have in the past. One is reminded of Walter Benjamin:

> Only that historian will have the gift of fanning the spark of hope in the past who is firmly convinced that *even the dead* will not be safe from the enemy if he wins. And this enemy has not ceased to be victorious. (Benjamin 1973: 257)

So the children of the future, if we and they are lucky enough, will have to fan the spark of hope by looking once again into their past, at what we do now, and what we will have done to provide for them. Maybe they will find friends among us, as I have found friends among writers, composers, artists, long dead, foreigners, whose work has helped me live. Figured in this way, the very experience of being human and living a life must necessarily entail a development of transitions from foreign to friendly relationships – not universal, not to be enforced, not in any sense uniform, but both given and chosen, inherited and selected – what we might describe as a series of natural and elective affinities.

If this is true of individual human beings, is it not also true of nations and states, or nation-states? And what of empires? And what would be the relations between individuals of potent authority and influence, and those families, larger social groups, tribes, clans, nations, states, über-nations, religious fanaticisms, defined in whatever way, who, collectively, in large numbers, might be willing to travel across foreign lands to deliver destruction upon others, at the behest of their rulers or for their own gain? We know too well how these things happen. We know how people in recent decades have committed atrocities upon those we would say they wished to define in perpetuity as "foreigners" – foreigners who can only be defined eternally as such in death. For life itself is always opposed to foreignness. Not to foreigners, which life welcomes. But to foreignness, which we are always being introduced to. We might say, perhaps, that we are obliged, by the fact of being alive, to try to understand that which at first seems foreign to us, this foreignness. And we might argue that the arts are our best means of understanding it. The sciences might help us control it, but what good is control without understanding? How often have we heard the notion that in poetry, the ordinary becomes extraordinary, the everyday becomes exceptional? It is so familiar as to be almost a cliché. Yet the truth in it might be understood legitimately as an active accommodation of otherness, an exploration of foreignness. Arts introduce us to other things. By their virtues, foreign things become familiar to us. But when such obligation is impossible, when that introduction to others leads to violence, and annihilation, or when the intrinsic optimism that inhabits curiosity is met with foreclosure and thwarted in its hopeful exercise, what then?

In our state generally, today, or in the as-yet-unrealised state-in-waiting from which I come, Scotland, what if I wished to consider elective affinities among those figures of the past who had become obscured by prevailing notions and priorities? How would I find friends beyond the army of clichés by which "Scotland" has been made familiar? Would I not be challenged by contemporary conventions just as the historians of the future will be challenged? What is the "enemy" in Benjamin's term? How do we fan a spark of hope in this place of foreigners and friends?

I am beginning with a kind of credo. Hugh MacDiarmid puts it most cogently. In his long poem "In Memoriam James Joyce" (1955), his central theme is the endless variety of languages in the world, the diversity of poetic and artistic expressions of human creativity, the limitations placed upon expressivity by political power and imperialism, and the need to balance energy and form. His is essentially a celebration of difference. He sums it up in a poem entitled "England's Double Knavery":

> The effort of culture is towards greater differentiation
> Of perceptions and desires and values and ends,
> Holding them from moment to moment
>   In a perpetually changing but stable equilibrium [...]
> (MacDiarmid 1992: 227)

This is a vision of utopian possibility, never to be fully achieved, because if it ever were achieved, the natural fact of the dynamics of human society would alter it, somehow. In any nation, the borders of languages are plural, porous, but real. To recognise this is to affirm continuing engagement with the people, history and geography of the nation as a viable state with a legislative structure which might endorse this inextinguishable human dynamic. The Nigerian Nobel laureate Wole Soyinka emphasised this in his 2004 musings on the fate of Algeria, where in 1992 a disillusioned electorate democratically voted for a dictatorship in perpetuity. Soyinka commented, "The perennial problem with that proposition of course is that this denies the dynamic nature of human society." (Soyinka 2004)

However, MacDiarmid has a counter-proposal to this vision of cultural possibility: the ethos of militarism:

> The deterioration of life under the regime
> Of the soldier is a commonplace; physical power
> Is a rough substitute for patience and intelligence
> And co-operative effort in the governance of man [...]
> (MacDiarmid 1992: 227)

He concludes: "The animus of war is to enforce uniformity / – To extirpate whatever the soldier / Can neither understand nor utilise" (MacDiarmid 1992: 227). This, of course, is an over-simplification. There is truth in it, but the world is a more complex place than a simple opposition between the effort of culture and the animus of war. War makes its own cultures, as Bertolt Brecht and Walter Benjamin knew too well. Culture wars are common enough, in universities as much as in commercial arts organisations and government funding bodies within nation-states or quasi-federal nations governed by an über-state or former empire, as we in Scotland know far too well.

But I'd like to emphasise that a simple dichotomy such as that just proposed is helpful. It is helpful because it polarises and we can see the extremes. On the one hand, there is the vulnerable friendliness of cultural complexity cradled in its ever-changing but stable equilibrium. On the other hand, there is the inimical foreignness of militarised death machines, whether mechanical conformity of human behaviours or literally manufactured weaponry and machinery bringing the uniformity of consumerism, sensationalism, information overload, and league tables for competing institutions. These are impositions of nightmare. These polarities are useful, but the world is more complex, and this is what the arts help us to understand. So let's consider a particularly complex man: Tobias Hume.

Tobias Hume (1569-1645) was a Scottish mercenary soldier and a significant composer, travelling through Poland and Russia in the 17th century with his *viol da gamba* and secret plans for a "Great Machine" of war, threatening to kill up to thirty thousand people. He played music, presumably to allay his melancholia. His life depended upon his loyalty to friends, women and men across the social strata and a range of different nations, and he was the subject of a curious, neglected novel, *Loot and Loyalty* (1955) by the Polish writer Jerzy Peterkiewicz.

Peterkiewicz himself is a fascinating figure. Born in rural Poland in 1916, during the First World War, he became well-known (in some respects, notorious) as a poet and polemicist, and then during the Second World War, he travelled to France and then to London, learning English and studying English literature at St Andrews University in Scotland, completing a doctorate at the University of London and becoming a professor of Polish language and literature there. He began writing his eight novels in English in 1953. *Loot and Loyalty* was his second. He was increasingly spending months in an adopted home in the south of Spain. He died in 2007.

Let me stay with Tobias Hume before I return to Peterkiewicz. His story opens to us, in the 21st century, questions of selfhood and survival, friendship and allegiance, art and militarism, neighbourliness and power, national identity and the value of music, literature and the arts: questions that are even more urgent now than they were four hundred years ago. Peterkiewicz, in his novel about Hume, addresses the same questions for a mid-20th century readership.

Hume published two books of music in 1605 and 1607, introducing the first of them with these words:

> I do not studie Eloquence, or professe Musicke, although I doe love Sence, and affect Harmony. My profession beeing, as my Education hath beene, Armes, the only effeminate part of me, hath beene Musicke; which in mee hath beene alwais Generous, because never Merecenarie. To praise Musicke, were to say, the Sunne is bright. To extoll my selfe would name my labours vaineglorious. Onely this, my studies are far from servile imitations. I robbe no others inventions, I take no Italian Note to an English Dittie, or filch fragments of Songs to stuffe out my volumes. These are mine own Phansies expressed by my proper Genius, which if thou doest dislike, let me see thine [...]. (Purser 2007: 137-138)

Blunt and unhoneyed words, but how suggestive they are! The oppositions there, between Arms and Music, between the generosity inherent in arts that give freely and the mercenary priorities of militarism that takes or sells itself to the highest paying contractor, between the masculinity implied by the profession of war, the "effeminate" sensitivity extolled as an essential component of music itself, and most tellingly, between the idea of a self-generated imagination providing works of art ("mine own Phantasies expressed by my proper Genius") as opposed to the business of theft (taking Italian notes for English "ditties") – this may have been a critical comment on the English composer of lute music John Dowland – these binaries polarise but also balance. They oppose but also connect. This brings together representations of art and politics, composer and mercenary, player and soldier. And professional soldier he was, serving as a captain in the King of Sweden's armies, leading the troops of the Emperor of Russia, travelling throughout Poland and Russia. It didn't end well for Hume. When he last was heard in 1642, it was in the words of his "True Petition presented to the Lords assembled in the high Court of Parliament" and imbued with pity and pathos: "I am an old and experienced Souldier, and have done great service in other forraine Countries as when I was in Russia, I did put thirty thousand to flight, and killed six or seven thousand Polonians by the art of my instruments of warre [...]," he writes. He concludes: "I am like to be starved for want of meat and drinke, and did walke into the fields lately to gather snailes in the netles, and brought a bagge of them home to eat, and doe now feed on them for want of other meate, to the great shame of this land [...]." (Purser 2007: 140) Three years later he died in the Charterhouse, on 16 April 1645.

Now, in the novel, *Loot and Loyalty*, Jerzy Peterkiewicz (or Pietrkiewicz as he was then) imagines Hume in southern Poland and Russia, in around 1605-06, becoming involved in a plot to put forward a young boy, Dmitri, as a stand-in for the murdered Tsar. In the central part of the novel, Hume is mistakenly arrested by his own soldiers. Isolated, a prisoner, he sets about constructing his "Great Machine" of war, the plans for which he has been carrying around concealed in his *viol da gamba*. The irony here is rich and layered: the composer, to allay his melancholy, plays his music; the soldier, hatching plans and trusting to the fortunes of war, has a master plan for a "Great Machine" that will deliver massive destruction through poison and pestilence – ultimately, this is chemical warfare attacking innocent people intimately, internally – and the plans for this machine have been with Hume hidden away in his musical instrument. The machine collapses but its malevolence seems to be effective: it appears that thousands of people are killed.

The pathos and drama of the story itself is evident, I think, but the central ambiguous symbol requires emphasis. The plans for the poisonous machine are hidden *within* the *viol da gamba*. Both are material objects, visible things, and both capable of releasing into the world invisibilities, either pestilence or music, the extreme options of devastation and death or enlivening sensibility, the quickening that art can bring. The musicologist and music historian John Purser says of Hume's Pavans that they are amongst the most profound music for solo instrument of any period. The great Spanish musician, Jordi Savall, performs these with mastery and Claude Chauvel describes several of the works as 'de la meilleure veine et d'une incontestable originalité,' adding that the Pavans are 'noble et austere.' Noble and austere indeed. Nothing quite so searching as this music for solo bass viol was to be composed for over a century, when it took Bach and his solo cello suites to stir those depths and reach those heights using no more than a single stringed instrument. (Purser 14 April 2017)

There is a curious afterlife to the novel. As well as being a music historian, John Purser is a Scottish poet, playwright and composer. Most importantly, he is the author and presenter of a BBC radio series entitled *Scotland's Music*. This was first broadcast in thirty 90-minute programmes in 1991-92 and then revised as fifty 30-minute programmes in 2007. When he was engaged in research for the series, Purser discovered the novel and through rather circuitous routes, made contact with Jerzy Peterkiewicz. They met and became friendly, discussing in meetings and in correspondence themes of shared interest: music and war, how to draw meanings from the past, how to try to make provision for the future. The histories of Scotland and Poland, nationalism and war in Europe, relations between nationalism and social life, art and the state, military precision and intuitive understanding, national identity and political purpose, entered into their dialogue, and in terms of how neighbours might be respected, or disrespected, are of evident concern to us here. With reference to the novel, John Purser wrote in a letter to Peterkiewicz, the following:

Loot and Loyalty – strange confederations gathering around a central figure whose innocence is alluringly complex and hovering over the dawn of evil. I have never been to those parts of Europe and you have fed me a vision of them full of clammy mists, foetid marshes and succubating mire and I begin to wonder what kind of people can possibly survive there with their souls intact. (Purser 12 March 1991)

But the reward was an acknowledgement of a prophecy. The scene of the Machine's collapse was the Pripet marshes, which lie all around Chernobyl, the still poisonous site of the nuclear catastrophe of 1986. At the end of his autobiography, *In the Scales of Fate*, Peterkiewicz says this:

In Purgatory or in Heaven – I still believe in them – we will be judged by the love of our friends. One of the secrets of Hell – if it exists – is that you will not find any friends there. No friend: no judgement.

I have been enriched by my friends: their love and loyalty have kept me away from the hellish traps of isolation. I sometimes wonder what kind of force it is in two people, which urges them to see their own reflection in another human being? [...]

Is it possible to befriend another land, find a region compatible with the mythical place of one's birth? I think I found such a place in the European South. It was not a castle in Spain, but a country house in the Andalusian style. [...]

I have become a European, loyal by birth and by adoption to two regions, one in the North, in the land of Dobrzyn, and another in the South, in Andalusia. Hampstead in London serves the purpose of a fulcrum. It balances the scales in my sign of Libra. (Peterkiewicz, 1993: 231-232)

This is an affirmation of doubleness, of ambiguity or ambivalence, a confirmation that any human being is capable of accepting and being nourished by the given facts of his or her inheritance and nature, and at the same time capable of making those "elective affinities" I spoke of earlier, according to preferences consciously worked through. Not "Loot and Loyalty" but the "love and loyalty" of friends. Indeed, it is a recognition of a requirement of balance: Libra holds her scales in perpetual co-ordination, the weight in each one responsive to the weight in the other. The fulcrum is where the balance is poised. It is a position of leverage and it can be an embodiment of power.

3. Bias and Thwart: George Osborne and Norman MacCaig

George Osborne, who in 2016 was the Chancellor of the Exchequer of the United Kingdom's Conservative government, was the Chancellor of the UK's coalition Conservative and Liberal Democrat government when he visited Scotland for a few hours on 13 February 2014, that is, seven months before the referendum on Scotland's independence on 18 September 2014. He was in Scotland to deliver a speech, recorded, televised, published and available online. He was there to tell Scots and the world of his opposition to an independent Scotland, and how his job as he saw it was to stop it coming into existence by ruling out of consideration the prospect of a continuing shared currency between Scotland and the rest of the UK.

Now, I'd like to close in on the rhetoric Osborne employed in a particular part of his speech, a moment burnt into the memory of many of us who remember that day. This is what he said to begin with: "In just over 7 months people in Scotland will decide whether or not to walk away from the United Kingdom. The stakes couldn't be higher or the choice clearer. The certainty and security of being part of the UK or the uncertainty and risk of going it alone. At the very heart of this choice is the pound in your pocket."

He escalated the rhetorical power as he went on (and if you look online at the government webpage where the speech is reproduced, it's fascinating to see how line-breaks are managed, as if the speech were a poem, presumably showing him as he was reading it where to pause for the greatest emphasis). This is what was at the heart of his speech:

> There's no legal reason why the rest of the UK would need to share its currency with Scotland, as the Treasury's publication today clearly shows.
> So when the nationalists say "the pound is as much ours as the rest of the UK's" are they really saying that an independent Scotland could insist that taxpayers in a nation it has just voted to leave…
> had to continue to back the currency of this new **foreign** country
> had to consider the circumstances of this **foreign** country when setting their interest rates
> stand behind the banks of this **foreign** country as a lender of last resort
> or stand behind its **foreign** government when it needed public spending support.
> That is patently absurd.
> If Scotland walks away from the UK, it walks away from the UK pound.

When Osborne uttered these words, a great deal was at stake. And the rhetoric made something unforgettably clear. He was saying that an independent country would be a foreign country, run by a foreign government. His opposition to that prospect – his absolute "unfriendliness" – uttered as it was in the erstwhile capital city of that country – was implicitly transferred to the country and city he was in. In other words, he was standing as a native of Britain, the UK, and creating in the imaginations of everyone watching him the context, for a moment, of being in a foreign and unfriendly nation, *their own nation*, beyond whose borders, and only beyond whose borders, safety and security lay. This is how he concluded: "There is an alternative, confident, future for Scotland": "It's a strong Scotland within a United Kingdom. / That is a future worth fighting for." (Osborne: 13 February 2014)

And after that, he walked swiftly out of the building and into a car, taking the quickest route back to London before anyone could draw breath to ask a question. This was not up for discussion and no reporter had a chance to say anything to him. He was off. He'd done the job. "Independent" from now on, the word itself, would mean "foreign." We – people living in Scotland – were now not to see ourselves as citizens, but as foreigners. This was an exercise in projection, a double or triple bluff, audacious, surely, and startling in its combination of sophistication and crudity, its appeal and its repulsiveness, its credibility and its absurdity.

There is an answer in a great poem by Norman MacCaig, one of that brilliant generation of Scottish poets – all men, I'm afraid, though that situation has changed completely now – who began writing through the Second World War and wrote their greatest works from the 1960s on. Each had their favoured location in Scotland, each one mapping out a territory, charging places with real, renewable value quite different from the economics that were maintained as the priority in the rhetoric of Osborne and many others of his stripe: George Mackay Brown in the Orkney archipelago, Sorley Maclean in Raasay and Skye in the Inner Hebrides, Iain Crichton Smith in Lewis and the Outer Hebrides, Edwin Morgan in Glasgow. For Norman MacCaig, Edinburgh was home but Lochinver, in Assynt, up in the far north-west of mainland Scotland, was the favoured place. And it came with its own geology and its own history. MacCaig returned there every summer for many years, so he was not a tourist or even visitor but, we might say, an intermittent but regular resident. And the poem I want to mention here, to answer Osborne's monstrous creation of the foreign country we call Scotland, is this: "Two Thieves" (first published in 1980). It begins in a particular location: "the Place for Pulling Up Boats" is its name in English. But in Gaelic, it was only "one word" and at the moment the poem enacts, "the tide is full." MacCaig describes it seeping over the grass "like a robber. / Which it is." It's a robber, MacCaig explains, because, as an old local woman has told him,

> that fifty yards stretch of gravel now under water
> was, in her granny's time, a smooth green sward
> where the Duke of Sutherland
> turned his coach and four.

MacCaig exclaims that this is an "an image of richness, a tiny pageantry / in this small dying place" because today, every house in the village is "lived in / by the sad widow of a fine strong man." He reflects that there were "fine strong men in the Duke's time." But the Duke, the aristocratic landowner, drove them to the shore then drove them to Canada. These Highlanders, people of Scotland's north-west, were subjected to brutal eviction, the Highland Clearances, in the 18th, 19th and on into the 20th centuries. And as for the Duke?

> He gave no friendly thought to them
> as he turned his coach and four
> by the Place for Pulling Up Boats
> where no boats are. (MacCaig 2005: 397)

This is a poem of incremental anger, making judgement on the callous indifference of the powerful and their (or in this case, his) legacy: not only the eviction of people but the loss of the Gaelic language, the devastation of an entire culture. No friendly thoughts were there in our own time either, from George Osborne, that day in Edinburgh. Foreigners indeed. But let's begin to draw to an end by returning to our friends.

4. Nationalism

To summarise, what we have been focused on and what my examples have, hopefully, kept before us, are questions of art, the arts, including music, and the priorities of economics which have their bearing in military priorities of expediency and practice. Whether that is given in terms of a 17th-century mercenary soldier and his legacy, or the verbal, mediated, propaganda warfare of the 2014 referendum on Scottish independence, or the long history of imperialism's oppression of linguistic diversity and what are called "minority languages" – in every case, the examples are and can only be, partial. They are contingent upon circumstance. The arts are never absolute and finished. As Brecht puts it most memorably, "How long / Do works endure? As long / As they are not completed." (Brecht 1976: 193) Equally, what seems like an absolute judgement from political or economic gurus, is part of a larger gambit, takes place in a continuing debate. Norman MacCaig laments the eviction of crofters and the loss of their Gaelic language, but since he wrote his poems, in various locations crofters have bought out big landowners and repossessed the land, and more people are learning Gaelic now than for generations.

If Tobias Hume lived and wrote his music in a pre-Enlightenment Europe, we might make the long journey through Enlightenment and Romanticism to Modernism and the 21st century very swiftly by noting the two strongest imperatives that sprang from the Enlightenment and grew into horrific distortions of themselves in their worst and most extreme forms: enthusiasm and nationalism. The liability in both is that the first could lead to isolationist fanaticism and the second to imperialist superiorism.

Yet fanatic devotion to their own art is a priority all artists know and of all people, artists have frequently been committed to and engaged in nationalism. This ambiguity is at the heart of the matter. Many of the greatest artists were nation-builders like Verdi and Wagner, Grieg, Sibelius, Pushkin, Borodin and Balakirev, the French Impressionists, and many were deeply aware of how national cultures interact with one another. Consider Debussy's reaction to German music. And more generally, consider how art reflects and represents a nation's self-esteem. Artists present their nation's culture to the world. This is perfectly evident in Italian neo-realist cinema, in Satyajit Ray's *Apu* trilogy, in Bergman's film visions of Sweden, and Kurosawa's of Japan. And alongside these we might register the significance of the displaced artists of the 20th century, Stravinsky, Rachmaninov, Schoenberg, and Bartok remaining true to their original cultures in all their travels and residences. *The Rite of Spring* may be a high-culture text, the paradigm of Modernism in music, internationally significant way beyond any concerns of "narrow" nationalism. And yet Stravinsky chose to give it a subtitle, emphatically present in its universal interpretation: "Pictures of Pagan Russia". These artists and composers cannot simply be described as "international" Modernists who came from nowhere in particular. It was important to return Bartok's remains to Hungary, for example, despite the fact that the name of the homeland he came from had long since disappeared. Poland would certainly not be what it is without Chopin. And Chopin visiting Scotland, performing in Glasgow, prefigures the strong connections between the two countries that were realised when so many Polish people settled in Scotland in the aftermath of the Second World War. That is, national identity is strengthened and enriched by the recognition of difference. Its value and purpose relies upon difference and distinction: foreignness, indeed. And the creative arts are the best ways in which that foreignness may be mediated internationally to beneficial diplomatic effect. This is not utopian, but merely realistic.

In the aftermath of the Second World War, the exclusion of Scottish art from the Edinburgh International Festival resonated for decades with the implication that Scottish art had no international calibre. And the centralisation of the Arts Council in London with a Scottish regional division also emphasised this idea that Scotland was no more than a region. Our institutional education system in Scotland neglected and oppressed literature in the Gaelic and Scots languages (with one glaring exception: Robert Burns), not to mention works of art and music by Scottish artists and composers.

Things changed radically in the second half of the 20th century, from the establishment of the Saltire Society, the Scottish Arts Council, the Association for Scottish Literary Studies, the Department of Scottish Literature at Glasgow University (preceded by the university-endowed Chair of Scottish History and the Chair of Scottish Literature) and the National Theatre of Scotland in 2006. Art galleries established in Stornoway, in Orkney, the new Shetland Museum in Lerwick – all these new initiatives since the Second World War herald new possibilities, new beginnings in particular localities far from the major cities. Yet the legacy of long-standing institutional neglect of, and hostility to, the full inheritance of the arts of Scotland is still with us.

"What is Scottish about Scottish art?" I was talking in Kirkcudbright about the artist J.D. Fergusson. "It's got nothing to do with Scotland," someone said. "It's all about rhythm and form. That's all." This is a familiar mantra. All art is universal. Nations don't matter. Especially Scotland because Britain is what counts (especially England) and Scotland is a minor component part of that.

The real and proper answer is, Hokusai is Japanese, Monet is French, Goya is Spanish, Turner is English, and so forth. So, William McTaggart, Charles Rennie Mackintosh, Margaret and Frances Macdonald, J.D. Fergusson, Joan Eardley, David Donaldson, Alexander Goudie, John Cunningham, Gwen Hardie, Ruth Nicol, and so on, are Scottish: they, and their best work, could have come from nowhere else.

And the key thing is this: each of them has possession in their work of particular aspects of Scotland, which their work *gives*, freely, to anyone willing and able to look at it, to read and enjoy it closely. In this way, they all make friends of foreigners.

For it is pre-eminently through works of art that the virtues of national, local and linguistic distinctions might be made public, given to people, universally, and freely. Foreignness, in this sense, is not a threat or an imposition, but a matter of curiosity, of optimistic enquiry, of engagement and extension of the human spirit. It is what Hume's music gives us, and what his Great Machine failed to do; it is what George Osborne never understood, and what Norman MacCaig so memorably captured in his poems. And it is at the heart of social and intellectual life, what characterises, for me, more than anything else, the unanswered question of Scotland's independence.

References

Benjamin, Walter. 1973. "Theses on the Philosophy of History." In: Hannah Arendt, ed. *Illuminations*. trans. by Harry Zohn. London: Collins / Fontana Books, 255-266.

Brecht, Bertolt. 1976. "About the Way to Construct Enduring Works." In: John Willett and Ralph Manheim, eds. *Poems*. London: Eyre Methuen, 193-196.

MacCaig, Norman. 2005. "Two Thieves." In: Ewen McCaig, ed. *The Poems of Norman MacCaig*. Edinburgh: Polygon, 397.

MacDiarmid, Hugh. 1992. "from 'England's Double Knavery'." In: Alan Riach and Michael Grieve, eds. *Selected Poems*. Harmondsworth: Penguin Books, 226-227.
Osborne, George. 13 February 2014. *GOV.UK*. Web. 15 April 2016.
Pietrkiewicz, Jerzy. 1955. *Loot and Loyalty*. London: William Heinemann Ltd.
—. 11 August 1993. Letter to John Purser. (Privately held. Quoted by permission.)
—. 1993. *In the Scales of Fate*. London/New York: Marion Boyars.
Purser, John. 2007. *Scotland's Music: A History of the Traditional and Classical Music of Scotland from Early Times to the Present Day*. Edinburgh: Mainstream.
—. 12 March 1991. Letter to Jerzy Peterkiewicz. (Privately held. Quoted by permission.)
—. 14 April 2017. "Tobias Hume: A Question of Identity." *The National*. (Daily newspaper, Glasgow).
Soyinka, Wole. 2004. "Lecture 2: Power and Freedom." In: The Reith Lectures. BBC Radio 4.

INDIA

CHAPTER TEN

HISTORY AND MEMORY: GENDERING THE OTHER IN JYOTIRMOYEE DEVI'S *THE RIVER CHURNING* AND AMITAV GOSH'S *THE SHADOW LINES*

NANDINI SAHA

The Muslims used to announce that they would take away our daughters. They would force their way into homes and pick up young girls and women. Ten or twenty of them would enter, tie up the menfolk and take the women. We saw many who had been raped and disfigured, their faces and breasts scarred, and then abandoned. They had tooth-marks all over them. Their families said, "How can we keep them now? Better that they are dead." Many of them were so young – 18, 15, 14 years old – what remained of them now? ... One had been raped by ten or more men – her father burnt her, refused to take her back. (Menon and Bhasin 2011: 32)

In the space of a few months, about twelve million people moved between the new, truncated India and the two wings, East and West, of the newly created Pakistan. By far the largest proportion of these refugees – more than ten million of them – crossed the western border which divided the historic state of Punjab, Muslims travelling west to Pakistan, Hindus and Sikhs east to India. Slaughter sometimes accompanied and sometimes prompted their movement; many others died from malnutrition and contagious disease. [...] As always there was widespread sexual savagery: about 75,000 women are thought to have been abducted and raped by men of religions different from their own (and indeed sometimes by men of their own religion). (Butalia 1998: 3)

1. Introduction

This paper examines the narration of history through a gendered reading of the Bangladesh partition with reference to its representation in two novels. The first is a Bengali novel translated in English as *The River Churning* (originally written in Bengali by Jyotirmoyee Devi (1894? –1988) in 1967 but published in 1968 and translated into English in 1995 by the noted translator and writer Enakshi Chatterjee). The second novel I will refer to here is *The Shadow Lines* (1988) by Amitav Ghosh, the globally acclaimed postcolonial writer of fiction and non-fiction. The two novels analysed in this paper are set against the backdrop of the Partition and the riots that erupted during this cataclysmic historical event and also those riots that took place around the issue of the demarcation of national boundaries between India and Bangladesh at other points of time. In India such historical disturbances have led to the generation of several categories and cultural stereotypes based on religious and national differences. These historical and cultural constructions of categories in India, which only tend to widen the rift created by the drawing of boundaries between nations, are at the central focus of this paper. All such stereotypes have evolved out of these historical moments and the tensions that brewed between various communities and religious groups and also out of the hatred that such historical crisis moments usually propagate. The paper underscores the most critically discussed aspect of Indian history – that of the Partition of the country in 1947 that divided the subcontinent into different countries and eventually led to the war of liberation of East Pakistan, now Bangladesh, in 1971.

The first epigraph at the beginning of this paper is from Ritu Menon and Kamla Bhasin's seminal work *Borders & Boundaries: Women in India's Partition* (1998 [2011]). This particular extract is from one of several such instances of horror that people told the authors about, recounting their horrific experiences of the Partition of India in 1947. While Menon and Bhasin recorded and documented real stories from people who witnessed the Partition, Indian English writing and literature in the various Indian languages (and translations of such literature into English) have mirrored all such stories of plunder, rape, and torture in innumerable works of fiction. However, very rarely is literature given its due for being an authoritative social document of any given time. Menon and Bhasin rightfully accord literature its due status:

> The abundance of political histories on Partition is almost equaled by the paucity of social histories of it. [...] Why has there been such an absence of enquiry into its cultural, psychological and social ramifications? There can be no one answer to this question, but what seems to have stepped in, at least partly, to record the full horror of Partition is literature. [...] In one sense it can be considered a kind of social history not only because it so approximates reality [...] but because it is the only significant non-official contemporary record we have of the time, apart from reportage. (Menon and Bhasin 2011: 6-7)

Menon and Bhasin are not the only ones to document these stories. Urvashi Butalia's *The Other Side of Silence* (1998), which is the source of the second epigraph, is also regarded as a landmark work in the field of Partition studies. There are several more of such non-fictional texts besides the large body of fiction created around the theme of Partition. It is with the aid of the two non-fictional works quoted above that this paper intends to analyse two fictional works – one in translation, *The River Churning* by Jyotirmoyee Devi, and the award-winning Indian English novel by Amitav Ghosh titled *The Shadow Lines*.

The state of West Bengal in India and its neighbouring country Bangladesh have experienced a traumatic and violent history of Partition. The geographical boundaries between India on the one hand and West and East Pakistan on the other, now Pakistan and Bangladesh respectively, were drawn majorly on religious lines under the British regime before the declaration of India's independence in 1947. All the categories and cultural stereotypes that will be explicated in this paper are a result of this religious divide, mainly between the Hindus and the Muslims, that was created during the Partition. The paper is divided into two sections. The first section will deal with a novel in which the stereotypes of religious groups determine the categories and processes of "othering" that affected human relationships during the events of the Partition. The next section will focus on another novel where the delineation of the "other" is shown to work not on religious categories as in the earlier novel, but gets defined and redefined through the events that take place either in Dhaka or in Kolkata during the riots. This paper also intends to evaluate the various ways in which the stereotypes of religion affect the gender discriminations that work in Indian society. The central focus will be how in several ways the construction of the "other" is gendered in India and how such social constructions then get reflected in literature.

2. History Gets Etched on the Female Body: *The River Churning*

The Partition of India and Pakistan is probably one of the most violent and disrespectful aspects of Indian political history. My argument is that this disrespect was not for any particular individual or group though it was played out between different religious groups – the Hindus and Muslims. Whatever may have been the epicentre of this tension, it was mainly played out against and through women – their bodies became the territories of power struggles between the various groups. As Bharati Ray points out, "all classes and castes on both sides of the border were victims of murder and forcible evacuation, but women were the worst affected. Through rape and abduction, women became central to the whole act of violence" (Ray and Basu 1999: 4). In the well-documented work of collected oral narratives of horror of the Partition of Pakistan in the North and North-Western parts of India, Urvashi Butalia and Ritu Menon and Kamla Bhasin in their publications point out how women were the victims most of the time when the different groups had to show their power. "A woman's body is a pawn even in the game of nation building. [...] At the moment of the birth of two nation-states in the place of one colonial state, the bodies of numberless women are brought under the control of their respective communities to complete the grand act of vivisection"[1] (Devi 1999: xxvi-xxxi). While the history of the 1947 Partition is well-documented, that of the twice partitioned Bangladesh is not. In very recent times, of course, there is an ongoing project that has been documenting and archiving stories of the Bangladesh partition and liberation, available on the website www.1947partitionarchive.org.

In 1947, while India rejoiced in its freedom, feelings of elation were also tainted with sadness, violence and bloodshed caused by the partition of the subcontinent into two distinct countries divided on religious lines. India was supposed to be a predominantly Hindu state and Pakistan – then East and West Pakistan – a Muslim country. Pakistan thus had two parts – one on the Western side, which is still known as Pakistan, and the other on the Eastern side where today we have Bangladesh as a separate country, which was then known as East Pakistan. Bangladesh wrenched its freedom from Pakistan in another bloody liberation war in 1971. For Bangladesh the horrifying experiences of the 1947 Partition was revisited in 1971–a dual experience of terror and bloodshed. While there are novels and stories in abundance on the Partition of India and Pakistan, the Partition stories of East Pakistan or Bangladesh are rare to find. "While historians and political scientists have until recently, focussed little on the impact of the Partition on private and family life, a number of creative writings [...] have ably and sensitively reflected the inner anguish and traumatic experiences of a generation caught in the crossfire of religious sectarianism."[2]

---

[1] Jyotirmoyee Devi's novel in English translation, *The River Churning* (first published 1995), includes an informative introduction by Jasodhara Bagchi. The original Bengali novel titled *Epar Ganga Opar Ganga* was first published in 1968. All references in the text will be to the translated version.

[2] Bharati Ray's essay in the book edited by her and Aparna Basu (1999) analyses Jyotirmoyee Devi's short story "*Chheleta*," translated from Bengali by Sukhender Ray as "The Little Beggar Boy," published in *The Impermanence of Lies*, Calcutta: Stree: 1998.

(Ray and Basu 1999: 3-4)

"Jyotirmoyee Devi (1894?–1988), was a feminist writer possessing an empathy and sensitivity towards women rare for an author of her time" (Ray and Basu 1999: 2). Born to a family of the Dewans to the Maharajah of Jaipur, Jyotirmoyee Devi did not receive formal education. Her education was achieved from the vast range of books that she got to read from her family library. Much as was the custom of those days in the upper caste Hindu society, Jyotirmoyee was married off at the tender age of ten. By the time she was 25 she was already a widow with six children. Her stories revolve around the lives of women – some that she saw in her growing up years in Rajasthan and then later in her life in Calcutta. To quote from the introduction by Jasodhara Bagchi to the translated text, "[W]ritten in 1967, published in book form a year later, Jyotirmoyee Devi's *Epar Ganga Opar Ganga* (*The River Churning*) is one of the rare examples of a Partition novel in Bengali written by a woman" (Devi 1999: xxvii). Jasodhara Bagchi introduces the author of the Bengali text thus: "[T]hroughout her life, Jyotirmoyee Devi wrote about marginalized, oppressed and destitute women, but it would be a mistake to trivialize her writings as a mere apology for social reform and social action, because Jyotirmoyee is alive to the processes of exclusion and marginalization of the women whom society constructs as 'deviant'" (Devi 1999: xxxi).

The translated text begins with a prologue by Jyotirmoyee Devi titled "Beginnings" and a brilliant "Introduction" by Indian feminist scholar Jasodhara Bagchi, where she summarizes the story of the novel:

> In a flashback we are transported to a night in 1946, when a sudden blaze of communal frenzy destroys the peace of a neighbourhood in a village in East Bengal, where Hindus and Muslims had lived in peace and amity. Within a few hours, there is complete havoc in the Hindu household. Before they have registered what is happening, the father disappears, the mother jumps into the pond to save her honour, the married sister disappears and the young adolescent girl, Sutara, loses consciousness under her assault and molestation. She is the only surviving member of her family to be nursed back to health by their Muslim neighbours. Through a haze of fear and physical pain she tries to piece together the nature of the outrage, since people are too embarrassed to answer her questions. Those who have been involved with riots and Partition will instantly catch on, that the trials of Sutara do not end with the assault on her body but are about to begin. (Devi 1999: xxx)

In *The River Churning*, Sutara is a Hindu girl who gets orphaned in the pre-partition Hindu-Muslim riots of 1946 in Noakhali in Dhaka, and finds shelter and love in the warmth and care of their Muslim neighbour's family. Tamijuddin Saheb, the Muslim neighbour who was also Sutara's father's friend, and his family realize soon enough that they will have to send Sutara to her "real" family – her brother and his in-laws, who reside in Calcutta. Tamij Saheb's wife wisely predicts how Sutara might not be accepted in her Hindu orthodox family for she had been sheltered in the Muslim household. This is because the rule of society demands that a Hindu girl cannot reside in a Muslim family, for that matter Hindus are known to get "tainted" and lose their religious purity if they touch or eat something given by Muslims. Sutara is treated like a daughter of their family, and her friend Sakina and Tamij Saheb's wife are also prepared with a solution for this extraordinary problem. She expresses her desire that Sutara be made her son's wife, her most loved daughter-in-law so that Sutara need not have to go back to her brothers. But Tamij Saheb is not so sure that is something Sutara's own family would approve of. Tamij Saheb makes arrangements to take Sutara to Calcutta himself and be safely transported to her brother's house. In a direct contrast to what history is wont to propagate–that the Muslims tortured and killed the Hindus and vice versa – Jyotirmoyee Devi shows how a Muslim neighbour shelters, protects, and showers love on a Hindu girl inspite of the fact that she has been violated. The fact of her being raped during the riots is only hinted at and not explicitly stated by the author. Sutara's own kin–her brother and his in-laws treat her like an untouchable because firstly she has been physically violated and thus been made impure; secondly she has spent months in the household of a Muslim.

> They reached Sanat's in-laws' home. [...] Boudi, carrying her child, Khoka, stoodnear the door and embraced her as Sutara touched her feet. Both began to weep. [...] She could overhear Boudi's mother's sharp tones, 'Are you out of your mind? Her clothes have been polluted by the touch of a Muslim household. Why did you have to go and take her in your arms?' [...] Sutara is offered a low stool, not a chair. [When Sutara comes to the kitchen to have tea with the other members of the family, she is treated as an untouchable–the "other."] To Bibha she [Bibha's mother] said, "See that she does not sit on the bed. She must be purified with Ganga water first. God only knows what kind of forbidden food she has eaten there.[3] (Devi 1999: 32-33)

Sutara is not allowed to sit and have food with the rest of the family. She is not even invited for social events where the whole family is supposed to

---

[3] Sanat is Sutara's elder brother who lives in his in-laws' house in Calcutta. *Boudi* is the term used to refer to one's sister-in-law in Bengali. Here *Boudi* is Sanat's wife Bibha and Sutara's sister-in-law.

attend. The author stresses the depiction of the marginalization and ill treatment that Sutara receives at her brother's house in contrast to the love and affection she receives at Tamij Saheb's house. The usual categories of the "other" that work on religious lines get transgressed and the fact that she is a woman and her body has been violated by members of the other religion now makes Sutara an "other" among her own family. The aspect of her "violation" and that Sutara is unable to accept Tamij Saheb's wife's proposal for marriage with her son because she knows that the men who raped her were Muslims comprise "silences" in the text. They seem to resound more loudly than the discrimination she faces at her brother's residence. Sutara is thus violated twice–by the men who rape her and violate her physically and by the members of her extended family who refuse to accept her back and constantly treat her as an untouchable, therefore violating her psychologically. The pertinent point here is that Sutara's "othering" happens because of her gender–she is raped by men on the other side of the border and she is sheltered by a Muslim family who nurse her back to health, but during the Partition all such girls with a similar fate would be wished dead rather than alive for having been "polluted." History then, through the Partition, gets etched on the female body of Sutara through her physical and psychological violations. In the process she gets "othered" because of her gender more than for being a Hindu.

Partition is supposed to have changed the relations between beloved neighbours and friends who lived like brothers (or sisters) earlier, irrespective of their religion. Indeed, Partition literature is replete with stories of such violence and rape against women of all ages.[4] Such literature also uses stereotypes of the women who were either abducted or raped or both and the various ways in which their dignity was violated firstly by the rioters and then by the rejection of their own families. "Thus riot victims like Sutara are hit twice by patriarchy: first by the male of one community who establishes his own 'identity' by exercising his territoriality over her body, second by her 'own' community which invokes compulsions of ritual purity to exclude her from the ritually pure domains of hearth and marriage, and drinking water." (Devi 1999: xxxii) Through her novel *The River Churning* Jyotirmoyee Devi helps to focus on this important aspect of patriarchal society.

---

[4] Saadat Hasan Manto's (1912-1955) oeuvre is full of such stories. The most poignant being "Khol Do" (Open It), mentioned later in this paper. Amrita Pritam (1919-2005) is another author who has written extensively on the Partition. Her Punjabi novel *Pinjar* (1950) deals with the partition abduction and the life after of a Hindu girl.

[I]n times of civil war or external war, it is the women who are singled out for particularly humiliating treatment– molestation, rape, abduction or forcible marriage–and it is they who have to suffer for the imposed ignominy. Women's bodies are considered by Indian men, Hindu, Muslim or Sikh, as the repository of men's honour. 'Power rape,' the raping of women to demonstrate and defeat rival men in patriarchal societies, is quite common in many parts of India, as indeed in many other areas of the world. The rape of a woman is akin to the rape of the community to which she belongs. (Ray and Basu 1999: 14)

Jyotirmoyee Devi's novel subverts the whole situation and shows how not Sutara's own family, but rather the "disrespected" Muslim neighbour is the one who takes care, nurses the physically and emotionally tortured back to health. And it is her own Hindu upper caste members of her family who then treat Sutara with disrespect and verbal abuse that she is supposed to deserve for being "polluted." "Jyotirmoyee presents the physical trauma of the young, adolescent girl. Her sexuality is the great "unspoken" in the novel, yet it remains the stake in the sinister game in which community teams up with nationhood, in order to keep alive the caste-class entente of the hegemonic group in independent India" (Devi 1999: xxvii). This is also a subversion of the process of "othering" – the Muslims who were supposed to be the "other" – for being the tormentor here becoming the protector. Sutara's brother or the other members of the family who were expected to provide care and protection to her are the ones who in reality become her tormentors – the "other." It is her horrific experiences of the riots that lead Sutara to reject not only Sakina's brother's proposal of marriage but also makes her decide to leave her own family and go away to a hostel to finish her education and go on to live alone and teach in a college in Delhi. Sutara, who has suffered because of the events of political history, finally emerges strong, managing to create a space for her own in Delhi. Sutara becomes a student of history and goes on to teach history in college. Ironically, one who studies and teaches history has lived history through her female body. Discussing the Partition, Bharati Ray in her article "Women and Partition" explicates the various demographic and geographic changes during the Partition that completely transformed the landscape of India in and around 1947 – the "streams of refugees entering India" and that the "most distressing aspect of Partition was the communal holocaust that accompanied and followed it" (Ray and Basu 1999: 3).

As mentioned earlier, literature is replete with stories of the torture and violation of women during the Partition. In recent times several films have been made around the same theme. In a Bengali film titled *Rajkahini*, released in 2015, there is a sequence which is a take-off from a short story by Saadat Hasan Manto. The scene depicts a girl who is so used to hearing her rapists order her to open her clothes that this is her first instant reaction when she hears the word "open," even when the doctor of the camp asks his junior to actually "open the window." The semi-conscious girl just responds to the word "open" and starts to open her clothes instantly. The extent of the torture the young girl and others like her might have suffered and the psychological effects of such a trauma are only depicted by such indirect yet forceful stories like Manto's "Khol Do."[5]

For a whole generation of Bengalis (and of course of the Punjabis in the North and North Western parts of India) as Bharati Ray observes,

> [T]he word Partition brings to mind the streams of refugees entering India, the squatting colonies and pavement shanties, the inflation, the rationing and black-marketing, the diseases, the nightmare that was Sealdah station, the political agitation and the extreme agony of the refugees – all such issues that were highlighted by official records in history and newspapers. The most disastrous and distressing aspect of the Partition was the communal holocaust that accompanied and followed it and the effects it had on several thousands of women and their lives. Partition riots have left indelible marks on the body and soul of an entire generation, but very few victims have kept records or diaries, perhaps because personal experiences were too harrowing to document. (Ray and Basu 1999: 3)

3. Bordering the "Other": *The Shadow Lines*

Amitav Ghosh's novel *The Shadow Lines* narrates the story of the Partition of 1947 and the riots in Calcutta and Dhaka of 1963-64 through the disintegration of families and relationships. Interestingly, Ghosh himself has commented that it was the 1984 riots in Delhi, which happened after the assassination of the then Prime Minister of India Indira Gandhi, that led him to write this novel. This was the novel that earned Amitav Ghosh the 1989 Sahitya Akademi Award, given by the Sahitya Akademi, India's National Academy of Letters. The categorization of the "other" in Ghosh's novel is of a more general kind, nonetheless influenced by stereotypes that characterize different groups. Contrary to Jyotirmoyee Devi's realistic representation of an incident during the Hindu-Muslim riots in Dhaka that brought out the worst in human nature and depicts the helplessness of women and the simple yet ruthless gendered ploy to "conquer" by physical torture of women, Ghosh's novel reflects on the interactions between personal and public histories. This documentation of history that the

---

[5] Saadat Hasan Manto (1912-1955) is famous for his stories in Urdu about the Partition. His oeuvre is a scathing criticism and a depiction of the harsh reality of the Partition. The story "*Khol Do*" has been translated as "The Return."

author deals with metaphorically and symbolically is explored through a mnemonic process of recovery. Being an anthropologist by training, Ghosh tends to interrogate the public chronicles of nations by highlighting and "recording the verifiable and graphic details of individual memories that do not necessarily tally with the received version of history"[6] (Mukherjee 1995: 255). While Ghosh's novel does not go into the detailed descriptions of the horrors of the riots on women, the women in this novel are at the centre of the narrative. It is through them that the effects of the Partition and other riots get mirrored in the plot of the novel.

At the focal point of interrogating the processes of history, questioning the justification and reasonableness of the Partition and the riots, is the character of the narrator's grandmother – "Tha'mma" as she is known in Bengali – whose experiences of the Partition enable the narrator to tread the path of negotiations with the past. Widowed at 32, the narrator's grandmother had moved to Calcutta to work in a school and provide for her family. Though she never speaks much about the horrors of the Partition, her quest for a house similar to the one she lived in at Dhaka is a reminder of the "silences" in her soul for the life she had been forced to leave behind. She had grown up in a large family with her sister and cousins who lived together in one house. But due to the "quarrel between the mothers" of the children of the two brothers, "things came to such a pass that they decided to divide the house with a wooden partition wall: there was no other alternative" (Ghosh 1995: 123). The partition of the 1/31 Jindabahar Lane house is a reflection of the Partition of India. The wall that was to be built within the family house is a metaphor for the Partition that divided the country which had lived for centuries like one family. The description of the way in which the wall was built in the grandmother's family home is a poignant depiction of the borders that were created to divide the country.

---

[6] The edition of Amitav Ghosh's *The Shadow Lines* which has been used in this paper, is an Educational Edition published by Oxford University Press in 1995. There are four important and extremely helpful essays that are included in this edition. This particular quote is from Meenakshi Mukherjee's essay that is included in this edition.

> But the building of the wall proved to be far from easy because the two brothers, insisting on their rights with a lawyer-like precision, demanded that the division be exact down to the minutest detail. When the wall was eventually built, they found that it had ploughed right through a couple of door-ways so that no one could get through them any more; it had also gone through a lavatory bisecting an old commode. The brothers even partitioned their father's old nameplate. It was divided down the middle by a thin white line, and their names were inscribed on the two halves – of necessity in letters so tiny that nobody could read them. (Ghosh 1995: 123)

This division of the Bose family home is an ironic representation of the division of the country along lines that seem equally absurd like the line that divided "an old commode" or even their "father's old nameplate." Such a division would leave both sides with some property but not the strength that comes from unity and a unified existence. The result of such a partition was the formation of "door-ways [...] that no one could get through any more" (Ghosh 1995: 123). This is an extremely potent suggestion of the ways in which the Partition of the country maimed the newly formed nations and shut the "doors" of development and progress for all.

On the one hand the physicality of the geographical boundaries is underscored by the presence of globes, an atlas, and maps at the centre of the narrator's imagination and the stories he hears and narrates. On the other hand, all such borders and boundaries are undermined by the memories of the narrator's grandmother and her rejection of all such imaginary faultlines that keep her away from her relatives. "For instance [...] she wanted to know whether she would be able to see the border between India and East Pakistan from the plane. [...] But surely there's something – trenches perhaps, or soldiers, or guns pointing at each other, or even just barren strips of land" (Ghosh 1995: 151). But when her son confirms that there is no marked demarcation of the border between India and Bangladesh, then known as East Pakistan, she is perplexed. "But if there aren't any trenches or anything, how are people to know? I mean, where's the difference then? [...] *What was it all for then–partition and all the killing and everything–if there isn't something in between?*" (Ghosh 1995: 151; emphasis added) The grandmother's search for the "differences" that would help to justify the Partition gets evoked when after the partition of their ancestral house both she and her sister make up stories about the "other" side of the house as the "upside-down house." (Ghosh 1995: 125). Because that "other" side was completely inaccessible and thus unknown to them after the partition of the house, they considered everything about that "other" as "wrong" – everything was done in a wrong sequence and hence "upside-down over there [...] their books go backwards and end at the beginning, they sleep under their beds and eat on the sheets, [...] [T]hey write with their umbrellas and go walking with pencils" (Ghosh 1995: 125-126). But with the historical event that divided their "homeland" – their country – the grandmother feels that "the strange thing was that as we grew older even I almost came to believe in our story" (Ghosh 1995: 126).

The Partition did not benefit any individual, community, or country. Much like the members of the Bose family who realized the absolute futility of the whole process of dividing their ancestral house which had housed their "big joint family [...] with everyone living and eating together" (Ghosh 1995: 121), the Partition has left Pakistan, Bangladesh, and India as neighbours who will live to fight all their lives. Tha'mma is shocked to learn how her ancestral house is now "occupied by Muslim refugees from India – mainly people who had gone across from Bihar and U.P." (Ghosh 1995: 134). Tha'mma felt the only "worthwhile thing left" (Ghosh 1995: 136) to do for her was to go to Dhaka and bring back her uncle safely to India with her. Ironically, while the refugees, complete strangers for her, tend to erase all memories of her childhood from her house in Dhaka, her uncle's harsh refusal to accept his own relatives but rely on these same strangers tends to muddle the nostalgia of the mnemonic process. The sisters' visit to their ancestral home was supposed to have been a trip down memory lane filled with fond memories. However, history and its events have altered not only the landscape of the Dhaka of Tha'mma's childhood, but also the relations between members of a family and also the meaning of family itself. The realization of the grandmother and her siblings is what most sensible members of the truncated countries would agree with. "They had all longed for the house to be divided when the quarrels were at their worst, but once it had actually happened and each family had moved into their own part of it, instead of the peace they had so much looked forward to, they found that a strange, eerie silence had descended on the house. It was never the same again after that; the life went out of it" (Ghosh 1995: 123). Much like the members of the Bose household there have been several thousands of people in these three partitioned countries who still long to go back and revisit their "homes." All categories of the "other" that were created during those years of the Partition – whether on the basis of religion or any other communal factor – do not hold true for any citizen of these countries any longer. There are advertisements, short films, long feature films, and documentaries that are constantly being made and literature that is still being written on the theme of loss and regret due to the events that preceded and followed the Partition.

Apart from the 1946-47 riots depicted in Jyotirmoyee Devi's novel, Bangladesh was torn by several such riots until its independence in 1971. The riots of 1964, which are described in Ghosh's novel to be "indelibly engraved" (Ghosh 1995: 264) in the memory of the characters, have "vanished without leaving a trace in the histories and bookshelves. They had dropped out of memory into a crater of a volcano of silence." (Mukherjee 1995: 214-215) The narrator finds he needs to dismantle the public chronicle of the nation because it threatens to erase the private stories. And it has been a successful postcolonial project to prove how private and individual stories are a repository of undocumented history that unfailingly gets left out of recorded history.

In this endeavour to record history through the private stories and memories of individuals, the house becomes an important metaphor. The house metaphor is relentlessly tied up with the Partition, as illustrated earlier. While most stories of the Partition narrate the victimization of women, Ghosh narrates the psychological effects of the Partition on the matriarch – the grandmother. The story of the Partition is depicted through the memories that the grandmother and May Price have of the violence of the riots and feelings of being torn apart. May Price is the daughter of the Price family who live in London. Her life gets intricately interwoven with the lives of the members of the narrator's family due to her presence with them during the riots in Dhaka, in which Tridib gets killed. The grandmother's expectation of the visibility of the border between India and East Pakistan grew out of her experience of the territorial division she had witnessed in her childhood. When her ancestral home, the Jindabahar Lane house in Dhaka, was partitioned, the brothers insisted on their rights with lawyer-like precision. That is also how seriously the borders were drawn when the Partition happened. The sense of "othering" that takes over during such historical events is evident in the grandmother recounting her childhood memories of seeing the other side of the house as the "upside-down house." In the Bengali film *Rajkahini* mentioned earlier, there is a scene where two childhood friends, who are now working for rival groups of governmental agencies, are employed to draw up the border for the two countries. So two children – one Hindu and the other Muslim – who grew up like brothers are now drawing the line that will divide them and their countries forever.

The Shadow Lines depicts the sense of othering that prevailed as an outcome of the Partition. Ironically, Ghosh's novel explores the divide that grew not only between people of different religious groups, namely the

Hindus and Muslims, but the rift that developed among members of the same family. The grandmother is one who believes in all sorts of categorizations and follows them in her life. So for her the bureaucrat brother-in-law would be a "Saheb," who she believes is a drunkard, and she regularly sniffs him to confirm whether he has been drinking. While the truth is that due to his position as a diplomat, he has to occasionally drink at official gatherings. Again, she hates both Tridib and Ila for reasons determined by different categories. Tha'mma is very conscious of time because she has been a witness to history and the way in which time has affected her and her family's life. This is why she hates Tridib who she regards as being guilty of "wasting time" because he, for the most part, wiles away his time in narrating stories. Ila according to Tha'mma, on the other hand, is a "greedy little slut" because she does not follow the dictates of Indian culture as to how she should dress and how she should behave. When the narrator explains that Ila lives in London because she loves her freedom, Tha'mma disagrees – "It's not freedom she wants [...]. She wants to be left alone to do what she pleases: that's all that any whore would want" (Ghosh 1995: 89). Tha'mma also believes in the gendered stereotypes of the masculine man. She would reprimand her grandson if he missed going out to play. For her all men must be strong and good at sports. However, it is the same grandmother who also questions the lines that divide India and Bangladesh and in turn therefore the "othering" that is an eventual consequence of it. The old lady, who accepts and swears by gender categories, fails to understand the logic and hence the stereotypes that keep people of a nation divided on religious and communal grounds.

The truth about how historical events tend to influence human relationship, in this case how the relations between members of the same family are soured because of the "drawing of lines," is explored throughout Ghosh's novel. The narrator's grandmother and her sister Mayadebi go to Dhaka, the land of their childhood, which they can hardly recognize any longer. They go there to bring their old uncle back with them to Calcutta because Dhaka is no longer safe for him. However, for the uncle, his family members and the children of his brother had long become the "other." The feeling of otherness for members of his family is evident in his conversation with them. When Tridib tries to intervene and explain to the hard-of-hearing old man: "We're your relatives; we've come to take you back. Do you remember your brother who lived in the other part of the house?" (Ghosh 1995: 214), the patriarch replies:

> I'm just waiting for them to come back, he said, so that I can drag them through every court in the land up to the Viceroy's Council. 'Possession is nine-tenths of the law' my cousin Brajen used to say, and he knew because he had taken his uncle's family through every court in the kingdom because they had taken away a handful of soil from the land on his side of the canal and added it to theirs. (Ghosh 1995: 214-215)

And Tridib "flinched from the festering malevolence in his bare, black gums" (Ghosh 1995: 214-215). All this rancour and loathing was for members of his family. Contrarily he had opened the doors of his house for members of the Muslim families who did not have shelter after the Partition. And now these Muslim families residing in his house are his family and the children of his brother who have come to take him to safety have become his enemies. That is the harsh reality of how the historical drawing of lines, metaphorically inside the ancestral house of Tha'mma, and geographically through the country, divided not only communities but families too. It is also an ironical statement about how the categories of the "other" shifted due to the situations created by historical circumstances.

Th'mma justifiably expected that the borders that divided India, the country she now calls home, and Bangladesh, the land she knew as home as a child, should be made explicit–that the lines should be clearly marked on the land by trenches or something. Her expectations seem befitting given that those same lines divided her family and led them to leave their home for good. Tha'mma had seen much violence and bloodshed during the Partition of 1947. She had also had to leave her ancestral home and the place where she grew up, only because of the partition of the country. All these tend to justify her constant awareness of the categories of "other" that she staunchly believes in and propagates. It is the border between the two countries of India and Bangladesh – how and to what effect it was drawn – that determines the process of othering in Ghosh's novel and simultaneously the lives of the women characters in the novel. Despite her insistence on the tidiness of separation we find Tha'mma disregarding the imperatives of the division when she goes through a great deal of planning and danger to rescue her uncle who however has developed a feeling of otherness for his own relatives – his nieces and their families. The categories of the "other" created by Partition, the Hindus for the Muslims and vice versa, are all fuzzy in Ghosh's novel. While the grandmother narrates how the "other side" of their house became the "upside-down house" after the ridiculous way in which the line was drawn in their house to divide the property, the upside-down house becomes a metaphor for the topsy-turvy world that most residents of the two countries found themselves being faced with. Nonetheless, when tension brewed anew during the 1964 riots, Tha'mma decides to go to Dhaka in Bangladesh, a land she had left with her family as a refugee, to bring her uncle back to safety. Her efforts are in vain because both Tridib and her uncle are killed in the riots. In the grandmother's disregard and rejection of divisions created by the state, "*The Shadow Lines* [...] questions the idea of nationhood that is consolidated through [...] wars or coercive state apparatus" (Mukherjee 1995: 265).

3. Conclusion

The two novels discussed in this paper – *The River Churning* and *The Shadow Lines* – both explore stereotypes and notions of the "other." However, the two novels approach the issue of the "other" from very different perspectives. Jyotirmoyee Devi's novel deals with an explication and realistic representation of the ways in which the stereotypes of religion and gender determined and instigated the violence and tortures that the women faced on both sides of the border during the Partition riots. Amitav Ghosh's novel, on the other hand, presents a complex web of all such stereotypes and relates it to the interrogation of the narratives and documentation of history. Both novels explore the categories of the "other" from differing positions. While the earlier novel is a feminist rendering of the events of the Partition, the latter is a postcolonial one. To conclude in the words of Urvashi Butalia: "it would seem that Partition was now over, done with, a thing of the past. Yet, all around us there was a different reality: partitions everywhere, communal tension, religious fundamentalism, continuing divisions on the basis of religion" (Butalia 1998: 7). While this rings so true for India, in the current state of world affairs, this holds equally true for the scenario around the globe and hence spurs my constant return to these texts of the Partition.

References

Bose, Brinda. 2003. *Amitav Ghosh: Critical Perspectives*. New Delhi: Pencraft International.
Butalia, Urvashi. 1998. *The Other Side of Silence: Voices from the Partition of India*. New Delhi: Penguin Books India.
Chatterjee, Partha. 1989. "The Nationalist Resolution of the Women's Question." In: Kumkum Sangari and Sudesh Vaid, ed. *Recasting Women*. New Delhi: Kali for Women, 233-253.
Devi, Jyotirmoyee. 1999 [1995]. *The River Churning: A Partition Novel*. Enakshi Chatterjee, trans. New Delhi: Kali for Women.

—. 1998. "*Chheleta.*" Translated from Bengali by Sukhender Ray as "The Little Beggar Boy." In: *The Impermanence of Lies*. Calcutta: Stree Samya.

Ghosh, Amitav. 1995 [1988]. *The Shadow Lines*. Educational Edition with four critical essays. New Delhi: Oxford University Press.

Kaul, Suvir. 1995. "Separation Anxiety: Growing Up Inter/National in *The Shadow Lines*." In: Educational Edition of *The Shadow Lines*. New Delhi: Oxford University Press, 268-286.

Menon, Ritu and Kamla Bhasin, ed. 2011 [1998]. *Borders and Boundaries: Women in India's Partition*. New Delhi: Kali for Women and Women Unlimited.

Menon, Ritu and Kamla Bhasin. "Recovery, Rupture, Resistance: Indian State and Abduction of Women during Partition." *EPW* 28.17, April 1993.

Mukherjee, Meenakshi. 1995. "Maps and Mirrors: Co-ordinates of Meaning in *The Shadow Lines*." In: Educational Edition of *The Shadow Lines*. New Delhi: Oxford University Press, 255-267.

Pandey, Gyanendra. 1994. "The Prose of Otherness." In: David Arnold and David Hardiman, ed. *Subaltern Studies VIII*. New Delhi: Oxford University Press, 188-221.

Ray, Bharati and Aparna Basu, eds. 2000 [1999]. *From Independence towards Freedom: Indian Women since 1947*. New Delhi: Oxford University Press.

Ray, Bharati. 2000 [1999]. "Women and Partition: Some Questions." In: Bharati Ray and Aparna Basu, ed. *From Independence towards Freedom: Indian Women since 1947*. New Delhi: Oxford University Press, 1-18.

Sangari, Kumkum and Sudesh Vaid, ed. 1989. *Recasting Women*. New Delhi: Kali for Women.

Sharma, B. K., ed. 2011. *The Fiction of Amitav Ghosh: A Postcolonial Perspective*. New Delhi: Sarup Books.

CHAPTER ELEVEN

"DWINDLING INTO SYMBOLS": THE POLITICS OF STEREOTYPING AFTER THE INDIAN PARTITION AND 9/11

CHRISTOPH SINGER

1. Introduction

Borders are scratched across the hearts of men
By strangers with a calm, judicial pen,
And when the borders bleed we watch with dread
The lines of ink across the map turn red.
—Marya Mannes,
Subverse: Rhymes for Our Times (George Braziller, 1959)

Marya Mannes short poem on the processes of devising and implementing borders recalls the Partition of British India into India and West- and East-Pakistan in 1947. The hand that held the "judicial pen" was that of the British Barrister Cyril Radcliffe. Yet, the Radcliffe-Line was the result of decades, if not centuries, of colonial identity-politics. With a million dead women, men and children and about 15 million refugees Partition drastically illustrated the bleeding borders as mentioned in Mannes's poem.

British divide and rule policies actively supported existing stereotypes that should help to break communities and neighbourhoods apart. This is not to say that British Imperialism created the differences between South Asia's manifold religions and ethnicities. However, as Ian Talbot argues, the census of 1881 set these stereotypes in stone:

> The colonial census which was introduced throughout India in 1881 formed the scientific basis for the stereotype of rigid religiously defined communities – a homogeneity which overlooked popular folk beliefs and practices and the influence of *Sufi* and *Sant* traditions which transgressed the boundaries of formal religion – and created the basis of religious

majorities and minorities. (Talbot 2009: 28)

Divide and rule policies led to an increased stratification of society as illustrated, e.g. by Bapsi Sidhwa in her novel *Cracking India*: "One day everybody is themselves – and the next day they are Hindu, Muslim, Sikh, Christian. People shrink, dwindling into symbols" (Sidhwa 1991: 101). This reduction to symbols and stereotypes can still be felt today.

Partition's bloody aftermath can still be felt. The relationship between Pakistan and India – both nuclear powers – shape the geo-politics not only of the Asian sub-continent but also of worldwide politics. It is no coincidence that the Obama Administration courts India's current government, while further alienating Pakistan. When the Obama Administration introduced the Af-Pak doctrine, it made very clear that Pak(istan) belonged closer to Af(ghanistan) than to India. After heavy criticism from the Pakistani government the Obama administration discontinued the use of this term.

The 1947 Partition of British India into Pakistan and India is – in a sense – still an ongoing event. The Pakistani historian Ayesha Jalal argues that Partition "was both the central historical event in twentieth-century South Asia and a historical process that has continued unfolding to this day." (Jalal 2013:148) Especially the violent conflict over Kashmir illustrates decades of rivalry. Consequently, Partition narratives invite an interesting look into the construction and deconstruction of stereotypes and their intersections with cultural memory. The daily and highly ritualized border closing ceremony at the Wagah border is a continued, symbolic expression of the nationalistic aspirations of both countries.

In the following, I will discuss two contemporary perspectives on the Partition of India. After a short history of Partition stereotypes, I will, firstly, analyse a song by the Hip-Hop Artist Heems from Queens, New York. Secondly, I will discuss an advertisement by Google India, entitled *Reunion* (Sharma 2013). Both examples share a deep investment in Partitionpolitics and use respective cultural memories for their specific purposes – that is criticism and consumerism. The following discussions are based on the premise that the Partition of India is used to make sense of current events, specifically 9/11, in Heems's case, and the proliferation of networks, in the case of Google's politics. Both cases are equally political, and both examples serve to illustrate the continuing (mis-)use and appropriation of an existing trauma for ulterior motives.

2. "Sawing through a Woman:" Introducing Partition Stereotypes

That the Partition of India was and is a traumatic event goes without saying (Singh, et.al. 2016). As a consequence, for decades, aspects of Partition were shrouded in silence, rendered unspeakable and taboo. Ali Sethi argues in an article on the Pakistani writer Saadat Hassan Manto that the "horrors of 1947 were well known, but few liked to talk about them. A collective trauma appeared to have silenced most people" (Sethi 2012) While there have been notable examples of Partition literature throughout the decades, specific themes have been addressed only relatively late: specifically, the terrifying experiences of women have found a voice in Urvashi Butalia's seminal study *The Other Side of Silence* (1998). And the *1947 Partition Archive* is building an extensive archive of histories from below. In form of short interviews this online archive counters the nationally shaped master narratives of Partition. Despite these important approaches, Suvir Kaul's impression from 2001 still rings true: "we remain, as a national culture, uncertain and anxious about the place of Parition in our recent history. In many ways, Partition remains the unspoken horror of our time" (Kaul 2001: 3).

These silenced histories have been increasingly addressed, and a focus on colonial politics indicates that the seed for Partition and its religious strife were planted long ago. As stated above, Hindu-Muslim relationships have been troubled for centuries. Kalid bin Sayeed argues sixteen years after Partition in his study *The Formative Phase*:

> There has never taken place a confluence of the two civilisations in India – the Hindu and the Muslim. They may have meandered towards each other here and there, but on the whole the two have flowed their separate courses – sometimes parallel and sometimes contrary to one another. (bin Sayeed 1968: 9)

At the start of the twentieth century, a time when Indian Independence first became truly conceivable, Hindus made up the majority in British India. Muslims made up the second largest religious group. The census of 1911, for example, lists 314 million Indians, of which 218 million were Hindus and 67 million Muslim (Gait 1913: 141). This imbalance led some Muslims to predict that the *Indian National Congress* Party (INC), which consisted mostly of Hindus, was likely to win in a nation-wide democratic election. This resulted in the troubling question as to how the Muslim minority would be treated under a Hindu majority. After all, the relationship between Hinduism and Islam had been problematic for centuries. Michael Mann explains:

> Dass es überhaupt zu einer solchen Eskalation zwischen zwei Religionsgruppen kommen konnte, hing mit der britischen Wahrnehmung der südasiatischen Gesellschaften zusammen. Die Kolonialbürokratie hatte sie in den vorausgegangenen Jahrzehnten auf Religionsgruppen reduziert. (Mann 2014)[1]

Winston Churchill "regarded the Hindu-Muslim feud as the bulwark of British rule in India" (Judd 2004: 155). The British Labour government under Clement Attlee, which succeeded Churchill's Conservative government, favoured a coalition between the INC and the Muslim League. But after years of divide and rule a coalition-government was no longer on the cards.

That the Partition would be dramatic and traumatic had been anticipated by political actors and commentators alike. It is for that very reason that Viceroy Louis Mountbatten decided to initiate India's independence one year earlier than planned. And commentators also anticipated the violent outcome as the cartoon below illustrates.

Fig. 1: "Sawing Through a Woman"

The cartoon "Sawing through a Woman" (Fig. 1, Kamra 2002: 77) introduces Partition's major political actors and their agendas. The cartoon, published on 9 July 1947 by a leading Anglo-Indian newspaper from Calcutta called *The Pioneer*, predicted the violence that would ensue five

---

[1] This escalation between two religious groups was only possible because of the British perspectives on these very groups. Colonial bureaucracy had reduced them to the very status of religious groups (my translation, CS).

weeks later once Independence was gained or granted. The five protagonists in the cartoon are either historical persons (Gandhi, Nehru, Jinnah) or personifications of either India (Mother India) or the British Raj (John Bull). The cartoon not only helps to illustrate the fundamental political divisions pre-Partition, it also shows how these actors were already reduced to stereotypes.

One of the most vocal Muslim supporters of Partition was Muhammad Ali Jinnah, leader of the *All Muslim League*. In the cartoon he holds the right handle of the two-man saw. His main political opponent, on the saw's left handle, was Jawaharlal Nehru. He was the leader of the *Indian National Congress Party* and was later to become India's first prime minister. While both agreed that Partition was inevitable, they differed with regard to where exactly the border between Pakistan and Hindustan should be. It was up to the newly elected Labour government to eventually take this fateful decision.

In the cartoon, the British rulers are represented by John Bull. Pictured as a stout middle-aged man wearing a tailcoat and light-coloured breeches, he anxiously, yet passively, observes the unfolding events. It would be incorrect, however, to assume that the British remained inactive. In postwar Britain, Britons were struggling with austerity, slowly abandoning their old Imperial pretensions and were being exposed to growing international pressure to leave India – this resulted in a departure that was rushed and ill-conceived.

In the cartoon, John Bull addresses the woman stuck in the magic box/coffin by saying: "I only 'ope nothing goes wrong Madam." The female assistant in this magic trick, facing being sawn in half, is Mother India. This motherly figure is a symbol of unity and warmth regardless of her children's religion, class and creed. In the end, no magic trick could save India from tearing itself apart after Partition. The cartoon clearly expresses a sense of impending doom and the inevitability that Mother India's blood will be soaked up by the sawdust.

The most iconic, yet most irrelevant character, Mohandas Gandhi, is consigned to the sidelines. Gandhi's peaceful civil disobedience campaign unified many Indians in their fight against the British Raj. In the cartoon he passively observes the two men performing their magic trick. His refusal to support Partition and his unwillingness to compromise left him mostly in the political limbo. This unfavourable presentation of Gandhi is taken up in contemporary representations as well. In Bapsi Sidhwa's *Cracking India* (1991), Gandhi is represented through the eyes of Lenny, the novel's young narrator. In Lenny's eyes, Gandhi is merely an irritating man focussed on dieting and enemas (Sidhwa 1991). And in Howard

Brenton's play *Drawing the Line*, Gandhi is presented as a man who enacts the negative sides of the iconic stereotype he has become: a religious leader, unwilling to compromise on anything, surrounded by young girls spending the days drinking goat's milk.

While the cartoon above shows what was happening at the time, it fails in explaining the reasons for the subsequent events. And while the violence, the bloodshed and the displacement was anticipated, the actual dimensions of the unfolding events came as a shock to many.

3. Heems: Partition as Post-9/11 Metaphor

The violence of Partition quickly invited historical comparison. After covering the atrocities of the Nazis, the American photographer Margaret Bourke-White was sent to Calcutta to report the communal riots in 1946. She stated that Calcutta "looked like Buchenwald" (quoted in von Tunzelmann 2007: 143). This simile intends to make sense of one event through another and recalls an argument by Jacques Derrida shortly after 9/11: "we do not recognize or even cognize that we do not yet know how to qualify, that we do not know what we are talking about" (quoted in Borradori 2003: 86). In the same vain as Bourke-White, Queens-based Hip-Hop artist Heems also uses a historic simile to express disorientation and anger in post-911 New York. He employs Partition as a foil to give those New Yorkers a voice who suffered under increased profiling, institutional racism and violence. The song's first bar sets the frame: "Product of Partition."

Heems – Himanshu Kumar Suri with full name – entered the music scene with his Hip-Hop group *Das Racist*. While *Das Racist* never made it into the mainstream, their idiosyncratic approach to politics did leave their mark. Their output was, on the one hand, absurd and demonstratively silly ("Pizza Hut"), on the other hand they gave voice to New Yorkers that were decidely transcultural in their outlook of the world. Heems, after all, was born to Indian parents and spenthis formative years in post-9/11 New York City where notions of multiculturalism were increasingly under scrutiny and under attack. In this light it is important to mention that Heems experienced the attacks on the World Trade Centre first hand. At the time he went to Stuyvesant High-School, located on Chambers Street in Downtown Manhattan. After the attack the school was used as a triage for the victims. In 2004, the Hip-Hoptrio *Beastie Boys* still stressed New York's unity: "Asian, Middle-Eastern and Latin / Black, White, New York you make it happen [...] Diversity unified" (Beastie Boys 2004). Heems's does the opposite. He illustrates how neighbourhoods in New York City disintegrate from the inside due to the proliferation of stereotypes and violent othering.

Heems's solo work, especially the album *Eat Pray Thug*, released in 2015, speaks for all of those who were victimized twice: firstly, as Americans who were attacked by foreign terrorists, secondly, as Americans that faced racial discrimination and attacks by their fellow citizens. This incomprehensible experience is central for *Eat Pray Thug*'s politics. The album's title is a nod to Two-Pac and Elizabeth Gilbert's novel *Eat, Pray, Love* (2007).

His song "Patriot Act" (2015) offers a biographical account of New York's changing neighbourhoods after 9/11. Heems expresses the shock of somebody that experienced the attack first hand – "Then the towers fell in front of my eyes / And I remember the principal said they wouldn't" – and was suddenly subjected to stereotyping, suspicion and scrutiny. The song's form mirrors the process of making sense of these experiences and transitions from a stream-of-consciousness into a coherent narrative. This process of attempting closure and cohesion recalls John Cleary's argument that "[t]rauma, in this sense, is as much about aphasia as it is about eloquence; it is as much a matter of repression, silence, sublimination and the difficulty of working a hurtful episode into coherent narrative as about speech or literary utterance" (Cleary 2002: 106). Heems's *Patriot Act* illustrates this attempt at narrative right from its jumbled beginnings to its coherent end:

> Product of partition
> Dripped in Prada for the stitching
> Proud of superstitions
> Got powder in the kitchen
> Powerful
> Superpowers be killing ya
> America, Britain, power for villains
> Powerful positions, power for the pigeons, powder for the chitlins
> Power for offshore drilling
> Pirates plunder, pillage, killing civilians
> Counting, currency's millions
> Politics make victim for income
> Parlor tricks, schism from system
> Babylon policing the people
> (Heems, "Patriot Act," 2015)

The song starts with a string of seemingly unconnected words: "Prada," "Superpowers," "Offshore-Drilling." For one, this impressionistic style forces the listener to create a sense of closure by her- or himself. At the same time this string of words forms two isotopes that stand in increasing contrast: the first semantic field alludes to the singer's Indian heritage, as he calls himself "a product of partition" and refers to "superstitions" and spices ("powder in the kitchen"). The second semantic field relates to global power politics. The "pigeons," the song implicitly implies, turn into the falcons that would shape post-9/11 politics, marked by foreign invasions ("superpowers be killing ya") and surveillance ("policing the people"). However, by indicating that the ensuing "schism [comes] from the system," the song implies that Heems is the product of two partitions: India's partition, as experienced by his ancestors, and the partition of the U.S.A. as implemented by the George W. Bush's *Patriot Act*.

For Heems the Patriot Act is also a means of divide and rule policies which create this "Schism for the System." This leads to mutual suspicion which in turn results in stereotyping: "And from then on they called us all Osama / This old Sikh man on the bus was Osama / I was Osama, we were Osama." This change of atmosphere is taken up by another song called "Flag Shopping." The song describes how everyone who looks suspicious is being labelled an "A-Rab," ("Flag Shopping") and signifiers of religious pride are being misread and used for insults. "They're staring at our turbans / They're calling them rags / They're calling them towels / They're calling them diapers" ("Flag Shopping"). The step from stereotyping to sectarian violence is a short one. The physical violence after Partition and 9/11 may not be comparable in scale, but in quality. Heems describes how "The neighbours threw rocks at the house [...] And our parents began to fear for our lives whenever we walked out the door / Because they read the news, and another cab driver was beaten to death" ("Flag Shopping").

The violence against U.S. American Sikhs continues to this day. In 2012 a shooter attacked a Sikh Temple in Oak Creek, Wisconsin, and killed six people (Yaccino 2012). In the fall of 2016 a Sikh man was attacked, beaten and his hair was shorn (Rocha 2016). It comes as no surprise that the U.S. Government prominently publicized photos of Simratpal Singh, a Sikh-American soldier for the U.S army. The most famous photo depicts Singh in uniform on Times Square in the heart of New York City. This photo is not only superficially reminiscent of Roland Barthes' seminal essay on myth. Barthes, however, wants to de-naturalize stereotypes and myths by analysing a soldier of colour in front of the French flag – as depicted on the cover of *Paris Match* (Barthes 1995). The image of Singh on Time Square wants to achieve the opposite. It is an attempt at naturalizing the Sikh soldier at what he is, an American and a serving member of the U.S.-army. That the photo does so by tapping into yet another stereotype – the Sikh man as a proud and valiant warrior – should not go unnoticed.

That these Americans with an Indian or Pakistani background are often anything but accepted becomes clear in the second part of Heems's "Patriot Act." As the song continues, the initial stream of consciousness is supplemented or contrasted, one should rather say, by a coherent narrative. It is this narrative at the end of "Patriot Act" that illustrates how, as a result of violence and constant attacks, people want or have to move. Neighbourhoods are breaking apart under institutional and peer-pressure

> And the FBI harassed one of my dad's friends so much
> he packed up his stuff and took his family and
> they moved back to Pakistan
> They would come at night and they would wake them up and make a mess,
> and the mess upset his wife
> Those giant metal birds in the sky brought my parents near
> and made things confusing
> And then crashed into those buildings and made things confusing
> But I guess it's okay because my dad wasn't deported
> And I still get to correct his English at dinner
> So he doesn't raise too much attention and get labeled a troublemaker.
> (Heems, "Patriot Act," 2015)

The song's final part, I would like to argue, reconnects the experience of post-9/11 America with the Partition of India. Ultimately, the comparison of Partition and 9/11 deconstructs the meaning of formerly positive signifiers of mobility, that is trains and airplanes. In Singh's novel *Train to Pakistan*, trains govern the temporalities of village life, they provide business, information and connection: "All this has made Mano Majra very conscious of trains" (Singh 1956: 4). Yet when the first trains with thousands of corpses arrive, this signifier of progress, prosperity and connectivity is turned inside out. A seed of doubt and mutual suspicion is planted in the villagers' minds, and the community quickly and violently starts falling apart.

The same is true for the airplanes in Heems's description: "Those giant metal birds in the sky brought my parents near and made things confusing / And then crashed into those buildings and made things confusing" ("Patriot Act"). The parallelism of these two lines indicates how deeply the suspicion of others has affected the perception and self-image of the suspected. By aligning two different planes so closely, the parallelism almost seems to invite a causal relation where none exists. It dissolves the boundary between the plane as a signifier of mobility and hope and as a signifier of death and terror.

Ultimately, the Patriot Act and stereotyping lead to a self-imposed form of cultural mimicry, a form of symbolic self-defence: "And so we rushed to buy flags for our doors / Bright American flags that read 'I am not Osama' / And we ironed our polo shirts and we combed our hair" ("Flag Shopping"). The American flag transforms into a mask. So do names: "They wanna shorter version / They wanna nickname / They wanna Toby us / Like we Kunta Kinte" ("Flag Shopping"). Heems's reference to the film *Roots* – yet another historical allegory – illustrates how diversity is being unwritten.

4. Google Reunion: Partition and Corporate Politics

Heems's way of referring to the Partition of India can be read as a rather straightforward way to make sense of another event. The following example is more complicated when it comes to the underlying politics. In 2013 *Google India* released a four-minute advertisement that quickly went viral. The advert, entitled "Reunion" tells the fictional story of two childhood friends who were separated after Partition: Baldevwas forced to move to New Delhi and Yusuf remained in Lahore. Many years later Baldev's tech-savvy Indian granddaughter organises – with the help of Google applications and Yusuf's Pakistani grandson – the reunion of both in Delhi. While the narrative is based on a historical event, the depicted characters are actors, the diary and photos are fake, and their stories are fictionalized. Google uses "histories from below" – as seen in the *1947Project* – to create an emotional tearjerker.

The advertisement was produced – for Google – by the Mumbai-based agency Ogilvy & Mather and was an instant Internet success. Over fifteen million views on YouTube to date and numerous articles on the video – ranging from *The Guardian* to *NPR* – are a testament to its public appeal. The reactions were mostly positive and uncritical, to say the least. There have been accusations that the producers stole the idea from a Pakistani short film called "Respect," but these accusations have mostly been disregarded. Google, it seems, managed to create a short narrative that is highly relatable to many Indians. One can only guess whether this success is achieved because or despite of on-going tensions between the two countries and the different ethnicities.

Google Reunion belongs to a specific subgenre that was perfected in Thailand. These advertisements present highly emotional narratives that usually resolve around characters that in the light of adversity – illness, poverty, social alienation – prove to be compassionate and selfless without a fault. The emotional impact of these advertisements is such that they spawned a popular competition on the internet: teary-eyed viewers watch these commercials, while trying not to be overtaken by emotions. Yet, hardly anyone can resist. This overtly emotional impact serves to advertise products that are anything but emotional: insurances, bank accounts, or in the case of Google, smartphone applications.

I would argue that this emotional approach to a highly complicated and traumatic subject neither heals nor consoles existing conflicts. Google's *Reunion* is an attempt at silencing existing stereotypes, differences and histories. This may – in and by itself – not be a bad thing. After all, by stressing the similarities rather than existing differences the advertisement strives for mending what have been ruptures. It provides a sense of order by pairing two nations, two cities, two gates and two generations: India and Pakistan, India Gate in New Delhi and Mochi Gate in Lahore, two elderly friends and their two young relatives.

And to be fair, the advertisement does not shy away from addressing the past. In a particularly emotional moment Baldev – sitting in a park close to Delhi's India Gate – relates to his granddaughter his flight from Lahore to Delhi, his lost friendship to Yusuf and his longing for home. The commercial at this point neither wants nor needs to allude to the sectarian violence that ripped apart communities and families. And here, I would argue, lies the catch. In a time where trigger warnings become increasingly central to violent narratives, the advertisement hits the unsuspecting viewer with an associative force that is unheard of in a commercial. Those who experienced Partition first hand are ambushed with a depiction of a history that is extremely personal and private at the same time. The following generations, however, are subjugated to a historical account that lacks any contextualization and background.

Surely it is not a commercial's responsibility to educate, but then again it seems highly unethical to encroach on cultural memory for the sole purpose of making money. Yet, this is where *Reunion* – technically speaking – is a class of its own. The greatest trick this commercial pulls is to make its viewers forget that it is just that: a commercial, a genre that is solely intended to sell goods. The advertisement may have a positive political message but raises some ethical questions concerning the intersections of corporations and cultural memory. To ask more provocatively: would Google – as a transnational, capitalistic agent – dare a similar approach in the context of the Holocaust, the genocide in Biafra, or the current humanitarian crisis in Syria?

Ultimately, the ad boils down a traumatic event to an emotional and fictionalised story. This focus on individual experiences is not the problem here since histories from below are an essential part of the larger narrative.

But Google milks every drop of emotion from a humanitarian crisis in order to endow their immaterial products with said emotion, in order to anthropomorphise algorithms.

Yet in the context of India, Google turns itself into a saviour of sorts. And the services provided by Google synthesize the two cultures that were formerly one. The borders between India and Pakistan are seemingly erased by Google. The separation ends thanks to a smartphone; the responsibility for this achievement is found on the citizens', not the politicians' side. It is only part of this inherent logic that the retelling of the painful past is staged in the public sphere and re-union is located in a private space. It is no coincidence that the advertisement was released exactly at that moment when the governments of India and Pakistan were discussing and negotiating changes in their visa regulations.

Apart from what is being depicted, the commercial is structured by what is omitted. And here lies the main difference to Heems's approach to Partition histories. Whereas Heems uses Partition to express the racism that he experiences as hidden by silences, Google's *Reunion* silences the very racism that partially made Partition possible in the first place. It is the absence of certain themes rather than the presence of others that I find telling as to how this ad works: the circumstances of Partition, the stereotyping, the sectarian violence and the mass migration are never touched upon. These omissions invite different interpretations.

The lack of women, e.g., I find especially striking, considering that Partition's violence specifically targeted women. On the one hand, it feels like the advertisement wants to gloss over a traumatic aspect of South Asia's history. On the other hand, this foregrounds the single female character. She, after all, initiates the reunion. In that sense she might be read as the Mother India – Bhārat Mātā. This motherly figure is a symbol of unity and warmth regardless of her children's class, caste and creed. According to Sukeshi Kamra, "'the people' are often embodied in the gendered form of Mother India [...]. As expected she is almost always silent and confined to the background, from where she anxiously watches the event being played out on the exclusively male stage." (Kamra 2002: 76) Mother India using Google to unify her children is quite an effective statement on the company's part.

This, however, only overshadows that it is Google that can provide the help or withhold it. Google, after all, is not a humanitarian institution. Google may proudly carry its motto: "Don't be evil." But evil is a relatively flexible concept and Google is relatively flexible when it comes to adapting to a foreign country's respective stance on "good" and "evil," legal and illegal. So while Google may not directly support censorship, it circumvents doing so by "launching country-specific versions [of YouTube] for Pakistan, Nepal, and Sri Lanka" (Cameron 2016).

Finally, what I listed as omissions are of course no omissions at all. They may not be mentioned explicitly, but they are still very present. As William Dalrymple argues, "[t]oday, both India and Pakistan remain crippled by the narratives built around memories of the crimes of Partition." (Dalrymple 2015) The Google advertisement taps deeply into cultural memory and in consequence triggers the connotations of the viewer without having to provide any historical context itself. When watching commercials an audience has, of course, to expect to be manipulated into consumption. But do they have to expect to be triggered into re-experiencing a painful past?

Where Heems employs the Partition narrative to shed light on the experience of minorities in a post-9/11 New York, the Google Ad silences these histories for a motif that is only superficially humanitarian. Admittedly, it does so in a very smart and effective way. Ultimately, advertisements and propaganda are brothers in kind. And similar to propaganda the Google advertisement confronts the critic with a seemingly innocent question: How can anyone be against such a positive portrayal of a reunion? How can you be so cold?

References

Barthes, Roland. 1995. "Myth Today". *A Barthes Reader*. Ed. Sontag, Susan. New York: Hill and Wang, 93-149.
Beastie Boys. 2004. "Ch-Check it Out." *To the 5 Boroughs*. Capitol Records.
Borradori, Giovanna. 2003. *Philosophy in a Time of Terror: Dialogues with Jürgen Habermans and Jacques Derrida*. Chicago: Chicago University Press.
Brenton, Howard. 2013. *Drawing the Line*. London: Nick Hern Books.
Cameron, Dell. 2016. "Google Appeases Pakistani Censors with Country-Specific Version of YouTube." *The Daily Dot* (12 January 2016). Web. 23 October 2017.
Cleary, John. 2002. *Literature, Partition and the Nation-State: Culture and Conflict in Ireland, Israel and Palestina*. Cambridge: Cambridge University Press.
1947 Partition Archive. Guneeta Singh Bhalla. Web. 23 October 2017.
Dalrymple, William. 2015. "The Great Divide: The Bloody Legacy of the Indian Partition." *New Yorker* (29 June 2015). Web. 23 October 2017.

Heems. 2015. "Patriot Act." *Eat-Pray-Thug*. Lyrics by Himanshu Suri. Megaforce. CD.
—. 2015. "Flag-Shopping." *Eat-Pray-Thug*. Lyrics by Himanshu Suri. Megaforce. CD.
Gait, E.A., et.al. 1913. *Census of India, 1911*. Vol. 1. Calcutta: Superintendent Government Printing. Archive.org. Web. 23 October 2017.
Gilbert, Elisabeth. 2007. *Eat, Pray, Love: One Woman's Search for Everything*. New York: Bloomsbury.
Jalal, Ayesha. 2013. *The Pity of Partition: Manto's Life, Times, and Work across the India-Pakistan Divide*. Princeton: Princeton University Press.
Judd, Denis. 2004. *The Lion and the Tiger: The Rise and Fall of the British Empire*. Oxford: Oxford University Press.
Kamra, Sukeshi. 2002. *Bearing Witness: Partition, Independence, End of the Raj*. Alberta: University of Calgary Press.
Kaul, Suvir. 2001. *The Partitions of Memory: The Afterlife of the Division of India*. Bloomington: Indiana University Press.
Mann, Michael. 2014. "Die Teilung Britisch-Indiens 1947: Blutiger Weg in die Unabhängigkeit." *Bundeszentrale für politische Bildung* (7 April 2014). Web. 23 October 2017.
Rocha, Veronica. 2016. "District Attorney Mulling Charges after Sikh Man was Beaten and His Hair Cut Off." *Los Angeles Times* (10 October 2016). Web. 23 October 2017.
Sayeed, Khalid bin. 1968. *Pakistan: The Formative Phase*. Oxford: Oxford University Press.
Sethi, Ali. 2012. "The Seer of Pakistan." *New Yorker* (30 August 2012). Web. 23 October 2017.
Sharma, Amit, dir. 2013. "Reunion – Google Advertisement." *YouTube*. Web. 23 October 2017.
Sidhwa, Bapsi. 1991. *Cracking India*. Minneapolis: Milkweed Productions.
Singh, Amritjit. 2016. *Revisiting India's Partition: New Essays on Memory, Culture, and Politics*. London: Lexington Books.
Singh, Kushwant. 1956. *Train to Pakistan*. New York: Grove Press.
Talbot, Ian. 2009. *The Partition of India*. Cambridge: Cambridge University Press.
Tunzelmann, Alex von. 2007. *Indian Summer: The Secret History of the End of an Empire*. London: Pocket Books.
Yaccino, Steven, Michael Schwirtz, and Marc Santora. 2012. "Gunman Kills 6 at Sikh Temple Near Milwaukee." *The New York Times* (5 August 2012). Web. 23 October 2017.

EUROPE

CHAPTER TWELVE

GOOD AND BAD NEIGHBOURS:
METAPHORS AND WORLD MAKING
IN U.S.-AMERICAN, GERMAN,
AND POLISH LITERATURES

PAULA WOJCIK

1. Ways of World Making: Cultural Stereotypes and the Conceptual Metaphor Theory

In his book *Ways of Worldmaking* (1978) Nelson Goodman argues that we never have direct access to *the* world but rather to different symbolic systems that he calls "world versions." Assuming that reality is not perceived objectively but is a cultural construct, Goodman, in accordance with the Conceptual Metaphor Theory, shares an interest in exploring the functionality of this cultural agreement. George Lakoff and Mark Johnson's seminal book *Metaphors We Live By* (1980) is prominent in the field of cognitive linguistics, but also opens new perspectives for other disciplines (literary studies, history and cultural studies, or sound studies) (Redling 2017).

The idea behind the Conceptual Metaphor Theory is that we can understand abstract entities or procedures only in terms of conceptual metaphors.

> The concepts that govern our thought are not just matters of the intellect. They also govern our everyday functioning, down to the most mundane details. Our concepts structure what we perceive, how we get around in the world, and how we relate to other people. (Lakoff and Johnson 2003: 3)

The conceptual metaphor that "argument is war" is a classic example:

Argument is war
Your claims are *indefensible.*
He *attacked every weak point* in my argument.
His criticisms were *right on target.*
I *demolished* his argument.
I've never *won* an argument with him.
You disagree? Okay, *shoot!*
If you use that *strategy*, he'll *wipe you out.*
He *shot down* all of my arguments. (Lakoff and Johnson 2003: 4)

Conceptual metaphors can be distinguished from linguistic ones. Linguistic terms such as "shooting," "strategy," "target," or "weak point" generate the conceptual metaphor "Argument is war" rather than, for instance, the metaphor "argument is a dance." A conceptual metaphor thus not only describes the way we *talk about* an argument but also affects the way in which we *behave in* an argument. According to Lakoff and Johnson it makes a significant difference in our everyday behavior whether we understand "love" as "war," or as a "journey."

What then is the connection between Conceptual Metaphor Theory (CMT) and cultural stereotyping? As I have argued elsewhere (Wojcik 2013) that a closer analysis of cultural stereotypes reveals their connection with basic conceptual metaphors. At the beginning of the twentieth century, for example, anti-Semitic metaphors such as "Jews are an illness," or "Jews are parasites," spread throughout Europe. These particular linguistic metaphors only "make sense" (subconsciously or otherwise) if we accept the underlying conceptual metaphor that a "nation is an organism." Only then do "illness" or "parasites" become a threat and need to be "cured." Andreas Musolff provided a detailed historical analysis of the use of such body- and illness- or parasites-metaphors in his book *Metaphor, Nation and the Holocaust: The Concept of the Body Politic* (2010). Tracing the long-standing conceptual continuity of thinking about nations as bodies, Musolff showed how thinking of Jews as a threat to the "body" in Nazi Germany goes back as far as the Middle Ages. A close look at a much more subtle concept by which whole groups of people are being externalized may be helpful here. Every time, for instance, we ask someone about their "roots" we imagine human beings as plants rooted in a specific place or soil. With this conceptual image in mind, it is then easy to consider cosmopolites or migrants as defective since they seemingly have no roots, or seem to have lost them. A third example is that of morality. We typically imagine moral and immoral behavior in terms of "black" and "white." This conceptual image is an example of what Lakoff and Johnson have called an "orientational metaphor" (Lakoff and Johnson

2013: 14): in this concept everything that is "up" – such as brightness or whiteness – is considered good or happy. Everything that is "down" – such as dirt or darkness – is metaphorically coded as something bad. "Heaven" and "hell" coincide with the orientational concept of "up is good" and "down is bad." Zoltán Kövecses explains that this concept even has had an impact on church architecture: "Christian churches are built in such a way that they point towards the sky, the assumed place, where God lives, which assembles the metaphor GOD IS UP" (Kövecses 2002: 58). These orientational concepts can be translated into colors on the screen as well: In western movies the good guy usually wears the white hat or/and has a white horse, while the bad guy's hat and horse are black as their supposed souls. To label individuals, or whole groups of people, as "black" and insinuating their immorality is a common strategy of xenophobic propaganda. The correlation between blackness=badness and a certain group of people (the Jews in the case of Nazi-Germany) becomes part of the habitual language use when it is spread by the media and is repeated often enough. Habitual language use can, however, become irritated in different ways. Literary language specializes in subverting habitual language and cognition by introducing new metaphors, disturbing common syntax or inventing new words, things, characters, etc. Thus, literature can violate the common way we use conceptual metaphors or disturb the seemingly evident connection between a particular metaphor and specific social groups.

Here, I will analyse three examples of how conceptual metaphors are used provokingly in U.S.-American, German, and Polish Literatures. I will start with the concept of "human beings as plants" in Jonathan Safran Foer's *Everything is Illuminated* (2002). The second example examines the concept of "morality as a chess game" in Michael Chabon's *The Yiddish Policemen's Union* (2006). Finally, this article will explore the conceptual metaphor that provides the title of this article – "nearby countries are neighbours" – in Sabrina Janesch's German novel *Katzenberge (Cathills,* 2010*)* and Olga Tokarczuk's Polish novel *Dom dzienny, dom nocny* (*House of Day, House of Night,* 1998).

2. The Concept of Rootlessness

Cultural practices of externalizing specific individuals or groups through stereotyping correspond with certain conceptual metaphors. A stereotype common in multiple languages and cultures is that of the "Rootless," "Wandering," or "Eternal" Jew (Ahasver). This stereotype goes back to the legend of the cobbler Joseph Cartaphilus, who refused Jesus a resting place on his way to Golgotha, and was condemned for this sin by having to travel the world eternally. It was not until the Middle Ages, however, that the story of Joseph the cobbler was turned into a story about a Jew, and therefore a story about Jewish sin against Christians. The legend of Ahasver quickly became popular and is known as the "Ewige Jude" in German, "Juif-Errant" in French, "Żyd wieczy tułacz" in Polish or "Juido Errante" in Spanish. In both literature and folklore Ahasver thus has a long tradition that over time transformed into the motif of the vampire and the revenant (Bodenheimer 2002, Körte 2000). The legendary character became a *pars pro toto* of the fate of the Jewish people. *The Eternal Jew* (1940) was also the subject of Fritz Hipper's Nazi-propaganda movie with the same title that fused the conceptual metaphor of "nation as organism" with the idea of rootlessness as a negative characteristic.

Rootlessness conveys an especially pejorative meaning if we think of human beings as plants, rooted in their natural environment, and embedded in their birthplace. In a cosmopolitan society, by contrast, territorial "rootlessness" would not necessarily be an insult, but could be understood as affirming the status quo instead. As long as we continue to think of our (intellectual) biographies as narratives with origins, and of organic entities as something with roots, however, the concept will stay valid. Some people claim to be "rooted" in a political or social movement, in philosophical ideas, music scenes, or social milieus. Although this particular idea negates that "territorial" means "rooted", it nevertheless confirms the conceptual metaphor that "human beings are plants," given that the frame is constant (Lakoff and Wehling 2008). Within the "roots" frame only the ground has shifted from the territorial to the immaterial.

Jonathan Safran Foer provides a playful view on the "roots"-metaphor in his award-winning novel *Everything Is Illuminated* (2002). The novel consists of two plots set in different historical times. In the novel's present, Jonathan Safran is undertaking a heritage tour to find his grandfather's place of birth, the former *shtetl* Trachimbrod in the Ukraine. The only trace he has, however, is a photograph of a woman called Augustine, who, so the family story goes, saved his grandfather's life. For this expedition Jonathan hires a translator, Alex, who speaks an obsolete form of English, and a driver – Alex' grandfather who is almost blind. It seems that the protagonist Jonathan Safran Foer takes the "roots"-metaphor almost literally when going on this expedition to locate his family's roots. The other narrative string of this novel is a chronicle of Trachimbrod, the place where the protagonist's ancestors were born. The village chronicle reaches back from the 1940s to the 18th century and the origins of the village, which will be extinguished by the Nazis more than 200 years later.

The history of the *shtetl* is closely connected to the history of the *shtetl's* river, the Brod: an accident marks the beginning of the *shtetl's* as well as the family's history: "It was March 18, 1791, when Trachim B's double axle wagon either did or did not pin him against the bottom of the Brod River" (Foer 2002: 8). Out of the wagon float different items like "a muddy hand mirror, the petals of some sunken forget-me-not, silt and cracked black pepper, a packet of seeds" and also a baby-girl born under the water to a dying woman who was stuck in Trachim B's double axle wagon, the protagonist's great-grand-grand-grand-grand-grand-mother who later will be named after the river. In this narrative scene the conceptualization of origin as somehow being rooted is subverted. This family tree's roots do not reach into the earth but arise out of the water. Thus, instead of presenting a stable, everlasting, and verifiable benchmark, in the form of a specific site and family tree, Foer's novel imagines origins as a dynamic, flowing, and historically blurred concept. And so the river becomes a symbol for historical change, and the impossibility to find the so-called "roots" of family trees. When the protagonist and his expedition finally arrive in his ancestor's birthplace, he does not discover any historical traces. Alex, the translator, describes it as follows:

> There was nothing. When I utter 'Nothing' I do not mean there was nothing except for two houses, and some wood on the ground, and pieces of glass, and children's toys, and photographs. When I utter that there was nothing, what I intend is that there was not any of these things, or any other things. 'How?' the hero asked. 'How?' I asked Augustine. ,How could anything have ever existed here? (Foer 2002: 184)

The protagonist, who is searching for his identity, realizes that the place's history was erased and that thus his roots cannot be found. Moreover, this insight is given an ironic undertone when the protagonist takes home some dirt from the non-existent *shtetl* to the U.S. in a zip-lock bag.

The novel evokes a special kind of metaphorical concept of being an individual with a biography and a family, and doubtlessly a beginning of a family's history. It is at once a very material and a very immaterial concept. If one had to define the counter-metaphor to "human beings are plants" in *Everything is Illuminated*, it would be "human beings are stories," which is not surprising in a novel. Foer's strategy, however, is to reveal the process of narrative creation itself, to emphasize the blending of fact and fiction, the ephemeral and the persistent. Thus the historical plot is revealed as a reconstruction that is a genuine creation because the story is put together from the artefacts the protagonist was able to find. Near the non-existing *shtetl* of Trachimbrod they meet a woman who seems to be the Augustine they are looking for, but is in fact an altogether different woman who has been collecting the material remains of all the former inhabitants. Her house has the character of a museum, or a warehouse, where she stores things in boxes of different sizes. She insists on giving a ring to Jonathan that belonged to the protagonist's ancestor Rivka. The following discussion is a meta-commentary on the role material culture plays in our cultural and individual remembering. The protagonist starts the discussion by stating that the ring

> 'would be a proof that she [Rivka] existed [...]. Evidence. Documentation. Testimony.' [...] 'But a ring is not needed for this. People can remember without the ring. And when those people forget, or die, then no one will know about the ring. [...] I think it was in case of this. In case someone should come searching one day. [...] The ring does not exist for you. You exist for the ring. The ring is not in case of you. You are in case of the ring.' (Foer 2002: 192)

Here we can see a clear shift from the ontological and passive notion of a concept of human beings as plants to an active and creative concept of a self-inventing and self-narrating individual. In the context of world making, Foer's novel disputes two possible worlds based on the two, mutually exclusive conceptual metaphors, but the dynamic and creative world version is clearly preferred.

3. The Concept of Morality as a Chess Game

Everything Is Illuminated is not the only contemporary novel that playfully deconstructs conceptual metaphors and stereotypes. Michael Chabon's counterfactual novel *The Yiddish Policemen's Union* (2006) introduces the metaphorical concept of "morality is a chess game" in the opening pages of the novel in which a disenchanted detective, Meyer Landsman, has to solve a chess player's murder case. In the victim's room the detective comes across a visual arrangement that will turn out to be the key to solving the crime:

> On the bedside table Lasker kept a chessboard. It looks like he had a game going on, a messy-looking middle game with Black's king under attack at the center of the board and White having the advantage of a couple of pieces. (Chabon 2006: 4)

At first, this might seem like the common setting and plot of a crime novel. However it is not, since this particular murder took place in Sitka, a fictional modern *shtetl* in Alaska, where three million European Jews had escaped from the Holocaust. Chabon's counterfactual narrative was inspired by a historical suggestion made in 1940 by Harold Ickes, Roosevelt's Interior Minister: to open Alaska to Jewish refugees from Europe. This suggestion becomes reality in Chabon's novel, where the survivors and their children, ruled by the Verbovers, a sect of Ultra-orthodox Jews, live in constant conflict both with the natives and with each other. The *New York Post* criticized Chabon's novel in a review entitled "Novelist's Ugly View of Jews,"

> 'The Yiddish Policemen's Union' [for] depict[ing] Jews as constantly in conflict with one another, and its villains are a ruthless, ultra-Orthodox sect that resembles the Lubavitchers [...] Chabon, who is Jewish, depicts some of his Jewish characters as willing to do anything, including massacring other Jews, in the cause of Zionism. (Johnson et. al 2007)

Chess is a leitmotif in *The Yiddish Policemen's Union*. The game, which was brought over from Europe by the first generation of refugees, is the last remaining link to Jewish-European history. In the novel, chess functions as a reference to fin-de-siècle Vienna and its café culture. In those days, chess was seen as a "Jewish game," and a Jewish chess player described as a *luftmensh*. Originally, this term was used to refer to Eastern Jews who were so poor that they seemed to live on nothing but air. But soon it became an insult for the chess-playing and non-working Jews hanging around in the cafés (Ehn and Struhal 1998; Berg 2005 and 2008: 31 f.). In the *The Yiddish Policemen's Union* almost all of the important characters have a connection to chess. Meyer Landsman's father is a passionate chess player, the detective himself seems to cultivate a love-hate relationship to the game, and the murdered Mendel Shpilman went by the pseudonym of Emmanuel Lasker, a German Jewish world chess champion who fled to the USA via the Netherlands, London, and Russia in 1933. Moreover, the name of the victim, who is the son of the Rabbi Heskel Shpilman, is reminiscent of a well-known Viennese chess player named Rudolf Spielmann. The genre of uchrony is considered by literary theorist to have a structural analogy with the chess game, because the plot of the alternate history depends on the "move" which was made before at the so-called "uchronic crossroad." At this point – in the case of Chabon's novel it was Ickes' suggestion – reality and story go at least two different ways. Chess offers a rich variety of associations in this novel that prove very suitable to approach the moral issue in terms of the dichotomy of colour-mapping.

Since *Yiddish Policemen's Union* is a crime novel, the moral frame of the novel revolves around the question of who is the bad guy. According to the conceptual metaphor of "morality is a chess game," black equals evil and white equals good. This is consistent with the orientational metaphor of up=good that was introduced above.

In fact, the members of the Verbover sect are called "the black hats" and the short description of the rabbi's origins is full of images that suggest darkness:

> Then the entire sect was *burned down* in the fires of Destruction, down to a hard, dense core of something *blacker* than any hat. What was left of the ninth Verbover rebbe emerged from those fires with eleven disciples and, among his family, only the sixth of his eight daughters. He [the rabbi] rose into the air like a *charred* scrap of paper and blew to his narrow strip between the Baranof Mountains and the end of the world. (Chabon 2006: 99, my markings)

This ironic quotation of the phoenix-motif plays on the opposition of bright/white versus dark/black. The rabbi character appears as a godfather who controls all criminal activities in Sitka. But what the authors of the NYP's review obviously did not realize is that the real villain who pulls the strings is someone else, and that the rabbi – the black king in the chess game from the beginning – is the character under attack. The murder of the rabbi's son is part of a conspiracy, planned in Washington, and carried out by a man named Cashdollar. Here is the scene in which the latter arrives in Sitka:

> They duck and pull back, and in their parting, a tall, slim, *fair-haired* man stands revealed. The new arrival, fresh from the hold of his *bright white* floatplane. The hair is really something, like a *flare of sunlight* on a sheet of steel. (Chabon 2006: 268, italics mine)

Though this character is constantly coded as white, bright, and clean, the colour-mapping in this case is not connoted with "goodness," "happiness" or "warmth" but rather with "coldness," "unscrupulousness," and "cruelty." Thus, when Cashdollar states that "the last thing he wants is any hint of a mess" (Chabon 2006: 268) the connotation of cleanness is not at all positive.

Throughout the novel the linguistic metaphors of darkness and brightness are connected to moral issues but not in a stereotypical way. While Foer introduces a counter metaphor to show how the arbitrariness of cultural concepts are based on metaphors, Chabon, on the other hand, simply inserts a new connotation within the concept of "morality is a chess game." When black appears together with white – as it does in a chess game – white is connoted positively. The connotation of "coldness" does not appear paired with black, but maybe with green or yellow, when we juxtapose a snowy landscape with a verdant lawn, or a sunny day. The association with "emotionlessness" arises when we compare a hospital's cleanness and its white walls with the cosy mess of a home. The unexpected moment in *The Yiddish Policemen's Union* is the unusual attribution within the conceptual metaphor "morality is a chess game." It emphasizes the cultural practice of associating colours with emotions or attributes and drawing conclusions from reality for such colour-related metaphors. Instead, in Chabon's alternative world version morality has many more complex shades than just black or white.

4. The Concept of Neighbourhood in the German-Polish Relations

The idea of neighbourhood provides a third metaphorical concept when we imagine "nearby neighbours". The abstract term "nation" is imagined as an entity with a concrete territory and a border, which marks the end of one's own homeland and the beginning of another. Unlike the metaphor "nearby nations are business partners" the neighbourhood metaphor emphasizes the everyday and emotionalism: neighbours share an area of action, they can help each other but they can also get into conflict with each other. The neighbourhood is a paradoxical situation of both being a community and being separate; of closeness and of distance. In contrast to the conceptual metaphor "nearby nations are friends" the neighbourhood-concept implies chance: we can choose our friends but we cannot choose our neighbours. Thus, nations as neighbours become the subject of prejudices and stereotypes because they have a status of foreigners. The difference between stereotyping Jews and stereotyping nations lies in this ontological status: Jews are construed as "others" within the same territory while the foreigner is coming from a territorially marked nation (Holz 2000).

One can also easily recognize that the idea of building "fences" between nations is inspired by the metaphor "nearby nations are neighbours" and not by "nearby nations are business partners" or "nearby nations are friends." It is this territorial aspect that stresses the neighbourhood-concept, and this is also the focus of two contemporary novels on German-Polish relations. I would like to explore the way, in which Sabrina Janesch's *Katzenberge (Cathills)* and Olga Tokarczuk's *Dom dzienny, dom nocny* (*House of Day, House of Night)* reveal a problem inherent in the metaphor "nearby nations are neighbors": what happens when borders between "estates" shift, i.e. when the "property" of one neighbour becomes that of another? This was the situation in the mid-1940s when the Poles were resettled from today's

Ukraine, or Belarus, to former German areas, and the Germans were displaced westwards. In the last few years many books have been published, both in German and in Polish literature that address the topic of flight and expulsion (see for instance Eigler 2014; Berger 2015; Niven 2014). Eigler and Berger both stress the nineteenth-century concept of *Heimat* and its geopolitical connotation within the literary discourse on flight and expulsion. *Heimat* is closely linked to the concept of "nearby nations are neighbours" insofar as within this concept, it marks the difference between the alter ego and the ego, one's own and the neighbour's territory, no matter whether it is an estate, a village, a city, or a nation. Of course, the metaphor can also emphasize relations between social spaces within one neighbourhood in the same way *Heimat* can be understood as a social community. Janesch's and Tokarczuk's novels work with this shift from territorial to social space within the neighbourhood-concept.

In *Katzenberge*, Sabrina Janesch demonstrates how "neighbourhood" is determined not only by a shared space but also by a shared history. Actually, the novel makes clear that the territorial notion of the metaphor remains meaningless if it is not filled with a social dimension. In *Katzenberge* the German-Polish first-person narrator, Nele Leibert, travels to Silesia after learning about her grandfather's death. From her Polish family, she hears about her grandfather's secret past in the former Galicia before he relocates to a village near Wrocław/Breslau, and she decides to recover the concealed pieces of his life. Her eastward journey parallels that of her grandfather's westward journey some fifty years earlier. Thus, the novel's plot unfolds in two regions in which the neighbourhood's borders shifted after the Second World War: The eastern part of Poland became Ukrainian, and the eastern part of Germany became Polish. The new borders do not, however, simply divide the space anew. On the contrary, the post-war spatial shift creates new correlations: The neighbours share a history that continues to have an effect on the present. This history is symbolized in a black beast that haunts the protagonist's family since the grandfather settled down in a house that had just been vacated by a German family. Above the front door there is a swastika, inside the house he stumbles upon their furniture, dishes, and old newspapers. Finally, he finds the owner of the house, who hung himself in the attic. This past is still alive in the family's history and the black beast can be interpreted as a post memorial trauma (Hirsch 2012). The estates of the nations as neighbours do not exist in a territorial way but via a still present history as vividly remembered places, or *lieux de mémoire* (Nora 1997-98). Janesch's narrative is "beyond fixation on loss," as Friederike Eigler sums up the historical development in literature on flight and repulsion (Eigler 2014:

1977), or if we wanted to be more precise we could say that it is "beyond fixation on loss of territory."

This idea of a diachronic neighbourhood is also the subject of Olga Tokarczuks *Dom dzienny, dom nocny*. The setting of this Polish writer's award-winning book is once again the former German area of Silesia. In her description of everyday life in a neighbourhood close to the Czech Republic, Tokarczuk introduces dreams, fantasies, legends of saints, the village history as a German area, and its present reality as a neighbourhood in post-communist Poland and mixes them together into a panorama of transnational narratives. The key scene in the book is when the German Peter Dieter visits the village where he spent his childhood. Too old to partake in the walking-tour, he suffers a heart attack on the Polish-Czech border, with one leg in Poland, the other in the Czech Republic. When the Czech border patrol finds him, they want to avoid the paperwork, and carry him to the Polish side. When the Polish border patrol discovers him there, they too want to avoid the paperwork and therefore carry him to the Czech side. And so: "Peter Dieter remembers his death before his soul vanishes as a mechanical movement from one side to the other, as a balancing act on edge, as remaining on a bridge."[1]

The German past, and the Czech and Polish present coexist in this image of being stuck on a threshold between past and present, Czech Republic and Poland, life and death. The symbolic threshold is the key to understanding how the novel plays with the territorial connotation of the concept of "nearby nations are neighbours." According to Arnold van Gennep, a threshold is a "spatial and symbolic area of transition" that can be found in all ceremonies "which accompany the passage from one social and magico-religious position to another" (Gennep 1960: 18). Gennep's phenomeno-logical approach to the threshold is a teleological one. The key concept of this passage is the transfer of an individual from one defined situation to another. In Tokarczuk's novel, by contrast, the threshold has gained an autonomous status. The characters are suspended between dream or fantasy and reality, like Krystyna who continues to hear the voice of a man called Amos in her head. She tries to find him and finally succeeds in tracking down a man called A. Mos who obviously belongs to the voice. But this encounter does not imply that the fantastic is transferred to reality: after having spent a meaningless night with Andrzej Mos Krystyna returns to her home village where she still hears Amos's voice. There is also the legend of the holy Troska (worriedness) written

---

[1] "Tak też Peter Dieter zapamiętał swoją śmierć, zanim jego dusza odeszła na zawsze – jako mechaniczny ruch, w jedną i w drugą stronę, jako balansowanie na krawędzi, stanie na moście. (Tokarczuk 1998: 95-96)

down by a neophyte called Joseph. While he is writing the history of Troska, who transforms into a transgender character resembling Jesus Christ, he starts transgressing gender borders himself. While for both characters being on this gender-threshold is quite pleasant, their social surrounding disapproves of this condition. Troska is in the end killed by her husband. In the context of the territorially motivated idea of nations as neighbours, the novel's focus shifts from the defined space and its borders to the border crossings. Thus, it is not important where someone is coming from, or where he or she is going to, only the process of transition is meaningful. In an in-between space the ground for stereotyping and the concepts of "self" and "other" become logically impossible.

Katzenberge and *Dom dzienny, dom nocny* reflect on the metaphor "nearby nations are neighbours" by demonstrating that nations are not stable entities with defined borders, but are constantly changing because of historical "accidents" like wars, occupations or unions. These novels also emphasize a paradoxical situation: while neighbouring nations depend on each other, creating one historical community and one area of action in a post-national Europe, they are still separated by national politics, national cultures or national identities. Thus, playing with Conceptual Metaphors in novels becomes a way of making a world in which transit areas, thresholds and transgressions are the dynamic forces that constitute the present neighbourhood of nations.

5. Conclusion

Lakoff and Johnsons stated that conceptual metaphors affect, or even manipulate, the way we think; partly because they are based on everyday language upon which we do not reflect. The purpose of this article was first to demonstrate to what extent metaphorical concepts are related to cultural stereotypes: either because they have normative implications (to be rooted somewhere is better that not to be rooted as in "human beings are plants"), or because they establish binary concepts (via the conventional relations between quality and colour as in "morality is a chess game"), or because they provide the categorical ground for stereotyping (establishing the self' and the 'other' via "nearby nations are neighbors"). The purpose was second to show the different strategies that literal texts introduce to alter the habitual application of metaphorical concepts either by introducing metaphorically a compelling concept (dynamic against a static meaning of being an individual in *Everything Is Illuminated*), by inverting the habitual associations within the conceptual metaphor (white as good and black as evil in *The Yiddish Policemen's*

Union), by evoking a different connotation of the same metaphor (interdependency against separation within the concept of neighbourhood in *Katzenberge*), or by shifting the focus from one aspect of a concept to another (from borders to transitions in *Dom dzienny, dom nocny*).

References

Berg, Nicolas. 2008. *Luftmenschen. Zur Geschichte einer Metapher.* Göttingen: Vandenhoeck & Ruprecht.
—. 2005. "Bilder von 'Luftmenschen' – Über Metapher und Kollektivkonstruktion." In: D. Diner, ed. *Synchrone Welten. Zeiträume jüdischer Geschichte.* Göttingen: Vandenhoeck & Ruprecht, 199-224.
Berger, Karina. 2015. *Heimat, Loss and Identity: Flight and Expulsion in German Literature from the 1950s to the Present.* Oxford: Peter Lang.
Bodenheimer, Alfred. 2002. *Wandernde Schatten. Ahasver, Moses und die Authentizität der jüdischen Moderne.* Göttingen: Wallstein.
Chabon, Michael. 2006. *The Yiddish Policemen's Union.* New York, London: Harper Collins.
Ehn, Michael and Ernst Stouhal 1998. *Luftmenschen. Die Schachspieler von Wien. Materialien und Topographien zu einer städtischen Randfigur 1700-1938.* Wien: Sonderzahl.
Eigler, Friederike. 2014. *Heimat, Space, Narrative: Toward a Transnational Approach to Flight and Expulsion.* Rochester, New York: Camden House.
Foer, Jonathan Safran. 2003. *Everything is Illuminated.* New York/London: Penguin Books.
Gennep, Arnold van. 1960. *The Rites of Passage.* Translated by Monika B. Vizedom and Gabrielle L. Caffee. London: Routledge.
Goodman, Nelson. 1978. *Ways of Worldmaking.* Indianapolis, Ind.: Hackett 2013.
Hirsch, Marianne. 2012. *The Generation of Postmemory. Writing and Visual Culture after the Holocaust.* New York: Columbia UP.
Holz, Klaus. 2000. "Die Figur des Dritten in der nationalen Ordnung der Welt." *Soziale Systeme* 1, 269-290.
Janesch, Sabrina. 2014: *Katzenberge.* Berlin: Aufbau.
Johnson, Richard, Paula Froelich, Bill Hoffmann, and Corynne Steindler. 2007. "Novelist's Ugly View of Jews." In: *New York Post.* Web. 20 June 2017.
Körte, Mona. 2000. *Die Uneinholbarkeit des Verfolgten. Der ewige Jude in der literarischen Phantastik.* Frankfurt/Main: Campus.

Kövecses, Zoltàn. 2002. *Metaphor. A Practical Introduction.* Oxford: Oxford University Press.

Lakoff, George and Elisabeth Wehling. 2008: *Auf leisen Sohlen ins Gehirn.* Heidelberg: Carl Auer. Imprint in English: *Your Brain's Politics: How the Science of Mind Explains the Political Divide.* Imprint Academic 2016.

Lakoff, George and Mark Johnson. 2003. *Metaphors We Live By.* Chicago, London: University of Chicago Press.

Musolff, Andreas. 2012. *Metaphor, Nation, and the Holocaust. The Concept of the Body Politic.* New York: Routledge.

Niven, Bill. 2014. *Representations of Flight and Expulsion in East German Prose Works.* Rochester, New York: Camden House.

Nora, Pierre. 1997-98: *Les lieux de mémoire. Volume 1-3.* Paris: Gallimard.

Redling, Erik. 2017. *Translating Jazz into Poetry. From Mimesis to Metaphor.* Berlin: de Gruyter.

Tokarczuk, Olga. 1998. *Dom dzienny, dom nocny.* Wałbrzych: Ruta.

—. 2003. *House of Day, House of Night.* Translated from Polish by Antonia Lloyd-Jones. Evanston, Ill: Northwestern University Press.

Wojcik, Paula. 2013. *Das Stereotyp als Metapher. Zur Demontage des Antisemitismus in der Gegenwartsliteratur.* Transcript: Bielefeld.

CHAPTER THIRTEEN

BETWEEN (SEMI-) ORIENTALISATION
AND (IMAGINATIVE) COLONISATION:
ON OTHERING THE ALLY IN POLISH
WARTIME RECOLLECTIONS

JOANNA WITKOWSKA

1. Introduction

The British declaration of war on Germany on 3rd September 1939 marked the beginning of the country's six-year wartime alliance with Poland. After the period of the "Phoney War" and the surrender of France (June 1940) many Poles arrived in Britain to fight for their country's freedom under British command. What was primarily aimed at military collaboration would also prove to be an effective channel of cultural exploration and, as such, a testing ground for cultural notions of the other.

The main thesis of the article is that, as presented in the recollections written by Poles, British perceptions of and attitudes towards the Polish other during the war bore the traces of a colonial discourse. The primary materials used for the analysis will be selected published wartime recollections of Polish soldiers, sailors and pilots. The theoretical framework is based on conceptual representations of Europe as elaborated on in Larry Wolff's *Inventing Eastern Europe. The Map of Civilisation on the Mind of Enlightenment*. Furthermore, references to Edward Said's *Orientalism* are also made.

2. A Brief Historical Background of Polish-British Relations

The first wartime encounters between the Poles and the British had already taken place on 1st September 1939, when the war began in Poland. It was then that Polish Navy destroyers reached the shore area of Leith, Scotland, in an operation to join the Royal Navy. Greater numbers of Polish servicemen started to arrive in the British Isles after the fall of France in June 1940. By the beginning of the Battle of Britain (July 1940), there were 4,700 Polish airmen there. Scotland, which expected a secondary invasion, initially welcomed 15,000 soldiers from Poland, who reinforced the modest British defence forces (Maresch 2006: 18-19, Siemaszko 2010: 35). Consequently, in the summer of 1940, Britain became home to over 30,000 Polish servicemen, the largest foreign national army (Olson and Cloud 2004: 95).

Allied operations and daily coexistence with the civilian population brought the two nations together, though bridging the cultural gap was not always possible, the process additionally hampered by the states' historical distance. Until World War II, there had been no significant encounters between the average John Smith and Jan Kowalski. They did not seem to have much in common either. Although geographically they were not that far apart, little connected the two countries politically, economically and culturally. They had different interests, development trajectories, strategic partners and foes. France, which Poland had traditionally allied with, was a historical enemy of the British. In the American War of Independence Poles, together with the French, supported the revolutionaries against the British crown. Although at times Russia posed a threat to British interests and in the time of the partitions[1] Poland hoped to play on this to gain independence from her dangerous neighbour, London was ready to criticise Russia at most but not risk the anger of such a powerful country and take military action against it. The national tragedies of Poland, which resulted in the loss of independence in the 19th century, coincided with Britain's greatest economic and imperial achievements. Even if some understanding and compassion for the Polish cause came from the British Romantic poets and public opinion, with the name of Tadeusz Kościuszko[2] on the lips of quite a few, this interest did not translate into a substantial relationship that would change the peripheral status of Poland in British

---

[1] Poland was partitioned between Russia, Prussia and Austria from 1772 to 1918.
[2] Tadeusz Kościuszko (1746-1817) – a Polish general and statesman. He was the leader of a national insurrection in Poland and a prominent participant in the American Revolutionary War. English Romantic poets were inspired by Kościuszko as an epitome of the struggle for freedom and referred to him in their poems. The poets included, among others, Samuel T. Coleridge (*Sonnet VII*), Thomas Campbell (Polish theme in Part I of the poem *The Pleasures of Hope*), Leigh Hunt (sonnet *To Kosciusko*) and George G. Byron (*Don Juan, The Age of Bronze*) (Gibińska 1992: 21-42).

politics. As Polish historian and politician Bronisław Geremek (2006: n.p) said, "up until World War I, the connections between the Poles and the nations of the United Kingdom were weak, at least in the sense that their mutual relations were devoid of moments of great emotion." The post World War I period did not bring about changes to this status quo. The British had no motivation to foster relationships or learn about the Slavs since their interests lay elsewhere. As Edmund Burke admitted: "Concerning our affairs, as a matter of fact, Poland can be located on the Moon" (Jasiakiewicz 2010: 91).[3]

3. Exoticisation of the Polish Ally

The Polish veterans confirmed that they were "terra incognita" for their ally, who was even unfamiliar with the geographic location of Poland. Complaints of exoticisation filled the pages of their recollections. Sometimes in an informative way, and on other occasions with bitterness and despondency, Poles reported being treated like an "exotic curiosity" [egzotyczna ciekawostka], as people coming from "a country infinitely more exotic than India or Canada" (Herbst 2013: 104, Pruszyński [1941] 2010: 43). The insufficient knowledge of Poland created a void which the British tried to fill by gaining first-hand experience of the ally. A peculiar "tourist trend" which verged on cultural voyeurism developed. Polish military camps became an attraction, with Britons from all over the country coming to see their allies (Leitgeber 1972: 63). Unwanted attention, also expressed in public places, occasionally provoked a playful response. A sailor from the veteran Eryk Sopoćko's recollections decided to teach the Britons, curiously staring at him in a restaurant, a lesson:

> I took a clean plate and put a peel of orange on it which I then cut into thin strips. Everybody stopped eating and waited, watching what I would do next. I asked the waitress to give me the tray with vinegar, salt and pepper back. [...] Having cut enough of the peel I poured vinegar on it, peppered and salted it. [...] As soon as I felt satisfied with the fact that the company [of staring people] had already been excited enough predicting the next course of events, I asked for the bill and left. [...] [A]fter this incident my next visits did not attract even the slightest attention. (Sopoćko 2010: 44-45)

Interestingly, these close encounters indicated that the information void about the Slavs was tinted with unfavourable myths. In accordance with

---

[3] Quoted in Jasiakiewicz (2010: 91), after the Polish translation by J. Feldman, *U podstaw stosunków polsko-angielskich 1888-1863*.

the etymology of the word *exotic*, coming from the Latin *exoticus* and the Greek *exoticos* meaning "outward," "foreign" (Skeat 1980: 175), perceptions of the Polish other had connotations of it being "different," "alien," "strange" and "unknown." On the other hand, combatants' narratives imply that from the Islanders' perspective, the signifier *exotic* represented not only the notion of the "unknown" but also that of inequality. This is because the exotic is not about essentialism but about an opinionated description which defines the rules of in- and exclusion, entangling itself in the politics of the ideologies which produce power relations:

> For the exotic is not, as is often supposed, an inherent *quality* to be found 'in' certain people, distinctive objects, or specific places; exoticism describes, rather, a particular mode of aesthetic *perception*—one which renders people, objects and places strange even as it domesticates them, and which effectively manufactures otherness even as it claims to surrender to its immanent mystery. [...] [A]t various times and in different places, it may serve conflicting ideological interests. [...] The exoticist rhetoric of fetishised otherness and sympathetic identification masks the inequality of the power relations without which the discourse could not function. (Huggan [2001] 2003: 13, 14)

Diarists felt that the British public perceived them not only as alien but also as backward. Discussing military strategy for the upcoming German invasion of the British Isles, the sailor Wincenty Cygan's colleague, expressed his conviction about the spirit of determination among the Britons who knew what was at stake, at the same time alluding to their failure to stand up for unknown Poland in September 1939: "One cannot withdraw at this point, there must be final desperation, Hamletian 'to be or not to be.' After all, it will be about Britain itself and not about France or Belgium or some unknown '*half-savage*' Poland" (Cygan 2011: 180-181, my emphasis).

The ally raised doubts about the technological development of Poland. Cygan remembered that the Scots were surprised at the good quality of Polish uniforms and could hardly believe they were produced outside Britain (2011: 202). Indeed, Poland could not rival the British textile industry[4] which had been the engine of the country's Industrial Revolution. However, it is worth noting that the industrial region around the Polish city of Łódź, created in the 19th century, was one of the biggest textile

---

[4] For example, in England in the years 1934-1938 the consumption of cotton per capita was 14 kilograms whereas in Poland it was 2-2.5 kilograms (Missalowa et al. 1970: 393).

industries in the world (Missalowa et al. 1970: 220). Known as the Polish Manchester, in the interwar period Łódź aspired to be the "uncrowned capital city of the world textile industry" ("Geneza włókiennictwa akademickiego"). After World War I, the textile sector was the biggest employer in Poland and was concentrated, apart from Łódź, in other regions also, e.g. the Częstochowa-Sosnowiec region or Żyrardów, the latter specialising very much in textile production (over 95% of Polish linen production, see Missalowa et al. 1970: 387-388). In 1923, almost every third person worked in the textile sector (30%) and in 1932 21% of people were textile workers (Missalowa et al. 1970: 391).

The British also questioned the mechanisation of the textile industry in Poland. In the 19th century, the sewing machine, "one of the first mass-marketed consumer durables as well as an industrial tool" (Coffin 1994: 750), became an important manufacturing product in Scotland. The production of Singer machines, one of the best known brands, made the Clydebank sewing-machine factory the largest in the world ("Clydebank. West Dunbarton-shire"). Although Poland did not have such a sewing machine production tradition, by World War I the machines had become quite common in Eastern Europe, the vehicle of popularization often being the Singer brand (Godley 2006: 266-267). Polish craftsmen, who held Singer machines in high esteem, would go to great lengths to purchase one. Hanna Zygmont, coming from a family with a sartorial history, evoked the story of her grandfather, Władysław Kołpacki, who already by around 1880 had come into the possession of a Singer sewing machine, which was quite an achievement taking into account that he was a village tailor (Zygmont 2014). This was possible because Singer made the machines more affordable via a merchandise system based on an instalment plan (Breneman 2001).

One can then understand the consternation of Stefan Bałuk, an SOE [Special Operations Executive][5] agent of the Polish Home Army trained in Scotland, when the Scottish host asked him about sewing machines: "One day, [...] while sewing something with a sewing machine she asked me 'Do you have sewing machines in Poland?' I jumped for a dictionary and after a while I asked her 'do you mean Singer navicular or cylinder machines?'. This time it was me who saw surprise in her eyes" (Bałuk 2007: 91).

---

[5] SOE was created in May 1940 by the British Government to support "'home-grown' subversion in occupied Europe" (Walker 2008: 145).

4. Eastern Europe as the Ideological Project of the Enlightenment

What Poles would not know was that their country had already been given an identity in the process of construction which was a part of a larger ideological project developed in 18th century Western Europe and aimed at Eastern European countries. In line with Foucault's "eighteenth-century epistemology, that 'all designation must be accomplished by means of a certain relation to all other possible designations'" (Wolff 1994: 92) the East of Europe was defined in relation to its Western counterpart, but on an unequal basis. Larry Wolff in *Inventing Eastern Europe. The Map of Civilization on the Mind of the Enlightenment* argues that "Eastern Europe was a project of philosophical and geographical synthesis" and "a cultural construction, an intellectual invention" of the people of the Enlightenment, suggesting that the East was created as the Orient of Europe, even though it never assumed the full set of characteristics attributed to the (mis)representations of Asia (1994: 356, 358). In other words, if the Orient, to use Edward Said's terminology and justification, had to be "Orientalised" ("created"), to give the Occident "flexible *positional* superiority which puts the Westerner in a whole series of possible relationships with the Orient without ever losing him the relative upper hand" (Said 1979: 14, 16) then Eastern Europe was similarly "orientalised" to become a mine of images of the other, a negative alter ego of the Occident in Europe, thus opening a plethora of vistas for Western identification and domination closer to home. The pattern of binary divisions known from Said's *Orientalism* was the major characteristic of this project with the civilization vs. savagery/barbarity opposition coming to the fore, exploited in various contexts and meanings. Poland was then perceived in the categories of savagery not only because it was unknown and strange but because the West wanted to find its negative copy there: "the Enlightenment [...] cultivated and appropriated to itself the new notion of 'civilization,' an eighteenth century neologism, and civilization discovered its complement, within the same continent, it shadowed lands of backwardness, even barbarism. Such was the invention of Eastern Europe" (Wolff 1994: 4).

This kind of othering complies with colonial discourse and its reliance on drawing boundaries along the lines of "identity and difference" where "[t]he colonizer's traditional insistence on difference from the colonized establishes a notion of the savage as *other*, the antithesis of civilized value" (Spurr 1993: 7). The discourse draws from a pool of rhetorical tactics "which all enter equally into the matrix of relations of power that characterizes the colonial situation," but David Spurr's analysis of its rhetorical tactics proves that there are "aspects of this language which survive beyond the classic colonial era and which continue to color perceptions of the non-Western world" (1993: 7, 8).

The practises of othering revolving around concepts of civilisation, modernity and progress show a great degree of persistence and continuity. Cygan's caustic comment about the ignorance of the wartime ally who imagined Poles as lacking cultural advancement, inhabiting "a savage country, wooded and of colonial culture" (2011: 202), testify that Western Europe's notions of its eastern fringes did not differ much from the images which had been promoted in the West two hundred years earlier. Eighteenth century travel books mapped Eastern Europe as a part of the world where natural landscapes prevailed over cultural ones. Full of morasses and forests, the scenery was proof of the agricultural backwardness of this part of Europe, whose inhabitants were deemed unable to cultivate the land. In the *Encyclopaedia of Diderot and also d'Alembert*, one of the sources of Enlightenment knowledge about Eastern Europe, a French scholar, Louis de Jaucourt, lamented on Polish economic impotence in a situation of natural resource abundance: "Nature has put in this state all that is needed to become rich, grains, pastures, livestock, wools, leathers, salt mines, metals, minerals; however, Europe has no poorer people" (quoted in Wolff 1994: 188). The image was replicated after the Enlightenment era. In his accounts of Poland from the 19th century, the journalist William H. Bullock confirmed that Britons' perception of Poland was that of a "howling wilderness," "peopled by wolves and bears," whose human inhabitants relied for food on roots or starved (Jasiakiewicz 2010: 62).

Wartime Britons imagined that their Polish allies were so backward that they did not even have proper housing. When due to military unpreparedness Scotland accommodated a number of Polish soldiers in camps with tents, some Scots drew the conclusion that tents constituted a part of the housing landscape of Poland: "'You still pitch tents sometimes in Poland, don't you,' asked the descendants of the Picts, reluctant to abandon the idea of a strange and exotic Poland," reported the soldier Ksawery Pruszyński (2010: 16). As civilisation is associated with urban settlements and its material expression in the form of buildings, tents brought to mind hunter–gatherer lifestyles and exemplified the lingering belief in the primitive existence or barbarian origin of the unknown allies. So did questions about modern means of transport or hygiene solutions which Poles were regularly asked about. Linking transport or hygiene with civilisation was understandable. Conquering nature by making good roads and the construction of means of transport aided civilisation processes. It helped to distribute goods and satisfy physical needs, thus fostering cultural needs[6] as well as the transformation of life patterns by triggering consumption, decreasing people's isolation and changing the class structure (Lewis 1936: 1, 3, 5).

Civilisation also stresses cleanliness. Historically, hygiene and health were inseparable; hygienic behaviour allowing humans to "win our evolutionary war against the agents of infectious disease" (Curtis 2007: 11). The progress was possible thanks to the advancement of medicine and individual concern about hygiene, with cleansing aids accompanying the process of privatisation of hygiene habits (Curtis 2007). An English historian, William Coxe, who travelled via Poland in the years 1778–1779, made comments about Polish illnesses, the presence of which was to him tantamount to backwardness and ignorance (Wolff 1994: 30, 31). Although Plica Polonica – the verminous matting of the hair which he talked about – was present in all Baroque and Enlightenment Europe, irrespective of the social strata, Coxe would only mention the condition in the context of Poland and other Eastern European countries[7] (Wolff 1994: 29-31, Widlicka). Bernard O'Connor (1666-1698), Coxe's fellow-countryman and Polish King's Jan III Sobieski's physician, was more objective, ready to point out that Poland was freer from some diseases than other countries (Hanczewski n.y.).

For Poles in wartime Britain, cleanliness was also a question of honour. Soldier Antoni Wasilewski (1978: 14-15) recalls being preached to by his Polish superiors that being a gentleman in Britain meant being clean. Servicemen were then encouraged to do their best to match the standards of the country that hosted them. National pride was also at stake. The veterans were told to follow practises that would reinforce a positive image of Poles and Poland abroad. As it turned out, the combatants were diligent students, ready to do their duty even if there was a price to pay for this:

> The duty officer asked about the reason for my late coming. 'Bath, lieutenant.' [...] Coming back to the bus station last night I asked a Scotswoman '*bas*,' thinking of *autobus* [Polish for *a bus*]. She invited me to her place, prepared a bath and then a cup of tea. I drank it, thanked her and left. In the street I asked another Scotswoman: *bas*. She also invited me to take a bath and to have another meal. This way I missed the last bus. 'But couldn't you explain to them?' – the officer asked. – 'I don't know

---

[6] On the other hand, "This does not mean that the art of transportation is always the cause of cultural development; indeed it is sometimes the result" (Lewis 1936: 1).

[7] It must be admitted though that the Western part of Europe was indeed more successful at fighting it (Widlicka n.y.).

English' – the soldier replied – 'and if I had declined, the Scotswoman could have thought that Poles are dirty.' (Tomaszewski 1976: 63)

Ready to convey favourable impressions, combatants were irritated and offended by queries about the most basic aspects of their lifestyle and culture and resorted to sarcasm as a coping mechanism:

- And do you have railways and aeroplanes? – they asked sincerely.
- Yes, we have, what is more, the railways which are not two hours late from Greenock to Glasgow due to one centimetre snowfall – I answered to one of them.

. . .

- Do you have bathtubs at home like we do?
- In cities and new homes there are bathrooms with bathtubs, but not in all villages . . .
- So where did those who do not have bathtubs or wash-basins wash? . . .
- I personally washed in the nearest river . . . and in the morning I went to work spick-and-span.

The Scot, apparently, understood the jibe because he would not ask any more questions again. (Cygan 2011: 202-203)

What was inscribed in the image of the uncivilised other was the invention of Polish traditions. Veteran Żegota-Januszajtis recalled the rumour spread among the Islanders about a tartar dagger being used in Polish cultural practises:

Poland? And where is it? – And is this true that walking with a tartar dagger kept crosswise in the mouth is a favourite traditional Polish custom? [...] Two years later my so called 'wartime mother' – a very nice temporary adoption by kind-hearted older ladies – confessed to me that she went to see our waterlogged campsite only with the purpose of seeing for herself that allegedly wild custom of ours. (2006: 30)

The demeaning overtone of this invention springs from the portrayal of Polish folklore as inferior ("wild"), the assumption underpinned by the association of the tradition with negatively defined peoples, here Tartars. Such denigration chimes in with the Enlightenment understanding of the concept of civilisation which was as much about economic issues as about the "refinement of manners," the ideas hitting French and English dictionaries in the second half of the 18th century (Wolff 1944: 12). Negative anthropological judgments were built upon these notions. An American sailor and explorer, John Ledyard, lumped Poles together with other "inferior" groups like Tartars, Russians and Jews on the assumption that they produced "Eastern Customs" characterised as "ridiculous" and "uncivilized" (Wolff 1944: 353).

Collating Poles with Tartars also goes back to the 18th century. William Coxe traced Polish pedigree back to Asiatic Tartars: "The Poles, in their features, look, customs, dress, and general appearance, resemble Asiatics rather than Europeans; and they are unquestionably descended from Tartar ancestors" (Wolff 1944: 29). The comparison had a twofold deprecating undertone – because of the Western construction of Asia and Tartars. As mentioned before, Asia, like Eastern Europe, was another binary opposition to match the Occident in which the latter acquired positive characteristics and defined itself as "dominating, restructuring, and having authority over the Orient" (Said 1979: 3). In the Western versus Eastern Europe division, on the other hand, Tartars were not only negatively constructed as belonging to the East, but they were also distinguished as the most inferior among its white inhabitants, with some representatives of the Enlightenment comparing them to the nations of Africa and the indigenous people of North America (Wolff 1944: 348, 346). John Ledyard was particularly keen on researching the similarities between Tartars and Africans as he linked race with civilisation, a relationship which, according to him, went in the West (of Europe) – East (of Europe) direction towards Asia (Wolff 1944: 347). His observation was that skin colour is of paramount importance in differentiating between the degrees of civilisation: "General Remark is that far the greatest part of mankind compared with European Civilisation are uncultivated and that this part of Mankind are darker Coloured than the other part *viz* European. There are no white Savages and few uncivilised people that are not brown or black" (Ledyard quoted in Wolff 1994: 347). The echoes of this reasoning would come back in wartime Britain with some doubting whether Poland were a part of European civilisation. Soldier Felicjan Majorkiewicz recalled Britons who "expressed their surprise that Poles have a white skin colour" (1983: 149).

5. Coloniser-Colonised Projections

If the British reaction to the "imperialism of the imagination" (Goldsworthy 1998: 2) was, even if unconsciously, the orientalisation of Poles, then the way Poles coped with the imperial tradition of their ally was the revival of the figure of the coloniser who, as the Polish pilots whose recollections are presented here claimed, performed their colonial practises on their ally from Poland. Interestingly, the reproduction of the coloniser–colonised roles took place mainly in the imagination of Poles.

What triggered the assumptions about the colonial nature of the relationships was the network of power relations which Polish pilots were subordinated to in the context of institutionalised military structures. Wartime circumstances naturally put the British in a superior position. After all, they were the hosts in the country the Poles had arrived in, as well as the bigger ally under whose operational command the Poles were placed. Consequently, the Polish army relied on the British in terms of, among other things, accommodation, provisions, equipment, training, dispositions and combat tactics. Though restless to resume fighting and see the formation of Polish only units, the airmen had to conform to the UK's regulations, its military traditions and potential first. To facilitate swift adjustment to the new circumstances, English language classes and training courses were organised. Poles were also members of British squadrons and representatives of British personnel joined Polish squadrons.[8] However, the British presence among Polish fliers meant to promote smooth cooperation sometimes had the opposite effect. The tension resulted from the initial Anglo-Polish air forces agreement (11 June 1940) which stipulated that senior squadron positions were to be staffed by Polish officers and their British counterparts but was unclear about the demarcation line of competences between them. "Nobody has managed to explain satisfactorily where the Englishman's command ends and where the Pole's begins" concluded one of the officers of 307 Polish Night Fighter Squadron (Zamoyski [1995] 2010: 99). What added to the friction were instances of more experienced and skilful Poles being instructed and commanded by less qualified Britons. Pilot Wacław Król from the 302 Polish Fighter Squadron complained:

> The actual squadron and wing commanders were to be Polish officers and the English their advisors only. Meanwhile the English took the power over the squadron at once and this caused our, the Poles, disagreements with and reluctance to the English, especially that – apart from the Squadron Leader Jack Satchell – all others represented lower level of training in comparison to Polish commanders. [...] They did not earn our trust, they were commanders less experienced in action, they could not keep cool in face of an overwhelming number of enemies and even in situations seemingly not much complicated. (1982: 8)

As a matter of fact, before they came to the British Isles, Król and his colleagues from the squadron had already achieved a record of 43 German planes downed over the skies of Poland and France (Zamoyski [1995]

---

[8] This was regulated by the agreements between the British government and the Polish government in exile on 11 June 1940 and then 5 August 1940.

2010: 77). Their British instructor confirmed their professionalism. One of them recalled they were "terrific pilots, more experienced than us" (Zamoyski [1995] 2010: 77).

If the direct reason for the activation of images of the colonial other could be flying know-how in combination with power relations, then equally constitutive were more distant, historical factors, responsible for the anchoring of such images in the first place. From a *longue durée* perspective, Poles were sensitive to the imperial gaze due to their own colonial past.[9] Not only did they want to avoid re-entering colonial schemata but they wanted to protect their own carefully created habitus. As Polish sociologist and cultural theorist Jan Sowa notes, out of the three powers that subjugated Poland in the 18th century, it was Russia which evoked the most negative emotions and whose role was most fundamental in the creation of this post-colonial habitus (Sowa 2011: 465). Poles defined themselves in opposition to what they linked Russia with, which meant ascribing negative binaries to their (former) occupier.[10] The moment they realised they were being negatively stereotyped, with the British military associating them with the inferior colonial other, Poles felt uncomfortable as it brought them nearer to Russia than to the West they identified themselves with more. As Sowa puts it:

> Our [Polish] resistance to the stereotypical perception [...] results from our desire to deny any resemblance between us [Poles] and our culturally inferior [as imagined by Poles] colonisers – the Russians. It is as uncomfortable for us [to be compared to the Russians] as for the British the similarity between them and a group of educated Westernised Hindus: it undermines a binary opposition of superiority–inferiority on which [our] identity was built. (Sowa 2011: 476)

Stefan Łaszkiewicz (1905-1998), the squadron leader of 308 Polish Fighter Squadron, devoted several pages of his book *Od Cambrai po Coventry* [From Cambrai to Coventry] to his and his colleagues' troublesome relations with the British, his squadron counterpart, John Alfred Davies, being one of them. He was a graduate of the Dęblin officers' school in Poland, which was a highly prestigious aviation institution, one of the best, if not the best, in the world (Zamoyski [1995] 2010: 13). To be accepted among its students was already a great achievement since there were sixty candidates

---

[9] Poland was partitioned three times – in 1772, 1793 and 1795, with the last partition bringing an end to the Polish state. Poland regained independence in 1918.

[10] Sowa (2011: 476) explains the relations in depth posing a "reversed mimicry hypothesis."

for one place and to graduate was another challenge, a test of endurance and knowledge of flying (Zamoyski [1995] 2010: 12-13). He was also a student of Wyższa Szkoła Wojenna [The Higher War School], a prestigious military academy. During the war he was retrained in France, taking command of the Montpellier Squadron which defended Cambrai. In June 1940 he shot down an enemy aircraft. In Britain he was among the first to establish the 308 Fighter Squadron (Rydołowski 2010).

His (308) Squadron counterpart, John Alfred Davies (1914-1940), in the 1930's served in the 1st City of London Regiment (Royal Fusiliers, second Lieutenant) and then in 604 Squadron, Auxiliary Air Force (Hendon). of which he became a Flight Commander in August 1939. Before joining 308 Polish Fighter Squadron on 18th September 1940, he was converted to Hurricanes in 6. Operational Training Unit RAF (Sutton Bridge) (Battle of Britain Archive 2007).

In his wartime recollections Łaszkiewicz presented a very negative picture of Davies, whose hostility resulted in the Polish pilot's removal from the squadron after he crashed in training. According to the Pole and the colleagues he refers to, the Englishman took advantage of wartime circumstances and his position in the squadron to abuse his power and harass Poles. In the narrative formula the veteran employs to account for this, Davies is consequently presented as the one who re-establishes the colonial order and subordinates Poles, thus reaching for negative imperial patterns and replicating master–servant relations:

> Kleczyński [Łaszkiewicz's squadron colleague] made me realise that Davies is a typical produce of the colonial policy, a high official or an officer – a '*pukka sahib*', literally 'a strong man', a kind of a 'sovereign prince'. He personified the authority of Great Britain and the certainty was in his blood that his orders or instructions will not be questioned. An answer different than 'yes, sir' could come only from an equal to him Englishman. A native who brought himself to it [to disagree with him] committed blasphemy. We, in the eyes of Davies, were such *natives in colonies* [emphasis mine, JW]. (Łaszkiewicz 1982: 267-268)

The "pukka sahib" term is given prominence by Łaszkiewicz, who makes it the title of one of his book chapters and drops frequent references to it in other parts of his recollections too. "Pukka" (*solid*), a borrowing from Hindi and Urdu languages, was used by the English speakers in the meaning of *genuine* (Merriam Webster Dictionary). In the post-colonial reality, together with "sahib" (*sir, master* – in reference to "a European of a social or official status") it had either a positive connotation, standing for *an elegant and refined gentleman* or a pejorative meaning denoting an *overbearing and pretentious* person (Merriam Webster Dictionary).

Łaszkiewicz makes it a synonym of colonial oppression, a shorthand for the spirit of the Western imperial mentality. Davies, a symbolic embodiment of this attitude, manifests it by displaying distance towards "inferior" Poles. He approaches them with reserve, haughtiness and disdain and most often indirectly via squadron commanders, thus remaining "invisible and inaccessible" (Łaszkiewicz 1982: 270).

In the narrative of his recollections, their antagonism is reflected in the ironic overtone of vocabulary that is supposed to generate the sense of hierarchy. The Briton is said to act like (a poor copy of) a "Roman proconsul" [rzymski prokonsul] and an "archpriest" [arcykapłan] who takes decisions about the fortunes of the British Empire (Łaszkiewicz 1982: 277). When talking to the squadron pilots he takes a "pontifical tone" [pontyfikalny ton] and when he meets them he is said to grant them "an audience" [audiencja] (Łaszkiewicz 1982: 276, 267).

The combatant explains the prejudice against the Poles in class terms. For a "pukka sahib," the non-English are just "poor bastards,"[11] that is "lower class beings" (Łaszkiewicz 1982: 269, 301). Put in a subordinate position they are believed to be lacking ability and in need of being educated. Łaszkiewicz's assertions about the competence of his 308 squadron pilot are thus received with disbelief (1982: 266).

The inferior other is assumed to be weak, undisciplined and deceitful and hence requiring constant control. Suspiciousness was the order of the day. The veteran reported Davies and his assistant, flight lieutenant Young's, humiliating practices of excessive monitoring of Poles, aimed at enforcing false accusations about them on the grounds of insubordination and ineptitude. British arrogance is compared to whiplashing which brings to mind injustices towards the treatment of slaves in colonies (Łaszkiewicz 1982: 276). Painful as it was, Łaszkiewicz (1982: 266) explains they were in no position to protect their reputation by opposing such treatment since the Polish authorities called for tact and concessions in mutual relations. Nevertheless, the Poles struck back in the privacy of their conversations in the Polish only environment and on the pages of their recollections. The British they found particularly malicious were discredited as people, commanders and pilots. "War, although the worst plague of the human kind, tends to tear the mask off people and vets them, revealing their true inside," Łaszkiewicz (1982: 277) reflected upon war psychology. Davies was said to be vengeful and deceitful, emanating artificiality and posturing (Łaszkiewicz 1982: 288, 292, 277). In the Poles' minds he appeared to be nothing more than a "knave" [kanalia] and a "scoundrel" [szuja] (Łaszkiewicz

---

[11] The veteran uses the English term and translates it into "biedny bękart."

1982: 328). He was dehumanized: "How could I think Davies was a human!" – Łaszkiewicz reprimanded himself when disappointed with the Englishman's conduct (1982: 285).

If the essence of humanity lies in the distinctness from the world of animals (Leyens in Haslam et al. 2013: 28), then the members of British personnel who made the lives of Poles miserable were degraded on the evolutionary ladder through being ascribed the features of animals. Among the latter were "demeaning animals" (here dogs); comparisons were used which led to the subject's "degradation," when humans were called "disgusting animals" (here reptiles), characteristic of the "revulsion" form of "animalistic dehumanization" (Haslam et al. 2013: 37). In Łaszkiewicz's book, Davies and/or flight lieutenant's Young "barked" [szczekać], "yaped" [ujadać], and "sniffed" [węszyć] (1982: 271, 287). On the other hand, similarly to reptiles, they "crawled" [pełzać] not walked, and "crept in" [wślizgiwać się] rather than mingled (Łaszkiewicz 1982: 271, 277).

Such "animalistic dehumanization" deprived one of uniquely human traits ("human uniqueness") acquired in the process of socialization, among them civility, refinement and morality (Haslam et al. 2013: 30). Historically speaking, this kind of "human uniqueness denial" is associated with the racial and ethnic stereotypes of the colonial era on which the "images of savages" were built and which are still taken advantage of today (Jahoda in Haslam et al. 2013: 35). Haslam et al. agree that their initial research confirms the correlation between the ideas of primitiveness/backwardness and closeness to animals (2013: 36). Ironically, Poles reversed the power relations scale. As (imagined) "colonial subjects" it was they who were vulnerable to dehumanization in the first place. On the pages of their recollections, they seized the opportunity and dehumanized their "colonizers" instead.

Apart from human uniqueness, another determinant of humanness which the veterans believed Davies and his like did not possess was "human nature," with its "deep-seated," *essentialized*, "emotion-related" and "culturally universal" attributes (Haslam et al. 2013: 28). Thus, if the lack of uniquely human traits changed them into animal-like individuals, then the lack of human nature turned them into "inanimate objects" (Haslam et al. 2013: 28). "They [such people or groups] are therefore represented as lacking emotion, warmth, desire, and vitality, and accordingly perceived as cold, inert, passive, and rigid. [...] [They] are seen as robotic or object-like: mere automatons or instruments" (Haslam et al. 2013: 30). Łaszkiewicz's Davies is such an inanimate object, a robot: "Each movement, each word seemed to have come not from a man but a mannequin [...][,] a mannequin ex officio and a wooden effigy in appearance" (1982: 277). The Briton lacked naturalness and smoothness in his movements. His legs were stiff and movements sluggish (Łaszkiewicz 1982: 277). The mask-like face is cold, the head still and the stare vacant, which impeded communication (Łaszkiewicz 1982: 265, 293). He is not portrayed as a whole person but as separate parts of a machine. Borrowing from photography, one can describe this type of character presentation as a "local processing style," that is "zoom[ing] in on the specific parts of another person or people," in contrast to "a global processing style" (Gervais et al. 2013: 8-9). It was not Davies who communicated messages but his lips, the latter "tapping" [wystukiwać] words rather than uttering them. Similarly, it was not his facial expression which informed the interlocutor (and the reader) about his reactions but the micro movements of the parts of the face: "His little moustache budged and stiffened. The lower lip, barely moving was tapping words" (Łaszkiewicz 1982: 286).

Davies failed not only as a human being but also as a professional airman. He did not even look like a good pilot: "in his eyes there was as much of a fighter pilot as of a boxer in a one-armed man" (Łaszkiewicz 1982: 277). Łaszkiewicz's intuition based on the flying experience told him that Davies' arrogance was to camouflage deficiencies of airmanship as his ways indicated poor perception, a slow reaction rate and slow movement (1982: 277).

But Davies was not an exception. There were other commanders whose talents were inferior to that of the Poles yet they claimed the right to teach them. "When he preaches us how to fly we sit in silence. It could have been funny if it were not exaggerated. He, who has been a pilot for a year, thinks that he knows about flying more than all of us together" – Łaszkiewicz (1982: 318) commented bitterly about flight lieutenant Thomas Roy Kitson.[12] The failure in combat of such fliers was only a matter of time, prophesied the Poles.[13]

Unqualified pilots could not make good commanders. They issued hazardous orders and supplied unprofessional instructions posing danger to other pilots' health and lives. Łaszkiewicz was the victim of poor

---

[12] Kitson was from No. 245 Squadron RAF to which Łaszkiewicz was transferred from his previous 308 Squadron.
[13] Actually, both Davies and Kitson were killed in action. J. A. Davies was killed on 16 October 1940 "after striking a barrage balloon cable above Coventry. [...] His Hurricane, P3999, dived into the ground at Whitley Stadium" (Battle of Britain Archive 2007). T. R. Kitson was killed on 13 March 1941.

commanders himself. The price he paid for obeying one of Davies' orders was his plane crashing and hospitalization.[14]

Incorrect decisions had disciplinary consequences. To save his reputation, Davies would uphold the legitimacy of his judgments, while harming his subordinates' careers. For Łaszkiewicz this equated with the undermining of his own flying skills, the loss of a commanding position and removal from the squadron. Nobody would take his own version of events seriously. The Poles felt helpless and discriminated against. Military discipline and wartime power relations favoured the bigger ally. Attempts to stand up for their rights could easily backfire. When Łaszkiewicz demanded a life vest from flight lieutenant Kitson, which he had the right to by law when airborne anyway, and said he would do without unless the lieutenant also decided not to wear it, the commander's reaction assured him that his moral victory would be short-lived: "He turned red and asked for a vest for me. His look assured me that he will remember this. One does not speak to an Englishman like this" (1982: 319).

6. Conclusion

World War II highlighted the cultural gap between Poles and Britons which the military alliance would not bridge. The gap often acquired an imaginative dimension, thus reflecting the creative power of nations to invent not only themselves but also the other. The examples presented above reveal the negative potential of such constructedness, which relied on intellectually grounded 18th century discourses of differentiation. One of the consequences of this was "the hierarchical encodings of cultural difference" (Huggan 2001: 15) which in a European context translated into "Western Europe defin[ing] its civilization with respect to the semi-Oriental backwardness of Eastern Europe" (Wolff 1994: 345). The reactions of the British to Polish servicemen were the continuation of the tradition. They fit the frame of otherness built on binary oppositions. Epistemological uncertainty was reduced by giving the inferior other an identity which was tailored to the expectations of their more powerful subject (Markowski and Burzyńska 2006: 557-558). The exoticism of Poles was then domesticated but on the conditions imposed by the Western ally. This, paradoxically, created the image of Poland which the Slavs

---

[14] According to Łaszkiewicz, he was made to take part in a training flight despite the malfunctioning of his machine, the validity of the claim being later confirmed in an official report from the factory about the reasons for the aircraft's failure.

historically assigned to their Eastern coloniser and which they wanted to avoid. In formal contexts, when military discipline and power relations imposed its regime of subordination, the Poles tried to resist the image by "going underground" and building their own counter-narrative. In the self-created alternative reality, they subverted the traditional master–slave relations which the British, as Polish pilots inferred, tried to contain them in. This allowed them to regain agency and put themselves in control when, by deconstructing British binary oppositions and power relations schemata, they constructed their own ones. From a psychological point of view, this helped them reclaim dignity. Historically and culturally, it enabled them to protect their (Western) identity.

References

Bałuk, Stefan. 2007. *Byłem Cichociemnym*. Warszawa: Wydawnictwo ASKON.
Battle of Britain Archive. 2007. "The Airmen's Stories – S/Ldr. J A Davies." Web. 11 February 2017.
Breneman, Judy Anne Johnson. 2001. "The True History of the Sewing Machine. Isaac Singer, Scoundrel or Genius." *History of Quilts*. Web. 16 March 2017.
Clydebank (West Dunbartonshire). "Scotland's Landscape". Accessed 16 Mar. 2017.
Coffin, Judith G. 1994. "Credit, Consumption, and Images of Women's Desires: Selling the Sewing Machine in Late Nineteenth-Century France." *French Historical Studies* 18.3, 749-783.
Curtis, Valerie A. 2007. "A Natural History of Hygiene." *Canadian Journal of Infectious Diseases and Medical Microbiology* 18.1, 11-14. Accessed 6 Jan. 2017.
Cygan, Wincenty. 2011. *Granatowa Załoga*. Gdańsk: Oficyna Wydawnicza FINNA.
Feldman, Józef. 1993. *U podstaw stosunków polsko-angielskich 1888-1863*. *Polityka Narodów*, 1.3,4.
"Geneza włókiennictwa akademickiego" Wydział Technologii Materiałowych i Wzornictwa Tekstyliów, Politechnika Łódzka webpage. Accessed 25 Apr. 2017.
Geremek, Bronisław. 2006. "Britain and Poland: The Neglected Friendship?" *Polski Instytut Spraw Międzynarodowych*. Web. 25 April 2017.
Gervais, Sarah J., Philippe Bernard, Olivier Klein and Jill Allen. 2013. "Toward a Unified Theory of Objectification and Dehumanization." In:

Sarah J. Gervais, ed. *Objectification and (De)Humanization: 60th Nebraska Symposium on Motivation.* New York: Springer, 1-24.
Gibińska, Marta. 1992. "'The Patriot's Virtue and the Poet's Song': Polish Themes in English Poetry of the Nineteenth Century." In: Wojciech Lipoński, ed. *Polish-AngloSaxon Studies.* Special issue on: Polish Themes in English and American Literature. 3-4, Poznań: Wydawnictwo Naukowe Uniwersytetu im. Adama Mickiewicza, 21-42.
Godley, Andrew. 2006. "Selling the Sewing Machine around the World: Singer's International Marketing Strategies, 1850-1920." *Enterprise & Society* 7.2, 266-314.
Goldsworthy, Vesna. 1998. *Inventing Ruritania. The Imperialism of the Imagination.* New Haven and London: Yale University Press.
Hanczewski, Paweł. "Choroby." Muzeum Pałacu Króla Jana III w Wilanowie webpage. Accessed 12 Dec. 2016.
Haslam, Nick, Steve Loughnan and Elise Holland. 2013. "The Psychology of Humanness." In: Sarah J. Gervais, ed. *Objectification and (De)Humanization: 60th Nebraska Symposium on Motivation.* New York: Springer, 25-52.
Herbst, Witold A. 2013. *Podniebna kawaleria.* Poznań: Zysk i S-ka Wydawnictwo.
Huggan, Graham. [2001] 2003. *The Postcolonial Exotic. Marketing the Margins.* New York: Routledge.
Jasiakiewicz, Wojciech. 2010. *"Woefullest of Nations" or "European America"? British Travel Accounts of Poland 1863.* Bydgoszcz: Wydawnictwo Uniwersytetu Kazimierza Wielkiego.
Jaucourt, Louis de. 1765. "Pologne." Encyclopedie, XII, 925.
Król, Wacław. 1982. *Walczyłem pod niebem Londynu.* Warszawa: Ludowa Spółdzielnia Wydawnicza.
Leitgeber, Witold J. 1972. *W kwaterze prasowej. Dziennik z lat wojny 1939-1945. Od Coëtquidan do „Rubensa."* London: Katolicki Ośrodek Wydawniczy Veritas.
Lewis, William M. 1936. "The Significance of Transportation to Civilisation." *The Annals of the American Academy of Political and Social Science* 187, 1-6.
Łaszkiewicz, Stefan. 1982. *Od Cambrai po Coventry.* Warszawa: Ministerstwo Obrony Narodowej.
Majorkiewicz, Felicjan. 1983. *Lata chmurne. Lata durne.* Warszawa: Instytut Wydawniczy Pax.
Markowski, Michał P. and Anna Burzyńska. 2006. *Teorie literatury XX wieku. Podręcznik.* Kraków: Znak.

Maresch, Eugenia. 2006. "Introduction." In: Eugenia Maeresch, ed. *Polish Forces in Defence of the British Isles 1939-1945*. London: Veritas Foundation Publication Centre, 12-20.

Missalowa, Gryzelda, Jan Fijałek, Bolesław Pełka and Wiesław Puś. 1970. "Koncentracja przemysłu w łókienniczego (1918-1939)." In: Irena Pietrzak-Pawłowska, ed. *Uprzemysłowienie ziem polskich w XIX i XX wieku. Studia i Materiały*. Wrocław, Warszawa, Kraków: Zakład Narodowy Imienia Ossolińskich Wydawnictwo Polskiej Akademii Nauk, 387-432.

Missalowa, Gryzelda, Jan Fijałek, Bolesław Pełka and Wiesław Puś. 1970. "Przemysł włókienniczy." In: Irena Pietrzak-Pawłowska, ed. *Uprzemysłowienie ziem polskich w XIX i XX wieku. Studia i Materiały*. Zakład Narodowy Imienia Ossolińskich Wydawnictwo Polskiej Akademii Nauk: Wrocław, Warszawa, Kraków, 219-276.

Olson, Lynne, and Stanley Cloud. 2004. *A Question of Honour. The Kosciuszko Squadron: Forgotten Heroes of World War II*. New York: Vintage Books.

Pruszyński, Ksawery. 2010 [1941]. *Polish Invasion*. Edinburgh: Birlinn.

"Pukka." 2017. *Merriam Webster Dictionary*. Web. 12 April 2017.

Rydołowski, Konrad. "Wspomnienie." *Wyborcza.pl Warszawa*. Web. 12 April 2017.

Said, Edward W. 1979. *Orientalism*. New York: Vintage Books.

"Sahib." 2017. *Merriam Webster Dictionary*. Web. 12 April 2017.

Siemaszko, Zbigniew S. 2010. *Polacy i Polska w drugiej wojnie światowej*. Lublin: Norbertinum.

Skeat, Walter W. 1980. *A Concise Etymological Dictionary of the English Language*. New York: A Perigee Book.

Sopoćko, Eryk. 2010. *Patrole "Orła"*. Gdańsk: Finna.

Sowa, Jan. 2011. *Fantomowe ciało króla. Peryferyjne zmagania z nowoczesną formą*. Kraków: TAiWPN Universitas.

Spurr, David. 1993. *The Rhetoric of Empire: Colonial Discourse in Journalism, Travel Writing, and Imperial Administration*. Durham, London: Duke University Press.

Tomaszewski, Wiktor. 1976. *Na szkockiej ziemi. Wspomnienia wojenne ze służby zdrowia i z Polskiego Wydziału Lekarskiego w Edynburgu*. London: The White Eagle Press.

Walker, Jonathan. 2008. *Poland Alone: Britain, SOE and the Collapse of the Polish resistance, 1944*. Stroud, UK: The History Press.

Wasilewski, Antoni. 1978. *W szkocką kratę*. Kraków: Wydawnictwo Literackie.

Widlicka, Hanna. "Plica polonica czyli kołtun polski." *Muzeum Pałacu Króla Jana III w Wilanowie webpage*. Web. 12 December 2016.
Wolff, Larry. 1994. *Inventing Eastern Europe. The Map of Civilisation on the Mind of Enlightenment*. Stanford, California: Stanford University Press.
Zamoyski, Adam. [1995] 2010. *The Forgotten Few. The Polish Air Force in World War II*. Barnsley UK: Pen & Sword Aviation.
Zygmont, Hanna. 2014. "Dziadek Władysław i trzej jego synowie - wszyscy szyli na miarę." *Nowosci Dziennik Toruński*. Web. 25 January 2017.
Żegota-Januszajtis, Jerzy Z. 2006. *Wspomnienia fotoreportera z Dywizji Maczka*. Kraków: Towarzystwo Słowaków w Polsce.

Chapter Fourteen

The "Other" in Contemporary Slovene Literature from the Trieste Region: A Case Study of National Stereotypes in Minority Literatures

Ana Toroš

1. Triestine Literature

The term Triestine literature has developed within Italian literary history (*letteratura triestina*) and denotes the literature written in Italian by authors living in Trieste. In Slovene Triestine literary history, which appropriated the term, Triestine literature is defined as the works written by authors from the Trieste area either in Slovene and (or) Italian, among other languages. In this case, the term has a wider context; or rather it is a flexible notion that lacks a single definition (Toroš 2014: 39-54).

The time aspect of the Slovene Triestine literature is also important: the literature has "existed"' or rather has been studied as a special chapter of Slovene literary history since the end of World War I, that is the fall of the Austro-Hungarian Empire, when the Trieste area was annexed by Italy and therefore separated from the Central Slovene space that came under Yugoslavian rule. This is the period when Slovene Triestine literary production begins in earnest and which has its own specific motifs, themes and ideas (Toroš 2014: 39-54).

For the purpose of this article I will define the term "Triestine literature" as the works of authors who live in the Trieste region and discuss it in their literature, in both Slovene and in Italian. The focus will be mostly on contemporary Slovene Triestine literature which will be compared to contemporary Italian Triestine literature. Our intent is to bring attention to the existence of national stereotypes (auto-stereotypes and hetero-stereotypes) in contemporary Slovene Triestine novels. At the same time, I will attempt to discern the reasons for their conception, longevity and the unrecognizability of their construction within the Slovene Triestine literary system in the Trieste area (Dović 2013: 38-44).

To better understand the existence of national stereotypes within Slovene Triestine literature, we must look back to the region's history, specifically the 19th century. It was during this period that tensions between the Slovene and Italian communities began, climaxing during the fascist era. It is therefore reasonable to take an interdisciplinary approach when studying Slovene Triestine literature, by way of two angles: cultural nationalism (Leerssen 2006: 559-578, Anderson 2007) and various concepts of memory (Halbwachs 2001). Based on this, I would like to propose a new research concept for Triestine literature, devised to be comparative and comprehensive. It compares the literary works of Triestine authors that are produced within various Triestine communities, written in various languages, based on various cultural memories and traumas. This will allow for uncovering the mechanisms behind the creation of stereotypes in Triestine literature.

Slovene Triestine literature and Italian Triestine literature can be put in the context of cultural nationalism as an international movement and the connected cultivation of culture (Leerssen 2006: 559-578). During this process, I will be interested in cultural and literary productions which were intended to fortify the Slovene, and/or Italian cultural identities in Trieste and in the region nearby. In literature, these tendencies manifested themselves in the creation of the Slovene or Italian collective protagonist.

During the 19th century, Italian literature in Trieste created the Triestine imaginary based on Italian irredentism, which strove to annex all the remaining areas with an Italian population to the Kingdom of Italy after its unification in 1861 (Ara 2007, Vivante 1984). One of the main priorities of the irredentist movement was Trieste. Consequently, the Italian Triestine literature had predicted Trieste's annexation to the Kingdom of Italy several decades before World War I. The irredentist literature helped influence the population by personifying *Trieste* as a beautiful Italian bride, waiting for an Italian prince to save her from the clutches of the Austro-Hungarian Empire. Both for the purpose of propaganda and for the invention of a cultural imaginary of Trieste as an Italian city, Italian literature was shaped by certain symbols and metaphors which were repeated by the majority of the Italian Triestine authors from that period. The only exceptions were artists like Umberto Saba, who did not submit to the norms of propaganda literature but tried to find their own voice. One of the mentioned symbols was the hill of St. Justus, where Ancient Roman artefacts were found, leading the hill to become a symbol of Roman presence within the Trieste area. Authors used the artefacts to substantiate the claims of the Kingdom of Italy on Trieste, depicting the city as an heir to Roman culture.

During this period, Italian literature fostered the image of Trieste as a former Roman city and the wish for it to become a future Italian city. As is evident, auto-stereotypes of Italians as heirs to Roman culture were shaped within Italian literature. The hetero-stereotype of the Other developed concurrently to the latter, delineating those who were not heirs to Roman culture, and therefore culturally backward and barbaric. The Other were also those who opposed the "marriage" between the beautiful *Trieste* and the Italian prince. They were depicted as the adversary, the antagonist, who could thwart their happy ending. The Other was the Slovene community in Trieste. The Italian irredentist literature of the time often alluded to people of the community using the racial slur *ščavo*, denoting a culturally backward person, speaking a Slavic language full of sibilants and post-alveolar consonants, which were completely unintelligible to the Italians.

The Other's (*ščavo*) role as antagonist was important within Italian poetry from Trieste up until World War I. After the annexation of Trieste to Italy and the implementation of fascism, the Other was eliminated from literature. In light of the intentional and violent Italianisation that took place in the Trieste area, the Slovene community should have been eradicated, and the literary discourse followed the lead of the anti-Slovene policy. After World War I and during the interwar period, Trieste was depicted in an idealised light, devoid of nationalist tension. Instead of continuing with the Roman depiction of Trieste, the interwar period saw Italian Triestine literature become saturated with a nostalgic Habsburg image of Trieste. What is relevant to this study is what kind of discourse was established in the Slovene Triestine literature of the time. For this purpose, I will look to Halbwachs's concept of collective memory (Halbwachs 2001). This study will touch upon the topic of memory within the Slovene Triestine community as a selective database existing in the community's consciousness. The community's image is based on this database, which has an integrative and cohesive function. I will also take into account the subsequent elaboration of the concept, which differentiates between communicative memory and cultural memory (Assmann 2011). Communicative memory is mostly passed on orally and lasts up to 100 years or rather three to four generations. The bearers of the communicative memory are all of the community's members. Cultural memory encompasses all the events to which the community assigns a substantiated value; they could have taken place further back in history and are passed on by textual coherence, symbolical codifying (monuments, depictions) and the elite (cultural intellectuals, authors) (Juvan 2005: 400). In this context a mimetic discourse, here literature, is seen to preserve the cultural memory (Johansen 2002), especially with canonised works.

The apex of the Slovene Triestine literary canon is represented by Boris Pahor (b. 1913) and Alojz Rebula (b. 1924). Based on their works (and the works of their slightly older contemporaries, born around 1900) we can observe that the period of Trieste during the fascist era is characteristic for these works. It encompasses the key elements of the cultural memory of the Slovene Triestine community such as the arson of the National Hall and the Bazovica killings. These two events are important settings serving as topographical mnemonics in their novels.

During the same period, a "mythical story" (mythicised memory) developed in Slovene Triestine literature of Trieste as a once Slovene city, which was captured by the Other, a foreigner, the enemy or rather the Italian speaking fascist. According to the myth this character effectively halted the cultural and economic development of the Slovene Triestine community. Consequently, the character became the main active antagonist within the Slovene Triestine literature during the interwar period. The Slovene community, now a collective protagonist, takes on the passive role of a helpless people, who observe and document the antagonist's cruel acts and crimes committed upon the Slovene population in Trieste.

Another relevant point of this discussion is the fact that these events were not only written about by the authors who lived and worked in the interwar period, but also by younger Slovene Triestine authors, who were part of the post-World War II generation and therefore did not experience the horrors of fascism. I feel confident in putting forth the theory that the younger authors, who read the older generation's works during their school years as mandatory reading material in Slovene schools in Trieste, absorbed the pattern for literalising the Slovene Triestine community and therefore infused their writing with elements of the community's cultural memory.

The memories of traumatic events were also passed on to descendants by parents and grandparents telling stories. Marianne Hirsch uses the term postmemory in this regard (Hirsch 2012). These intimate tales had a greater emotional impact on the younger generation than the literary works which may have also spoken about the same events in the Trieste area. The contemporary generation of Triestine authors still has access to this oral tradition.

2. Traumatic Experiences

In the following chapter we will try to explain how these traumatic events and the postmemory of these events influenced the specifics of Slovene Triestine literature (including the longevity of national stereotypes). We will begin with Freud's findings on trauma processing in the human subconscious: when a person loses a loved one or a "homeland" or "freedom," they can react with grief, which is resolved when the person successfully works through the pain and accepts the loss. Sometimes the loss is too great and the person is unable to process it and reacts with melancholy. The past constantly invades the present, keeping the link to the traumatic event alive. Literature is a space, where nostalgia is mirrored by what was and what was lost (Boulter 2013).

Seeing literature as a space where trauma can be vented helps us understand why writing about the Slovene Triestine community which lived under the fascist regime with a sense of loss was so important for the authors of the interwar period, who established the foundations of Slovene Triestine literature. In order to explain the obsessive repetition of the mythicized memories of the Slovene Triestine community characteristic of the generation of Slovene Triestine authors born after the end of the fascist regime, I must look to transgenerational transmissions of the (fascist) trauma, which passes down to the second and third generations through a child's early subconscious identification with important people – usually parents, especially mothers – and their traumatic history (Jurić Pahor 2004: 47).

This study is based on the hypothesis that the fascist trauma has had a great deal of influence on Slovene Triestine literature since its beginning almost one hundred years ago. Due to the mechanisms of establishing cultural and communicative memory and its reflection in literature as well as the transgenerational transmission of fascist trauma, which results in the need for constantly mentioning the traumatic period in literary works, a clear distinction between Us (Slovene, good) and Them (Italian, evil) was established in the Slovene Triestine literary discourse. This can clearly be seen by looking at literary characters in Slovene Triestine novels. In novels written by well-known Slovene Triestine authors like Boris Pahor, the Slovene characters are usually nationally conscious and possess positive personality traits. Italians characters on the other hand are usually portrayed in a negative light, even if they are not actively committing crimes against the Slovene Triestine community. It is enough that they are part of the Italian speaking community, whom the literary discourse indiscriminately links with fascist imagery. Boris Pahor's novel *Parnik trobi nji (The Steamer Sounds a Horn for Her,* 1964 is a good case in point, where the protagonist is a Slovene girl from Trieste. She arrives in Trieste after World War I and falls in love with a Slovene boy. Both of them are nationally conscious and actively fight fascism as part of an illegal organisation. In one scene, the illegal organisation holds a ball for its members. When an Italian coincidentally walks in on the ball, all of the Slovene women refuse to dance with him. The Italian as an individual did nothing insulting or violent to the Slovenes, and yet he still does not have the narrator's empathy. His very presence fills the setting with a tense atmosphere.

A similar depiction of Slovene and Italian characters can be found in the novel *Burjin čas (Time of The Bora,* 2009) written by the Slovene Triestine author Vilma Purič (b. 1966). This novel also deals with the fate of the Slovene Triestine community during the fascist era and World War II. The main story line revolves around a young woman who falls in love with an Italian man. In the end, she finds herself imprisoned and tortured. The Slovene community does not approve of her relationship with the Italian and in the end they are proven correct as the Italian leaves the Slovene woman.

It is important to note that stereotypical divisions between characters – here "good" Slovene protagonists, there "bad" Italian antagonists – in Slovene Triestine novels are not questioned by Slovene literary critics and therefore are not considered a construct. There is a lack of critical reflection upon the stereotypes.

3. The Other

A different narrative of the Slovenes in Trieste could be observed in the novels written by Fulvio Tomizza (1935-1999) from Istria, who moved to Trieste after World War II. He therefore identified with neither the Slovene nor the Italian community in Trieste. He had a culturally hybrid identity (Slovene-Croatian-Italian identity) and saw the Slovene community from the outside, from a different perspective, allowing him to create different Slovene characters than in the Slovene Triestine literature. In this light, the most relevant of his novels is *Frančiška (Franziska,* in Italian), which is also set in the early 20th century and in the Trieste region as Pahor's aforementioned novel *Parnik trobi nji*. I will use it to conduct a comparative imagological analysis.

The protagonist Frančiška is a Slovene woman, who after the First World War falls in love with an Italian soldier in Trieste. The novel follows her personal drama, the miserable love affair which is the result of complex personality traits in both lovers and unpleasant circumstances. The main difference that separates it from the previously mentioned Slovene Triestine novels is the narrator's attitude towards the Slovene woman, who does not actively fight for a Slovene Trieste and decides to pursue a love affair with an Italian man. She is not portrayed negatively due to her life choices, she is not the bearer of negative personality traits, nor is she judged by the narrator. Her life choices are not commented upon, nor are they the subject of any deeper reflection or are in any way presented as a problem. In other words, the plot is not based on the mythicised memory of the Slovene Triestine community. Concurrently and unlike the Italian Triestine literature, the novel does not oppose this matrix, but it offers an alternative perspective of an Italian from Istria who came to Trieste and saw both the Slovene Triestine and Italian Triestine communities from the outside. In this vein, neither do we find the stereotype of the cruel Italian in his novels. The Italian officer's decision to leave Frančiška is not rooted in his cruelty or fascist ideology, but can be explained by his personality traits.

As we can observe, we are dealing with two novels and two authors who belong to roughly the same generation and who write about the Slovene Triestine community during the interwar period, yet belong to two different cultural and communicative memories and different traumatic events. In this comparison, seeing the difference in the characters' depiction in both novels, it is easier to recognise the stereotypical narrative model (nationally conscious Slovene characters and their Italian antagonists) in Pahor's novel that is typical for the Slovene Triestine literature.

An indicator of the longevity of this narrative model in Slovene Triestine literature is its presence in novels written and set in 21st century Trieste, which apparently do not directly update the collective mythology of the Slovene Triestine community within which we find the aforementioned national stereotypes. In this context, I can highlight the Slovene Triestine author Evelina Umek, born in 1939. Her novels are a novelty in Slovene Triestine literature, as she broke with the tradition of portraying characters with a fixed Slovene identity (Pertot 2014). Her novels coincide with the latest scientific research which uncovered an ever more fluid identity among Slovene Triestine secondary school students. Umek's prose typically includes a whole array of characters from different generations (parents, children, grandchildren) who, at least partly, identify as Triestine Slovenes. Her novel *Zlata poroka a litržaški blues* (*Golden Anniversary or The Triestine Blues,* 2010) gives centre stage to this problematic question of identity. Despite the author's effort to showcase the cracks in the Slovene Triestine auto-stereotype which includes a nationally conscious, morally righteous Slovene Triestine with a fixed Slovene identity, a more in-depth analysis of her characters reveals that the author's empathy is with those characters who primarily identify with being Slovene. The characters' traits, their bodily features and the dark or bright atmosphere of their living places (Stekar 2015: 17-25) are subtle indicators of the author's narrative strategy.

It is evident, that the given novel nevertheless maintains the nationally conscious Slovene with a fixed identity as the desired model along with its antithesis, which is the hetero-stereotype of the cruel Italian. It is somewhat modified due to the 21st century setting, but nevertheless holds on to the basic attributes: not knowing or caring to know the Slovene language, a haughty attitude towards Slovene culture and using the racial slur *ščavi* to refer to Slovene people. The most negative character in the novel is an Italian from Istria called Fiore, who came to Trieste as a boy, when his family decided to leave Istria during the Istrian exodus after World War II. Evelina Umek uses this character to weave the novel's key plot, which is symbolically a battle between Slovenes and Italians. Fiore, who has Slavic ancestors and whose original name is Cvetko, is married to a nationally conscious Slovene woman. Their marriage if full of national tension, to such an extent that one child is raised solely by the mother within the Slovene tradition, goes to a Slovene school, has a Slovene name and spends time with his Slovene grandparents; whereas the other child is raised solely by the father in the Italian tradition. Fiore is filled with anger by the perceived injustice against his father who had to leave all of his earthly possession behind in Istria. He suffers a trauma and embraces Italian nationalism in a bid to win back his father's land.

The author does not dedicate much attention to the fate of the Istrian refugee. Due to his anti-Slovene stance, Fiore is the novel's antagonist more so than he is a representative of Istrian refugees and consequently fills the role that Italian characters usually assume.

From the second half of the 20th century onwards, the Istrian refugees' literary image represents the third important minority community in the Triestine literary discourse, the first two being the Slovene Triestine and Italian Triestine communities. The aforementioned author Fulvio Tomizza is the most important Istrian author who moved to Trieste. His novel *Materada* (1969) speaks about the topic of the Istrian exodus. In it he highlights the trauma of the Istrian community, especially the farmers', which was caused by the confiscation of their land after World War II during the Socialist regime in Yugoslavia. Consequently, this led to a second traumatic event, the exodus itself, which meant farewell to their birthplace. In conclusion, this novel supplements Evelina Umek's image of the Istrian refugee and allows us to see the issue from a wider perspective through the dialogues of literary discourses originating from different (traumatic) memories.

To enhance the previous observations, I will summarise Russell Scott Valentino's findings on the nature of Istrian identity. According to him, Istria has a characteristic regional identity, which transcends ethnic and national identities (Slovenes, Croats and Italians) and connects the person with their living environment on an intimate level. In the realm of literature, it is precisely in Fulvio Tomizza's novel *Materada* where he finds this Istrian identity. Scott Valentino explains the transgenerational trauma transmission, to use Marija Jurić Pahor's terminology, of the Istrian exodus, whilst taking into account the socio-political circumstances, based on the deep connection between the Istrian people's identity and their living environment. The Istrians' choice to either stay or leave deeply affected the lives of their descendants. The people faced with this decision had lived in their houses for generations and had worked hard for their own piece of land. To leave meant to abandon the ambitions and hard work of generations of their ancestors. It was also an enormous social risk, as the emigrating population was not well off and therefore had little freedom of choice as to where and how to live. Those who chose to stay did so to preserve their way of life, passed on to them by their ancestors, and certain elements of their Istrian identity (language, culture, cuisine). Life in Istria changed dramatically after the Second World War owing to migration and new political borders and ideologies. With the changes, the former image of Istria disappeared and with it a complementary Istrian identity. Those that stayed had to adapt or were forced into internal exile as the concept of *Italian-ness* of the Yugoslavian regime was linked to fascism (Scott Valentino 2000: 7-19). In both cases the Istrian identity could only be preserved through memory, as a yearning after something that is forever lost but is verbalised in literary discourse.

We can conclude with Michael Rothberg's thought, which offers a different concept to understanding collective memory as a multidirectional memory rather than a competitive memory. The latter perspective is mutually exclusive, deriving from the premise that it is only possible to preserve a certain community's memory (and therefore the community itself) by eliminating the memory of another community. The other point of view places a discursive space centre stage, where memories from different eras and cultures can coexist (Rothberg 2009: 5).

Such a comparative approach, indicated many times throughout the article, is especially useful to research and understand Triestine literature, which is based on the traumatic memories of various Triestine communities (Slovene Triestine memory, Italian Triestine memory, Istrian memory), resulting in a comprehensive review of all regional literatures. Triestine literary works are constantly engaging in symbolic dialogue, in the sense that they are from the same time period and from the Trieste region. In this sense they supplement each other in certain areas, in others they radically oppose each other, but they always give us a comprehensive view of "Triestine memories" within the Triestine literary discourse. Based on these confrontations, it might prove easier to identify, understand and overcome certain stereotypical depictions of the Other and of ourselves.

References

Anderson, Benedict R. 2007. *Zamišljene skupnosti: o izvoru in širjenju nacionalizma*. Alja Brglez Uranjek and Andrej Kurillo, trans. Ljubljana: Studia humanitatis.
Assmann, Jan. 2011. *Cultural Memory and Early Civilization: Writing, Remembrance, and Political Imagination*. Cambridge/New York: Cambridge University Press.
Ara, Angelo and Magris, Claudio. 2007. *Trieste un identità di frontiera*. Torino: Giulio Einaudi Editore.
Boulter, Jonathan. 2013. *Melancholy and the Archive: Trauma, History and Memory in the Contemporary Novel*. London: Bloomsbury Academic.
Dović, Marijan. 2013. "Kulturninacionalizem, literatura in Enciklopedija romantičnega nacionalizma v Evropi." In: Boža Krakar-Vogel, ed. *Slavistika v regijah*. Ljubljana: Zveza društev Slavistično društvo Slovenije, 38-44.
Halbwachs, Maurice. 2001. *Kolektivni spomin*. Ljubljana: Studia humanitatis.
Hirsch, Marianne. 2012. *The Generation of Postmemory: Writing and Visual Culture after the Holocaust*. Columbia: Columbia University Press.
Johansen, Jørgen Dines. 2002. *Literary Discourse: A Semiotic-Pragmatic Approach to Literature*. Toronto: University of Toronto Press.
Jurić Pahor, Marija. 2004. "Neizgubljivi čas: travma fašizma in nacionalsocializma v lučinuje po obdobju latence in transgeneracijske transmisije." *Razprave in gradivo: revija za narodnostna vprašanja* 44, 38-64.
Juvan, Marko. 2005. "Kultura in spomin in literatura." *Slavistična revija* 53. 3, 379-400.

Leerssen, Joseph Theodoor. 2006. "Nationalism and the Cultivation of Culture." *Nations and Nationalism: Journal of the Association for the Study of Ethnicity and Nationalism* 12.4, 559-578.

Pahor, Boris. 1964. *Parnik trobi nji.* Ljubljana: Cankarjevazaložba.

Pertot, Susanna and Kosic, Marianna. 2014. *Jeziki in identitete v precepu: mišljenje, govor in predstave o identiteti pri treh generacijah maturantov šol s slovenskim učnim jezikom v Italiji.* Trst: Slovenski raziskovalni inštitut SLORI.

Purič, Vilma. 2009. *Burjin čas.* Trst: Mladika.

Rothberg, Michael. 2009. "Introduction: Theorizing Multidirectional Memory in a transnational age." In: Mieke Bal et. al., eds. *Multidirectional Memory: Remembering the Holocaust in the Age of Decolonization.* Stanford: Stanford University Press, 1-29.

Scott Valentino, Russell. 2001. "Utopian Dreams and the Nostalgic Impulse: Fulvio Tomizza's Materada and the Continuing Istrian Diasporic Discourse." *Ricerche sociali* 10, 7-19.

Stekar, Daniela. 2015. "Sestavljene narodne identitete v romanu Eveline Umek Zlata poroka ali Tržaški blues. *"Jezik in slovstvo* 60.2, 17-25.

Tomizza, Fulvio. 1969. *Materada.* Milano: Mondadori.

—. 2002. *Franziska.* 4th ed. Milano: Mondadori.

Toroš, Ana, 2014: "Triestinità and Tržaškost: Common Points and Differences." *Slovene studies* 36.1, 39-54.

Umek, Evelina. 2010. *Zlata poroka ali Tržaški blues.* Trst: Maldika.

Umek, Loredana. 2010. "Odprtost kot izraz stiske jezika ali bega iz družbene osame." In: Evelina Umek, ed. *Zlata poroka ali Tržaški blues.* Trst: Mladika, 143-154.

Vivante, Angelo. 1984. *Irredentismo adriatico.* Trieste: Edizioni Italo Svevo.

CHAPTER FIFTEEN

FEMALE REBELS UNDOING OTHERNESS
IN FATIH AKIN'S *AUF DER ANDEREN SEITE*
AND *GEGEN DIE WAND*

FUNDA BILGEN STEINBERG

1. The Spectrum of Female Representation in Hollywood Movies as Social Practice

In Hollywood, stereotyping often manifests itself in the form of an ideology aimed at keeping women in "their place" (see Mulvey 1975, Johnston 1973). She appears almost like an object of fetish, and is characterized by various genre specific types and "the acts of objectifying, fantasizing, sexualizing, dehumanizing, and sexually violating women are clearly interconnected in the fictional world of mainstream film" (quoted in Cuklanz 2015: 37). Be it Victorian angels in the 1910s and 1920s or overtly sexual seductresses (e.g., femme fatales of the traditional male fantasy, especially in film noir movies starting in the 1950s), the stereotypical woman is identified with beauty and youthfulness. In romantic comedies, it is her so-called "admiration" of the male hero, in horror movies her victimization, or her appearance in the film noir tradition as the man-hating, monstrous, femme-fatale types opposite the common loner male/wolf/cowboy figure (e.g., in Clint Eastwood movies), whom the evil woman wishes to "tame" (Edwards 2015: 43). These images of femininity not only underline male masculinity and power, but stabilize the position of the female as an object to be looked at by men, thus serving the ideological power represented by a certain group. As "the male and masculine cannot bear the burden of sexual objectification" (Edwards 2015: 44) these traditions also reinforce the activity/performativity of the male while reinforcing the passivity/spectatorship of the female.

On the other side of this radical spectrum, more often than not, in contemporary mainstream media, the empowerment of women is identified with sexual assertiveness, buying power, and an individual economic control over their lives that is one-dimensionally sexual. In these contemporary representations of femininity, female liberation is artificially diminished to women's sexual freedom and activity, and one can generally see representations of "assertive, sexually active, career-focused" white, middle class women – as in the examples of *Ally McBeal* and *Sex and the City* (Lumby 2015: 604). Even though in movies and TV series such as these women look like they have control over their destiny, it is not surprising to find out their happiness still depends – one way or another – on a male character.

In addition, in some contemporary films, women are also made to seem like they desire violence. And the desire of these "violence-seeking" female characters serves to justify male violence over women, revealing the underlying misogyny of our century, as critics like Cuklanz (2015: 39) have described in detail. This is explicitly displayed in horror movies, as most focus on female characters as the victims, rendering the movie more graphic by stressing the victimized female characters' identification with "abject" terror. Not only are women objectified to the degree of victimization and degradation in contemporary media culture, besides the so-called "female desire" for violence, female characters in these movies seldom appear as the primary protagonists. In mainstream media, especially movies and television shows, as well as videos and video games, they almost never appear as the heroine. When they do appear so, the qualities attributed to them is more often than not radically different. In mainstream media, men are presented to perform heroic deeds a part of their character so they do it naturally, whereas female characters do so because of other motivations. For example, "Sarah Crisby (2004) similarly shows how female heroines [...] can take on roles of violent heroism reserved for male characters but within certain proscribed limits: the heroines do not enjoy these roles and perform them out of a sense of altruism and care for others" (quoted in Cuklanz 2015: 39). In other words, this essentialist inclination according to which men, by being strong and heroic, are presented as if they are just fulfilling their natural potentials – i.e., "what they are supposed to be" – is further evidence of how women are excluded from certain domains of behaviour and characteristics due to patriarchal structures in the media.

However, fresh questions challenging these representations are posed due to recent global phenomena such as postmodernism, transnationalism, and digital and new media. Starting with the foundation of Intersectional Media Studies in the late 1960s and early 1970s, the interaction between various biological, social, and cultural categories such as gender, race, class, and identity started to be studied to show how gender is not the only determining element on women's "fate" (see Aulette, Wittner, and Blakely 2009, Thomson and Armato 2012). It has increasingly been emphasized "how gender(s) intersect sexuality, class, race, nationality, or citizenship; and/or illustrates [sic] how gendered representations in the media are significant in the production of social, political, or cultural inequalities (Molina-Guzman and Cacho 2015: 75).

Structured forms of knowledge and memory determine the social practices and everyday dynamics of power which can be observed through written, oral, and visual texts and contexts. Just like Barthes noted (1973) that ideology has the effect to make its signs appear part of the natural order, feminists point to how dominant filmmaking practices transmit the ideological codes of patriarchy to construct a fixed image of a woman. Post-structuralism and semiotics have opened the way for feminists to conduct a theoretically rigorous analysis of how a film's ideological operation constructs the idea of woman within its textual or semiotic practices (McCabe 2004: 17).

In *Discipline & Punish: The Birth of the Prison*, Foucault (1975) describes how social bodies are determined through discourse, and how they shape societies, lives, and personae; Foucault analyses the failures of essentialist approaches and their focus on "natural," given ascriptions. Likewise, racist, gendered, populist discourses, and many more examples of such serve to the construction and intensification of this "natural" impression of cultural, social, and gender regimes. Foucauldian explanations of power and ideology are interested in "de-mystifying ideologies and power through the systematic and retroductable investigation of semiotic data (written, spoken or visual)" (Wodak and Meyer 2009: 3). This model of hegemony and its focus on the dissemination and implementation of power through fear, anxiety, domination, and exploitation are what dictate the everyday dynamics of action, behaviour, and relationships – though the machinery of semiotic power-construction remains invisible most of the time.

Likewise, a contemporary male director, Fatih Akin, points out the significance of understanding how power relationships, structured around dominant ideology, make the marginalized perceive the schemata suggested to and imposed on them – as the absolute, neutral and without alternative truth, especially when it comes to racism and sexism. By pointing this out, Akin aims to delineate how physical and symbolic oppression and violence in everyday narratives can be deconstructed as negative forces by focusing on female stereotypes in his critically acclaimed feature films *Auf der anderen Seite* (2007, German Film Awards

2008, European Film Awards 2007, Cannes Film Festival 2007) and *Gegen die Wand* (2004, Berlin International Film Festival 2004, European Film Awards 2004, Nuremberg Film Festival 2004).

2. Challenging Archetypes as Determiners of Truth

Jung (2014) suggests that archetypes play a determining role in the individual and collective unconscious. On the other hand, Foucault argues discourses fundamentally influence the production of social, political, and personal bodies. The difference between Jung's and Foucault's approaches to how gender and sexuality are turned into social constructs is of great interest to this study. As Lumby asserts in reference to Foucault, power and knowledge are never inseparable, adding that "there is no way of 'speaking the truth' as an outsider to power"; therefore, "all speaking positions – dominant, submissive, victimized, or ostentatiously reasonable – are always laced with their own claims to authority" (2015: 608). Under the effect of these claims that determine the dominant discourses, how the marginalized – who in this case is the women – are turned into the products of male fantasy can be explicitly seen in the male-dominant cinema tradition. As McCabe (2004: 69) states:

> [...] stereotyping functions to normalize an image of the Other. This is achieved by initiating knowledge that oscillates between what is already known and somehow fixed, and something which must be anxiously and compulsively replicated in order to maintain credibility.

In addition, stereotyping is more often than not in the minds of the individual as he or she is made to believe his actions and interactions are constantly monitored (van Djik 1993: 257). Controlling discourses involves one or more of these categories, e.g. determining the definition of the communicative situation, deciding on the time and place of the communicative event, or on which participants may or must be present, and in which roles, or what knowledge or opinions they should (not) have, and which social actions must be achieved by discourse (van Djik 1993: 356).

It is Akin's intention to create awareness, to challenge and to change these social practices instead of only trying to understand or explain them which is, as I will point out, what makes his cinema especially valuable, as it makes the invisible visible again. It is of importance to figure out where this invisible force, which has so much power on the collective unconscious' governing modes of behaviour and thinking, comes from. Jung (2013: 3) claims:

> [...] the personal unconsciousness rests upon a deeper layer, which does not derive from personal experience and is not a personal acquisition but is inborn. This deeper layer I call the *collective unconsciousness*. [...] The contents of the collective unconscious, on the other hand, are known as *archetypes*.

These *a priori* archetypes have no time, space and context. Only their representations do. However, this kind of approach carries its potential risks of diminishing, in a very radical fashion, human behaviour to nothing. In contrast, Judith Butler stresses the "performativity" of humans and social interaction. In order to tackle such a limiting approach and its discourse, Akin uses multi-faceted and powerful female characters that can be considered as counter-archetypes. These counter-archetypes aim, through their rebellion and by embracing a feminist agenda, "to get engaged in an attempt to find rival and challenging female archetypes to help feminist conclusions" (Goldenberg 1976: 448). In the selected movies by Akin they appear in terms of the counter mother archetype, they display anima and animus characteristics as suggested by Jung, but in a subversive manner, thus creating images of femininity which disturb the patriarchal order and are opposed to the male (cult) hero.

One of the archetypes that is essential to Jung's theory is the mother archetype, which also embodies a lot of conflicting representations. According to Jung, "the specific appearance of the mother-image at any time cannot be deduced from the mother archetype alone but depends on an innumerable number of other factors" (Jung 2013: 13). The mother-archetype is worth discussing in depth in this study because of the parallelism in the dual nature of the characteristics attributed to the mother-archetype and to women in male-dominated societies and its cultural products.

> The qualities associated with it are maternal solicitude and sympathy; the magic authority of the female; the wisdom and spiritual exaltation that transcend reason; any helpful instinct or impulse; all that is benign, and that cherishes and sustains, that fosters growth and fertility. The place of magic transformation and rebirth, together with the underworld and its inhabitants, are presided over by the mother. On the negative side the mother archetype may connote anything secret, hidden, dark; the abyss, the world of the dead, anything that devours, seduces, and poisons, that is terrifying and inescapable like fate. (Jung 2013: 15)

Both positive and negative meanings that are assigned to the mother/women archetype emphasize the duality of female nature. Just like nature itself is depicted to have dual characters, female nature is portrayed to be both nurturing but also violent and uncontrollable. The power exerted on the children of these female characters does not come from the archetype itself, but rather through the meanings projected upon it (Jung 2013: 16). These carry potential risks since too much burden and too many meanings are attributed to femininity, which over the course of time become repeated discourses, serving the power of the dominant, male, white, western, and elitist discourse. They become so neutralized that they become the reality of the collective unconsciousness. However, in Akin's movies, this tendency is counteracted by Akin paying special attention to socially discriminated and marginalized groups, and draws attention to the mechanisms used to control them through dominant, specifically male discourses.

3. Creating Counter-Discourses in *Auf der anderen Seite* and *Gegen die Wand*

The challenging of the mother archetype by Akin can be exemplified through Yeter in *Auf der anderen Seite*. First of all, despite Muslim societies' strict sense of morality and judgment of women by categorizing them as either good or bad/fallen, Yeter is a representation of rebellion as she lives her own choice concerning the issue of what to do about her body. Even though there is moral pressure from the conservative Muslim men chasing her and threatening to kill her if she does not quit her way of living, Yeter continues to do what she believes to be true: to support her daughter's education on her own. When she is approached by one of her regular visitors, Ali, an older guy who invites her to live with him and demands that she has sex only with him, she accepts it. However, it is crucial to notice that she does not give up her freedom and still speaks up for herself. When Ali tries to abuse her sexually, and starts to abuse her with his paranoid thoughts about Yeter and his son Nejat having an affair, she rebels and says, "Fuck you and your money. You do not own me (00:25:42)." Even though the fight between Yeter and Ali ends with Yeter's death, Yeter is a very crucial example of a rebellious woman who first of all stands against her own society in Turkey, and comes to Germany, and then refuses – by taking on prostitution as an occupation – to accept the role of "moral" woman and the mother image imposed upon her by the male-oriented society. Next, she rebels against Ali's humiliation of her and tries to leave him. It can be inferred that she will live up to her choice, which is prostitution as her job, but will not tolerate a man trying to treat her as *his* prostitute by psychologically and physically abusing her. Yeter is not looking for the comfort and safety of a man's psychological "ownership" exercised by his financial power, but rather strives for her freedom and respect.

With this striking and non-conformist mother figure, Akin suggests an alternative discourse not only to male hegemony but also to Orientalism. Ayten is a woman of the "eastern" culture working as a sex labourer in the German "host" culture. On the other hand, a German mother, Frau Staub, who is a strong defender of the EU and the systematic structure, feels violated by the arrival of the uninvited stranger Ayten in her domestic "sphere," intruding into her "western" way of life. With reference to Said, Adi suggests that "orientalism is instrumental ideas that constitute an 'enormously systematic discipline' by which European culture 'manage(s) and produce(s) the Orient politically, sociologically, militarily, ideologically, scientifically, and imaginatively'" (Adi 2010: 15; see Said 1979: 3). Frau Staub attempts to judge and "handle" Ayten and this is highly symbolic of western discourse. Even though she lets go of her harsh idealism about her daughter's involvement with Ayten, it is not until she leaves her comfort zone, that is, her house and her country, and goes to the "east" that she experiences the "eastern" culture as different from her prejudices (i.e., she believes Ayten is fighting politically just because she enjoys it) in the beginning of her encounter with her.

The second male-oriented discourse which Akin challenges in his movies is characterized by the marginalization of women through the attribution of and identification with certain characteristics such as domesticity, reproductivity, morality and irrationality that put them in the position of the secondary sex.

> Controlling discourse involves one or more of these categories, e.g. determining the definition of the communicative situation, deciding on time and place of the communicative event, or on which participants may or must be present, and in which roles, or what knowledge or opinions they should (not) have, and which social actions must be achieved by discourse. (Van Djik 1993: 356)

According to Jung, the identification with the mother image/the feminine inner personality, which he names the "anima," can have different results on male and female children. The over-identification with the anima, one of the two essential elements of the collective unconscious according to Jung, can result in "hypertrophy." A lesser identification with it can result in "atrophy." These two concepts will be further analysed through this study as they play an important role in explaining the male's projection of himself as the superior sex, or the female resistance to motherhood, child-bearing, marriage with intellectual and creative power. Here it is of great significance to look at the fact that whether a woman is liberated of traditionally assigned roles or whether she has the capacity of intellectual thinking and creativity depends upon the positioning of her intrinsic "male" characteristics, which Jung calls the animus. However, Akin combats this sort of essentialist and simplifying attitude by creating complex female characters that are anarchistic lesbians, suicidal brides, and sex labourers, such as in the case of Yeter.

In contradiction to rational thinking and strength, that is, "logos," connected to the existence of the animus in a woman's psyche, Ayten, the main character in *Gegen die Wand*, comes to the foreground as a homosexual warrior who with her group is fighting globalization to create a world of more educational and social justice. Furthermore, Ayten is not only a political rebel, but she also rejects any kind of power being exercised on her. She stands against male subjugation, especially in terms of financial dominance. In addition, she resists to Lotta's mother as she does not respect her ideals. Ayten embodies change itself and creates an alternative reality which cannot be explained with the innate characteristics that a (heterosexual) woman borrows from the male psyche. The only thing that does not go away is her homosexual relationship with Lotta, which is also a powerful form of rebellion. She subverts the dominant male discourse underestimating the female psyche as defined by "Eros."

As for *Gegen die Wand*, the main protagonist Ayten's rebellion against her cultural background – represented by her family – stands for her multidimensional challenging of the power dynamics stabilized by the discourses of her patriarchal environment. To avoid the oppression of her conservative family, Sibel's offer to Cahit Tomruk, the male protagonist, can be seen in contrast with her desire to be free as it looks like a wish to have a life abiding by the rules of another male figure. However, she marries Cahit only under the condition that she will be free to live her life, and this freedom for her especially means her sexual freedom. She even attempts to take her own life rather than living as a prisoner in her marriage. Sibel's fierce attitude is "ferociously demonstrated by her willingness to slit her wrists with a broken beer bottle rather than face the oppression of her unwaveringly dogmatic Turkish family" points out she is ready to pay whatever price she needs to fight for her freedom, even if it means killing herself (Isenberg 2011: 57).

Therefore, she rebels against the restrictive norms of her society which manifest themselves through her family in Germany to gain sexual liberation. In order to do so, she also rejects the bourgeois notions of romantic relationships with men. Furthermore, her rebellion against any kind of restrictive force can be observed through her relationship with her cousin, Selma, who gives her a hand when Cahit is in prison but turns out to be a rather restrictive figure in her life. Selma as a manager of a big hotel in Istanbul with a bourgeois and orderly lifestyle symbolizes the modern individual whose aims are to make money to buy freedom; however, she ends up being a slave to it, that is, everything Sibel, whose biggest concern in life is her freedom, stands against. Therefore, even at the cost of ending up at a bartender's house and getting raped by him, or being beaten up by a couple of violent, macho men in the middle of the street, Sibel opts out of the safety and comfort Selma would offer her.

To sum up, in both movies Akin creates powerful, radical, courageous women who are open to transition and spiritual "rebirth" and end up with different forms of individuation even after traumas with passive, weak, close-minded, psychologically and mentally rigid, and traditionally retrogressive male characters. Different to the male-centred cinema tradition, the disturber – and here the hero – is the woman in these movies. However, female characters in Ayten's films rather appear as anti-heroines, as in the case of Yeter, who is murdered as she does not surrender to male hegemony in return for security; similarly, Sibel attempts suicide to avoid her family's oppression, and Ayten is a political outcast in order to stand for her values and beliefs. This can be observed best through Cahit Tomruk in *Gegen die Wand*, Ali Aksu in *Auf der anderen Seite*. The weight of society's discourse can be heavily felt in both movies through some characters that represent a social phenomenon in Turkey. Especially in recent years, this voice, representing the moral values and judgments of a certain group vocalized through a group of local people in Turkey and the pressure it evokes, is referred to as "mahallebaskisi" – literally translated as "pressure coming from within society."

To begin with Cahit Tomruk in *Gegen die Wand*, though he shows some progress in rehabilitation as he is also suicidal like Sibel at the beginning of the movie, he gets taken over by his "macho" drives and ends up killing someone because as his jealousy builds up with Sibel's flirts and dates. The fact that he was born and raised in German culture, with his drug addiction and "junkie" attitude he appears to be sharply in contrast to the conservative Turkish-Muslim community Sibel is involved with. Nonetheless, he cannot help but act upon the patriarchal discourse of his ethnic roots when it comes to "competing" with other men about his love and her "honour." Likewise, Ali in *Auf der anderen Seite* tries to abuse Yeter sexually and eventually beats her to death once he understands he will not be able to "own" her soul and body. The practices of the dominant male discourse, like all other discourses, aims at determining the holders and the application of power, can also be clearly seen through Sibel's family, especially her brother who wants to legitimize the power abusing discourse on women as he is the male (superior) of the family and considers it is his right to decide about Sibel's chastity and life. Likewise, in *Auf der anderen Seite*, the group of men cornering Yeter on the way to her house from work, threatening her about her "corrupt" lifestyle and demanding that she, as a Turkish Muslim woman, quit, serve the same purpose. "Discourse structures enact, confirm, legitimate, reproduce, or challenge relations of power and dominance in society" (van Djik 1993: 353). This voice of the male, regardless of who it specifically belongs to, turns later into the common voice, the keeper of the (moral) "order," the eye of the guard keeper, the centre of the panopticon prison model suggested by Foucault.

In conclusion, with his unique female characterization, Akin challenges the deeply-rooted grand narratives that depend on the archetypes that are buried in the collective unconscious. These grand narratives not only solidify the gender injustice and inequalities through the discourses in media and culture, but also create new ones in such a normalized way that they are accepted as the continuum of everyday norms, judgments, and practices. This article aimed at showing how, especially in *Auf der anderen Seite* and *Gegen die Wand*, Akin achieves his objective of stripping these discourses from their meanings and thus exposes the tools of ideology and power behind them. Akin replaces them with feminist discourses suggesting that it is possible to explore and experience new "realities" – freed from mechanisms of surveillance, punishment and imprisonment for women, especially in male-oriented societies and media.

References

Adi, Bambang T. 2010. *Critical Discourse Analysis (CDA) of Terrorism in Newsweek Magazine: Uncovering Connections between Language, Ideology and Power*. Saarbrücken: Lap Lambert.

Akin, Fatih, prod. and Fatih Akin, dir. 2007. *Auf der anderen Seite*. Istanbul: Anka Film.

Aulette, Judy R., Judith Wittner, and Kristin Blakely. 2009. *Gendered Worlds*. New York: Oxford University Press.

Cuklanz, Lisa M. 2015. "Mass Media Representation of Gendered Violence." In: Cynthia Carter, Linda Steiner, and Lisa McLaughlin, eds. *The Routledge Companion to Media and Gender*. New York: Routledge, 32-42.

Edwards, Tim. 2015. "Lone Wolves: Masculinity, Cinema, and the Man Alone." In: Cynthia Carter, Linda Steiner, and Lisa McLaughlin, eds.

The Routledge Companion to Media and Gender. New York: Routledge, 42-51.

Foucault, Michel. 1995. *Discipline and Punish: The Birth of the Prison*. Alan Sheridan, trans. New York: Vintage Books.

Goldenberg, Naomi R. 1976. "Feminist Critique of Jung." *Signs: Journal of Women in Culture and Society* 2.2, 443-449.

Guzman, Isabel M. and Lisa M. Cacho. 2015. "Historically Mapping Contemporary Intersectional Feminist Media Studies." In: Cynthia Carter, Linda Steiner, and Lisa McLaughlin, eds. *The Routledge Companion to Media and Gender*. New York: Routledge, 71-81.

Isenberg, Noah. 2011. "Fatih Akin's Cinema of Intersections." *Film Quarterly* 64.4, 53-61.

Johnston, Claire. 1973. "Women's Cinema as Counter-Cinema." In: Sue Thornham, ed. *Feminist Film Theory: A Reader*. New York: New York University Press, 31-40.

Jung, Carl. 2013. *Four Archetypes: Mother, Rebirth, Spirit, Trickster*. Trans. R. F. C. Hull. London: Routledge Classics.

Jung, Carl. 2014. *The Archetypes and the Collective Unconscious*. Ed. Sir Herbert Read Michael Fordham, and Gerhard Adler. Trans. R. F. C. Hull. New York: Routledge.

Lumby, Catharine. 2015. "Post-postfeminism." In: Cynthia Carter, Linda Steiner, and Lisa McLaughlin, eds. *The Routledge Companion to Media and Gender*. New York: Routledge, 600-610.

McCabe, Janet. 2004. *Feminist Film Studies: Writing the Woman into Cinema.* New York: Columbia University Press.

Mulvey, Laura. 1975. "Visual Pleasure and Narrative Cinema." *Screen* 16.3, 6-18.

Said, Edward W. 1979. *Orientalism*. New York: Vintage Books.

Thompson, Martha E. and Michael Armato. 2012. *Investigating Gender: Developing a Feminist Sociological Imagination*. Cambridge, Mass: Polity Press.

van Djik, Teun A. 1993. "Principles of Critical Discourse Analysis." *Discourse & Society* 4.2, 249-283.

Wodak, Ruth. 2009. "Critical Discourse Analysis: History, Agenda, Theory, and Methodology." In: Ruth Wodak and Michael Meyer, eds. *Methods for Critical Discourse Analysis.* London: Sage (2nd revised edition), 1-33.

CONTRIBUTORS

Funda Bilgen Steinberg is a researcher on literature, film, and media studies and a university lecturer. She completed her BA in English Language and Literature at Bilkent University and her MA in English Literature with a focus on gender and cultural studies in Middle East Technical University. Her master's thesis was entitled "An Ecofeminist Approach to Atwood's Surfacing, Lessing's The Cleft and Winterson's The Stone Gods". She has been working as a lecturer since 2005, including her visit as a Fulbright scholar at Mercyhurst University in the USA. Currently she works at Ankara University and is a doctoral student candidate at Filmuniversität Babelsberg KONRAD WOLF.

Brygida Gasztold, Ph.D, D. Litt. holds an MA degree, a Doctorate degree, a D. Litt. from Gdańsk University, and a diploma of postgraduate studies in British Studies from Ruskin College, Oxford and Warsaw University. She is an Associate Professor at Koszalin University of Technology, Poland. Her academic interests include contemporary American literature, American Jewish literature, Canadian Jewish literature, as well as the problems of immigration, gender, and ethnic identities. She has published *To the Limits of Experience: Jerzy Kosiński's Literary Quest for Self-Identity* (2008), *Negotiating Home and Identity in Early 20th Century Jewish-American Narratives* (2011), *Stereotyped, Spirited, and Embodied: Representations of Women in American Jewish Fiction* (2015), and essays on immigrant literature and ethnicity.

Eva Gruber is Assistant Professor of American Studies at the University of Konstanz. Her research interests include Indigenous North American literatures and film, conceptualizations of race in 20th- and 21st-century American literature, and the field of literature and terrorism. She is the author of *Humor in Native North American Literature: Reimagining Nativeness* (2008) and the editor of *Thomas King: Works and Impact* (2011) and *Literature and Terrorism: Comparative Perspectives* (with Michael Frank 2011). She has also published on space in Caribbean-Canadian writing and on the politics of translation. Her current project is entitled "The Realities of Race: Black and White in the American Novel After 2000."

Katarzyna Jaworska-Biskup is an assistant professor (adjunct) in the Department of Celtic Languages and Cultures at Szczecin University. Her major academic interests include Welsh and Scottish literature, law and legal translation. Her current research project concerns reflections of Scottish and Welsh law in selected literature from Wales, Scotland and England.

Frank Obenland is a senior lecturer of American Studies at the Johannes Gutenberg University in Mainz. He is the author of *Providential Fictions: Nathaniel Hawthorne's Secular Ethics* (2011). More recently, he has also published articles on the dramatic works of William Wells Brown, Suzan-Lori Parks, and Cherríe Moraga. His post-doctoral research interests focus on the importance of transatlantic performance traditions in American ethnic drama. He is particularly interested in how theatre and drama serve as platforms for commenting on the social construction of racial identities as well as the problematic implications that follow from such constructions. He is also the co-editor of a collection of essays on recent developments in cultural theory together with Oliver Scheiding and Clemens Spahr (*Kulturtheorien im Dialog: Neue Positionen zum Verhältnis von Text und Kontext,* 2011).

Eva-Maria Orth is a lecturer at the Department of English and American Studies at the University of Jena where she teaches English Literature and British Cultural Studies. She is the author of a study on the dialogical monologue as a means for the representation of consciousness and has published articles on English narrative fiction, drama and biography. She is currently particularly interested in short fiction.

Albert Rau teaches English Canadian Drama and literature at the University of Cologne. He is a founding member of the Association for Canadian Studies in German-speaking countries. His articles and publications discuss aspects of Canadian drama and deal with the didactics of English Canadian literature for the ESL (English as a second language) classroom as, for example, *Glimpses of Canada* (1991), an anthology of literary texts, *Study Notes* for Margaret Atwood's *The Handmaid's Tale.* (2006) and an anthology of short stories with Albert-Reiner Glaap, *Short Stories from Canada.* (2006) He also co-edited the *Canadian-German-Hungarian Cultural Reader* (2011) and *A Cultural Reader on Aboriginal Perspectives in Canada* (2013). In May 2011, he was awarded the *Certificate of Mérit* by the International Council for Canadian Studies.

Alan Riach Born in Lanarkshire, Professor of Scottish Literature, Glasgow University. Books include poetry: *The Winter |Book* (2017), *Homecoming* (2009) and *Wild Blue: Selected Poems* (2014); criticism: *Hugh MacDiarmid's Epic Poetry* (1991), *Representing Scotland* (2005), and co-authored with Alexander Moffat, *Arts of Resistance: Poets, Portraits and Landscapes of Modern Scotland* (2008), described in the *Times Literary Supplement* as "a landmark book", and *Arts of Independence: The Cultural Argument and Why It Matters Most* (2014). Riach and Moffat are also the co-editors of the annotated edition of J. D. Fergusson's radical manifesto-book *Modern Scottish Painting* (1943; new edition, 2015).

Caroline Rosenthal is Professor of American Literature at the Friedrich Schiller University, Jena. She has published on Comparative North American Studies; Canadian literature, culture, and literary theory; city fiction and spatial theory; American Romanticism; and Gender Studies. Her books include *Narrative Deconstructions of Gender in Works by Audrey Thomas, Daphne Marlatt, and Louise Erdrich* (2003), *New York and Toronto Novels after Postmodernism: Explorations of the Urban* (2011) as well as the co-edited essay collections *Probing the Skin: Cultural Representations of Our Contact Zone* (with Vanderbeke 2014) and *Fake Identity? The Impostor Narrative in American Culture* (with Schäfer 2014). Her current research interests are related to mobility studies, transarea studies, and ecocriticism.

Nandini Saha is Professor at the Department of English, Jadavpur University, Kolkata, India. She has been teaching at Jadavpur since 2009. Previously she taught at the Department of English, University of Kalyani, West Bengal, India between 1995 and 2009. She did her PhD on John Fowles's fiction and is currently working on a project on women Dalit writers from Bengal. She is also working on some projects in translation studies.

Christoph Schubert is Full Professor of English Linguistics at the University of Vechta, Germany. He received his PhD and his postdoctoral degree (*Habilitation*) from the University of Würzburg. His main publications are a PhD thesis on the complex sentence in English poetry (2000), a postdoctoral study on the cognitive constitution of space in descriptive texts (2009), and a book-length introduction to English text linguistics (2nd ed. 2012). He recently co-edited two collections of essays, *Variational Text Linguistics: Revisiting Register in English* (2016) and *Pragmatic Perspectives on Postcolonial Discourse: Linguistics and Literature*

(2016). He has published widely in the areas of discourse analysis, text linguistics, stylistics, cognitive linguistics, and pragmatics.

Christoph Singer is an assistant professor in the Department of British Literary and Cultural Studies at the University of Paderborn, Germany. In 2012 he finished his dissertation on literary representations of shorelines as liminal spaces. He published anthologies on intersections of Middlebrow & Modernism with Kate Macdonald and the iconography of Dante & Milton with Christoph Lehner. Currently he is working on a project on narrative temporalities.

Ana Toroš is an Assistant Professor at the School of Humanities and a research fellow at the Research Centre for Humanities (University of Nova Gorica). Her main research and teaching domain is literature along the border between Slovenia and Italy. Within this research area she published two monographs: In 2011, she published a monograph (*The Image of Trieste and its surroundings in the Slovenian and Italian Poetry of the first half of the 20th Century*) and received an award by the Republic of Slovenia Government's Office for Slovenians Abroad. She published her second monograph in 2013, *O zemlja sladka: kamen, zrno, sok. Alojz Gradnik ter romanski in germanski svet* ("Alojz Gradnik and the Romance and Germanic Worlds"). She is currently leading the EDUKA 2 project activities at the University of Nova Gorica.

Laurenz Volkmann is Full Professor of Teaching English as a Foreign Language at Friedrich-Schiller-Universität Jena, Germany. He has published widely on literature, culture and media studies, from Shakespeare to Gender Studies to Intercultural Learning. Major publications are *Homo oeconomicus: Studien zur Modellierung eines neuen Menschenbilds in der englischen Literatur vom Mittelalter bis zum 18. Jahrhundert* (2003), *The Global Village: Progress or Disaster* (textbook, 2007), *Englische Fachdidaktik: Kultur und Sprache* (2010) and *Teaching English* (with Nancy Grimm and Michael Meyer, 2015).

Joanna Witkowska is a lecturer at the University of Szczecin, Faculty of Languages. Her research focuses on Polish-British cultural relationships. She has published on anti-Western propaganda and Polish-British relations during WWII. Her publications include *The Image of The United Kingdom in Poland During the Stalinist Period* (Szczecin 2009) and "'Absence' of War in World War II Polish Veterans' Recollections" in: Wojciech Drąg, Jakub Krogulec, Mateusz Marecki, eds. *War and Words: Representations* *of Military Conflict in Literature and the Media* (Newcastle Upon Tyne 2016)

Paula Wojcik is assistant professor for German and Comparative Literature at Friedrich Schiller University, Jena). In her PhD-thesis she analyzed the dismantling of anti-semitic stereotypes in contemporary Polish, German, and US-American Literature. The thesis was published in German as *Das Stereotyp als Metapher. Zur Demontage des Antisemitismus in der Gegenwartsliteratur* (Transcript, 2013). In her next book, she is working on a functionalist theory of the classics.

Uwe Zagratzki is Professor of Anglophone Literatures and Cultures and the Chair of Literature at the Institute of English at Szczecin University, Poland. He has held various posts at the Universities of Osnabrück, Greifswald, Halle-Wittenberg, Rostock and Oldenburg and has worked as a Visiting Professor at the Universities of Brno, Czech Republic and West Georgia, USA. A growing interest in Canadian Studies has been funded by several scholarships from the International Council of Canadian Studies. He has widely published in his main fields of interest: Scottish, English and Canadian Literature and Culture, Cultural Studies and War and Literature. He is also a co-editor of *Deutsche Schottlandbilder* (1998), *Das Blaue Wunder. Blues aus deutschen Landen* (2010), *Us and Them – Them and Us: Constructions of the Other in Cultural Stereotypes* (2010), *Ideological Battlegrounds – Constructions of Us and Them Before and After 9/11. Vol.1: Perspectives in Literatures and Cultures* (2014) as well as *Despite Harper: International Perceptions of Canadian Literature and Culture* (2014) and *Exile and Migration: New Reflections on an Old Practise* (2016). He is a co-founder of the Szczecin Canadian Studies Group.

Jutta Zimmermann is Professor of North American Studies and Director of the Center of North American Studies at Christian-Albrechts-University, Kiel. Her publications include monographs on metafiction in Canadian literature and on the gender issue in American realist fiction. She has co-edited essay collections on Canadian postcolonial literatures and recently *Atlantic Islands in the Americas: Sites of Cultural Contact and Identity Formation*. Among her research interests are cultural memory and trauma, multicultural and ethnic literatures, and regional literatures in North America.

INDEX

A

African American, 27, 41-61
African American theatre / drama, 41-61
Akin, F., 234-244
Alamo myth, 23-40
Ally McBeal, 235
Anglo-Norman writing, 114-126
Anzaldúa, G., 33
Asian American, 62-78
Asian Canadian, 97-112
Attlee, C., 176

B

Bangladesh, 157-172
Barri, G. de, 114-126
Barthes, R., 180, 236
Beastie Boys, 178
Beckett, M., 127-139
Benjamin, W., 142-144
blackness, 41-61
Boswell, S., 125
bottom-up effect, 3, 4, 11
Breaking Bad, 2-22
Britain, 202-222
British imperialism, 173
Bush, G.W., 180
Butalia, U., 171
Butler, J., 238

C

Canada, 80-112, 204
Canadian First Nations, 97-112
caricature, 47, 140
Cash, J., 25-35
Chabon, M., 190-196
Chinatown, 97-112
Chinese American, 62-78
Chinese Canadian, 97-112
Chomsky, N., 88
Choy, W., 100
Churchill, W., 176
Civil Rights Movement, 32, 43
cognitive model, 3, 7
cognitive-linguistic perspective, 5, 188
cognitive representation, 8
Conceptual Metaphor Theory, 188-201
Counselor, The, 3-22
Critical Discourse Analysis, 2, 4, 6, 8,
Culpeper, J., 3, 4
cultural memory, 23, 24, 174, 183, 184, 226

D

Day After Tomorrow, The, 19
Derrida, J., 178
Desierto, 19
Devi, J., 156-172
Devious Maids, 19
Dowland, J., 145
Du Bois, W.E.B., 46

E

Eastwood, C., 234
Englishness, 116
Emmerich, R., 19
Escape to Gold Mountain, 100-110
Eurocanadian, 97-112
Everything I Never Told You, 62-78

F

Fairclough, N., 2, 4
Farkas, E., 93, 94
Foer, J.S., 190-193
Forgetting the Alamo Or Blood Money, 37, 38
Foucault, M., 33, 207, 236, 237, 243
France, 145, 202, 203, 212, 213
Freud, S., 227
Friedan, B., 73
frontier, 26, 30, 32, 33, 35, 65

G

Gaelic, 150-152
Gandhi, M., 176, 177
Gates, L.H. Jr., 44
gender representations, 31, 234-244
Gennep, A. van, 198
Germany, 189-199, 202, 239-241
German-Polish relations, 196-198
Gilbert, E., 179
Goodman, N., 188
Google India, 174, 182-186
Gosh, A., 157-172

H

Halbwachs, M., 224-232
Hall, S., 42, 49
Hancock, J. Lee, 25, 35, 36
Heems, 174-185
High Noon, 31
Hindu, 156-170, 173-186
Hume, T., 141-153
Huntingdon, H. of, 115-119

I

imagined community, 24, 35
India, 156-171, 172-186
in-group / out-group, 8
Ireland, 114-126, 127-139
Irish Troubles, 127-139
Israeli-Palestinian relationship, 80-95

Italy, 223-233

J

Jameson, F., 33
Jacobs-Jenkins, Branden, 41-60
Janesch, S., 190-199
Jewish identity 80-95
Jewish Canadian, 80-95
Jinnah, M.A., 176, 177
Johnson, S., 125
Jung, C.G., 237-241

K

Kiely, B., 128, 129

L

Lacan, J., 52, 55, 56
Lakoff, G. and Johnson, M., 188-201
Last Stand, The, 2-22
Latin American, 2-22
Lee, J.S., 97-112
Lee, Y.J., 46, 47
Lone Star, The, 34, 35

M

Machete, 19
Mamet, D., 50
Mannes, M., 173
Manifest Destiny, 8, 29
Manto, S.H., 162, 163, 175
Maracle, L., 97-112
MacCaig, N., 148-153
MacDiarmid, H., 141-153
McCann, E, 129
Mexican, 2-22, 23-40
Mexican American stereotypes, 2-22
Mexican American border, 2, 5, 17
Mexican identity, 2-22
multiculturalism, 32, 35, 178
Muslim identity, 156-172, 173-186, 239-243

N

Nathans Plays, 80-95
9/11, 35, 36, 173-186
Neighbors, 41-61
Nehru, J., 176, 177
Newburgh, W. of, 115, 118, 123, 124, 126
Ng, C., 62-78

O

Obama, B., 41, 44, 48, 174
O'Neill, E., 50
Orientalism, 201, 207, 240
Osborne, G., 148-153

P

Pakistan, 156-172, 173-186
Pérez, E., 36-38
Peterkiewicz, J., 144-148
Poland, 144-152, 188-201, 202-222
post-black / post-blackness, 41-61
post-colonial, 41, 45
post-ideological, 41-61
prototype theory, 3, 6
Purser, J., 145-147,

R

Rajkahini, 163, 168
Roots, 182
Russia, 144, 146, 194, 203, 210, 213

S

Said, E., 88, 202, 207, 240
Savages, 2-22
Scotland, 114-126, 140-154, 203-222
Sex and the City, 235
Sherman, J., 80-95
Shipment, The, 46
Sicario, 2-22
Sidhwa, B., 174, 177

Sikh, 156, 163, 174, 180
Slovenia, 223-233
Souaid, C.M., 93, 94
Soyinka, W., 143, 144
Spanglish, 19
Stowe, H.B., 50

T

telecinematic discourse, 2-22
telecinematic narrative, 2-22
Texas, 23-40
Tokarczuk, O., 190-201
Tomizza, F., 228-233
top-down inferencing, 3, 4, 8, 11
Traffic, 2-22
Trevor, W., 127-139
Triestine literature, 223-233
Trump, D., 8, 18, 19, 21, 32, 33, 38
Turner, F.J., 30
Turkey, 234-243

U

Umek, E., 229, 230
USA, 2-22, 23-40, 41-61, 173-185
US television series, 2-22

W

Wales, 114-126
Wales, Gerald of, 114-126
War on Terror, 36
Wayne, J., 25, 30, 31, 32, 35
William the Conqueror, 114-126
Wilson, A., 46
Wong, D.H.T., 100

Y

Yee, P., 100, 104-11
Yugoslavia, 223, 230, 231

Z

Žižek, S., 49, 52, 53, 55, 58, 61